The Black Book of Bosnia

The Black Book of Bosnia

THE CONSEQUENCES OF APPEASEMENT

BY THE WRITERS AND EDITORS OF *THE NEW REPUBLIC*

Edited by
NADER MOUSAVIZADEH

Afterword by
LEON WIESELTIER

BasicBooks
A Subsidiary of Perseus Books, L.L.C.

Grateful acknowledgment is made for permission to reprint the following:

Maps on pages *xiv–xvi:* Copyright © 1992/1995 by The New York Times Company. Reprinted by permission.

"After Srebenica," copyright © 1995 by Zbigniew Brzezinski.
"Beyond Words," copyright © 1995 by Fouad Ajami.
"Dateline Macedonia: Fear," copyright © 1994 by Misha Glenny.
"Dateline Sarajevo: Back on Track," copyright © 1994 by Zlatko Dizdarevic.
"Dateline Sarajevo: Greater Serbs," copyright © 1995 by Samantha Power.
"Dateline Sarajevo: War and Peace," copyright © 1994 by David Rieff.
"Europa Nervosa," copyright © 1993 by Niall Ferguson.
"Falling Down," copyright © 1993 by Slavenka Drakulić.
"In Europe's Shadow," copyright © 1994 by Fouad Ajami.
"Love Story," copyright © 1993 by Slavenka Drakulić.
"See No Evil," copyright © 1993 by Patrick Glynn.
"The Nation That Wasn't," copyright © 1992 by Aleksa Djilas.
"The One and the Many," copyright © 1991 by Istvan Deak.
"The Parable of the Stripper," copyright © 1994 by Arthur Miller.
"War Crimes," copyright © 1995 by Michael Lewis.

Library of Congress Cataloging-in-Publication Data

The Black book of Bosnia : the consequences of appeasement / by the writers and editors of The New Republic ; edited by Nader Mousavizadeh ; afterword by Leon Wieseltier.
   p. cm.
"A New Republic book."
Includes index.
ISBN 0-465-09835-5
1. Yugoslav War, 1991- 2. Yugoslavia—Ethnic relations.
I. Mousavizadeh, Nader.
DR1313.B58 1996
949.702'4—dc20   95-50103

98 99 ❖/RRD 9 8 7 6 5 4 3

Contents

PART III
Indecision and Impotence

Sarajevo

Now, when a revolution is really needed, those who were once fervent
are cool.

While a country, raped and murdered, calls for help from the Europe
it trusted,

While statesmen choose villainy and no voice is raised to call it by its
name.

It was a sham, the rebellion of the young who cried for a new earth,
and that generation has written the verdict on itself,

Listening with indifference to the cries of those who perish
because they are just barbarians killing each other

And the lives of the well-fed are worth more than the lives of the
starving.

It is revealed now that their Europe has been, since the beginning,
a deception, for its faith and its foundation is nothingness.

Nothingness, as the prophets keep saying, brings forth only nothingness
and they will be led once again like cattle to slaughter.

Let them tremble and at the last moment let them comprehend that the
word *Sarajevo* from now on will mean the destruction of their sons and
the debasement of their daughters.

They have prepared it by repeating "We at least are safe," unaware that
what will strike them ripens within them.

Czeslaw Milosz
(translated by the author and Robert Hass)

Preface

This is a book of documents, but it is also an elegy. An elegy not for the death of a people—for there remains a Bosnian people, however tortured and decimated—but an elegy for the death of an idea. The idea was simple: that within Europe, in Bosnia, a multiethnic people could exist in peace and tolerance. With the collapse of Yugoslavia this idea was set upon, not by a host of unfathomable and ancient hatreds and resentments, but by the soldiers of a Greater Serbia. A fundamentally racist war was conducted from Pale and Belgrade with the aim of eliminating all signs of Muslim life from the Balkans.

That war, with its mass killings, rapes, and expulsions of millions, may at this writing be coming to an end. And if the architects of a Greater Serbia find their edifice somewhat unfinished, if their "ethnic cleansing" has left a few spots still uncleansed, it would be a crime to forget just how efficient they really were. What remains, largely, is the debris of an incomplete genocide, with its record of families dismembered and cities destroyed. The evidence of this war of genocide has never been hidden from the world. Nakedly, unsparingly, it has been brought before us, day after day, on television and in newspapers, in images of bombed-out mosques and leveled libraries, of rubble where there once were villages, of mass graves where there once were quiet fields.

One merciful day the memories of Bosnia will become history—their history as well as ours. The memories of Bosnia will haunt America, too, for this is the country to which the Bosnians appealed for help, and then found too little help too late. The documents in this book, which are presented here as they appeared in *The New Republic,* are assembled for two purposes: as a contribution to the historical narrative of the crime in Bosnia, and as a cautionary record. They serve as a chronicle of warnings not heeded and testimonies not heard, of opportunities missed and of judgments ignored. They explain the complexities of this war, and they reveal the simplicity of this war.

We have called this collection of essays, reportage, and editorials *The Black Book of Bosnia* because we wish to make an analogy. The original *The Black Book* was a record of the Nazi murder of Jews in the Soviet Union, carefully and ambitiously compiled by the Soviet writer Ilya Ehrenburg. It constitutes a remarkable archive of aggression, containing hundreds of testimonial documents, diary entries, letters, eyewitness accounts, and memorial essays. The first English edition was published in New York in 1946. Ehrenburg and his fellow editor Vassily Grossman set themselves two goals with their work:

> *The Black Book* should become a memorial placed over the innumerable graves of Soviet people viciously murdered by the German Fascists.
>
> *The Black Book* is intended to serve as material for the prosecution of the Fascist villains who organized and participated in the murder of millions of old men, women, and children.

It was a terrible project, with terrible hopes. And though one may look back at Ehrenburg and Grossman's work with the knowledge that those murdered by the Nazis are remembered today, and that some Nazis were indeed prosecuted, the war in Bosnia has served not least as a reminder of forgetting. It has disabused us of the idea that the world would never again stand by. This century has taught us too often that the survival of smaller peoples simply is not worth the bother.

Since August 1992, and the editorial entitled "Rescue Bosnia," Bosnia has been an obsession of *The New Republic.* It has been an obsession because the struggle for Bosnia is the struggle for difference and ethnic pluralism, in Europe as everywhere. And it has been an obsession because Bosnia, from the beginning, represented nothing less than a test of Western will. If we would not intervene there—on the border between East and West and in the heart of Europe, with force and with determination, on the side of the victim—then nothing the West had ever said about the lessons of appeasement would mean anything. And who today can look back at Bosnia and say that it did?

The Black Book of Bosnia has been assembled thematically as well as chronologically. The first section, titled "The Legacy of the Balkans," begins with Arthur Miller's short account of an evening in a Balkan bar where small prejudices become metaphors for larger hatreds. The review-essays by Istvan Deak, Aleksa Djilas, and Fouad Ajami carefully explore the history of ethnic strife and ethnic sanity in the Balkans, exposing the myth of eternal conflict, and explaining the origins of this particular conflict. Anthony Lewis concludes this section with a larger examination of the many betrayers of Bosnia, from the United Nations to Europe to America. Part II, "A People

Destroyed," assembles the best and the most vivid of *The New Republic*'s reports from the shattered landscapes of Yugoslavia. In these accounts, the fear, the hatred, the sorrow, and the despair of the ordinary men and women engulfed in the war are brought to life. "Indecision and Impotence," the third part of the book, is a selection of articles that analyze the conflict in strategic and political terms. And we end the book with a selection of the magazine's own editorials under the heading "The Abdication of the West." The title of this section evokes the theme of *The New Republic*'s editorial of February 28, 1994, "The Abdication," which was one of the most influential commentaries written on the Bosnian conflict. These editorials, almost all of which were written by Leon Wieseltier, provide a call for action and a chronology of outrage. It is hard to read them without bitterness. For they remind us that what could not, perhaps, have been predicted could have been prevented; what could not, perhaps, have been prevented could have been stopped. They remind us that we, too, have the blood of Bosnia on our hands.

The making of this book has benefited from the interest and the dedication of many people, inside and outside the magazine. It was Martin Peretz who conceived the idea of *The Black Book of Bosnia*. Leon Wieseltier offered invaluable advice about the selection of essays and articles. Over the last four years, a number of editors—Leon Wieseltier, Andrew Sullivan, David Shipley, Margaret Talbot, Ann Hulbert, Weston Kosova, David Greenberg, and Alexander Star—have commissioned and improved these pieces. At Basic Books, Paul Golob worked tirelessly to make a book out of an archive. Without the efforts of Laura Obolensky and Melanie Rehak, the archive could not have been assembled. Finally, we owe our greatest debt to those writers and correspondents whose dedication to reporting the truth about the Bosnian war opened our own eyes, and the eyes of our readers, to its horrors. What they wrote will not soon be forgotten.

Nader Mousavizadeh
Washington, D.C., November 1, 1995

The Balkan Borders in the
Twentieth Century

(*The New York Times*, May 3, 1992)

Areas of Control, October 1995

The Bosnian Serbs
Serbian leaders in Bosnia say their people fear life under Muslim domination, and had looked to Serbia for support for their rebellion, but are now reduced to seeking a semi-autonomous region. The political leader, Radovan Karadzic, and the military leader, Ratko Mladic, have both been indicted for war crimes and have lost Serbia's support for their war aims.

Serbia
A majority of Serbia's 10 million people are Orthodox Christian Serbs, but the country also includes restive Albanian and Hungarian minorities. At first the undisputed powerhouse of the region, Serbia and Montenegro retained the name of Yugoslavia, an entity not widely recognized by other countries. President Milosovic fanned the flames of nationalism, but the dream of a Greater Serbia has wilted.

Croatia
Mainly Roman Catholic, with a population of nearly 5 million, Croatia has fought to regain its territory, with support from the West, which sees it as a counter-balance to Serbia. Now in an uneasy alliance with the Bosnian government, its main immediate goal is to secure the return of eastern Slavonia, seized by Serbs in 1991.

Bosnia and Herzegovina
When it broke from Yugoslavia in 1992, Bosnia's population of 4.6 million was about one-half Muslim — mainly Slavic people who adopted Islam under Ottoman rule — one-third Serb and one-fifth Croat. The government, dominated by Muslims, says it is committed to a pluralistic society, and it now hopes that international backing will preserve its borders.

Bosnian-Croat Federation
At American urging, Bosnian Croats and government forces stopped fighting each other in 1994 and forged an alliance to battle the Bosnian Serbs. The federation is to govern about half of Bosnia under the peace settlement, but the government is alarmed by indications that local Croats are deepening their ties to Croatia.

KEY
● Original U.N. "safe areas"

AREAS OF CONTROL
Bosnian Government
Croatian
Serbian

(*The New York Times*, October 10, 1995)

Peoples and Territories of the Former Yugoslavia, November 1995

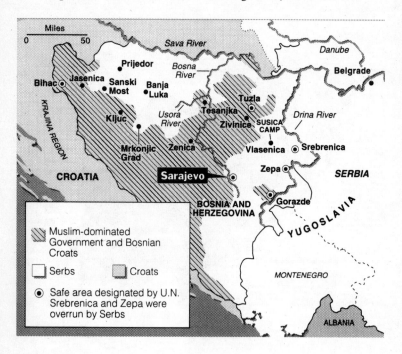

(*The New York Times*, November 1, 1995)

PART I

The Legacy of the Balkans

The Parable of the Stripper

ARTHUR MILLER

The Yugoslav catastrophe raises, for me, an especially terrible and comical memory. In the 1960s I presided over the Congress of International PEN that was held in Bled, a beautiful resort town built around a crystal clear lake high in the lovely mountains of Slovenia. Bled had been the watering hole for generations of Europeans, a fairy-tale place. And it was already more than a decade since Tito had broken with Moscow.

Marxist intellectuals in Yugoslavia were remarkably open in their criticisms of the economy and politics of the country. That the system needed deep changes was taken for granted, and new concepts were being floated that would free individual initiative while retaining the social gains of the Communist system. Worker ownership of factories was being tried, and identical consumer products, such as radios, were given different names in order to spur competition between factories, in the hope of raising quality and lowering prices. Yugoslavia was prodding the limits of socialism; and to come there from the dictatorships of Hungary, Czechoslovakia, East Germany, not to mention Russia, was to experience the shock of fresh air. In the '60s Yugoslavia the place seemed filled with enormous energy. These were the proudest, friendliest people I had met in Europe, and the most frank and open.

There was one taboo, unmentioned but obvious: the ethnic nationalism that Tito had ruthlessly suppressed. I knew, of course, that Slovenians, Bosnians, Serbs, Croatians, Montenegrans, and other nationalities made up the Yugoslav delegation to the PEN Congress, but to me they all looked alike and conversed in a mutually understood language, so their differences might be no more flammable than those separating the Welsh and the English, or maybe even Texans and Minnesotans. And when I asked an individual, out of curiosity, if he was Croatian or Slovenian or whatever, and the question caused a slight uneasiness, it seemed minimal enough to be dismissed as more or less irrelevant in this rapidly modernizing country.

Then one evening a group of four writers, one of them a Serb journalist friend called Bogdan, invited me out for a drink after dinner. Two of my companions were poets, a Croatian and a Montenegran, and one a Slovenian professor. We walked down the road to the local nightclub that usually catered to tourists. The room was very large, like a ballroom. There were maybe fifty bare, plastic-covered tables, only a few of them occupied by stolid, square-headed Alpine types. The cold night air was not noticeably heated. The place had the feeling of a big Pittsburgh cafeteria between meals.

Then a three-piece band took its place on a platform up front and began tootling American jazz standards, and a woman materialized and stood unsmilingly facing the audience. Small and compact, she wore a matching brown skirt and jacket and a shiny white rayon blouse. In a businesslike way, she began undressing, in what I was informed was to be a delightful striptease. The scattered audience of men and their chunky women silently gulped beer and sipped slivovitz as the dancer removed her suit jacket, her shoes, her blouse, and her skirt, until she stood looking out upon us in her pink rayon slip and bra. It was all done rather antiseptically, as if preparing for a medical examination. Each garment was tidily laid out and patted down on the piano bench, there being no pianist.

Then she stepped out of her slip, and in her panties did a few routine steps in approximate time to the music. She had very good legs. Things were heating up. From somewhere she picked up a heavy blue terry cloth robe and, wrapped in it, she slipped off her bra and flashed one breast. My fellow writers broke off their dying conversation. I don't know what got into me, but I asked a fatal question; "Can you tell from looking at her what her nationality is?"

My Serb friend Bogdan, depressed by his wife's absence in Belgrade, since it had left him for the entire week to the mercies of his melancholy mistress, glanced across the room at the stripper, and gave his morose opinion: "I would say she could be Croatian."

"Impossible!" the Croatian poet laughed. And with a sharpened eye and a surprising undertone of moral indignation, he added, "She could never be Croatian. Maybe Russian, or Slovenian, but not Croatian."

"Slovenian!" The mocking shout came from the Slovenian literature professor, a tall, thin fellow with shoulder-length hair. "Never! She has absolutely nothing Slovenian about her. Look how dark she is! I would say from the South, maybe Montenegran."

The dark-skinned Montenegran poet sitting beside me simply exploded in a challenging "Ha!" Just a few minutes earlier, he had been ethnically relaxed enough to tell a joke on his own people. Montenegrans are apparently famous for their admirably lethargic natures. One of them, said the poet, was walking down a street when he suddenly whipped out his revolver and, swiveling about, shot a snail on the sidewalk behind him. His energetic Serbian friend asked what the hell he had done that for. The Montenegran explained, "He's been following me all day!"

When it came to the stripper, however, humor had noticeably evaporated, as each of the men kept handing her over to somebody else. And in the middle of this warming discussion of ethnic types, I noticed that the dancer had left the platform in her thick terrycloth robe, with her clothes cradled neatly in her arms. She was just about to pass us when I stuck out my arm and stopped her. "May I ask where you come from?" With a wan, polite smile, she replied "Düsseldorf," and continued on her way.

None of the writers allowed himself to laugh, though I thought one or two blushed at the irony of the situation. A bit tense, struggling awkwardly to reconstruct the earlier atmosphere of comradely warmth, we strolled through the dark Balkan night, the president and four distinguished delegates of the writer's organization established after World War I by H. G. Wells, George Bernard Shaw, Henri Barbusse, and other war-weary writers as an attempt to apply the universalist tradition of literature to the melting down of those geographical and psychological barriers of nationalism for whose perpetuation humanity has always spent its noblest courage, and its most ferocious savagery.

(JANUARY 3, 1994)

The One and the Many

ISTVAN DEAK

I

As these lines are being written, Yugoslavia has a presidency, a government, a Parliament, and a federal army. Its economy and its currency, although weakening, are far from prostrate. Much of Yugoslavia is quiet and, along the Adriatic coast, extraordinarily beautiful. And the vast majority of its citizens desire nothing more than to live in peace and harmony with one another.

It is also true, however, that the presidency, the government, and the Parliament have all been in precipitous decline for quite some time, that the individual republics are less and less prepared to trade with one another, that the federal army has suffered a humiliating defeat at the hands of the ragtag militia of Slovenia, one of Yugoslavia's smallest member states. Croatia and Slovenia have declared their independence, people are getting killed every day in the regions with neighboring Serbs and Croats, and some opposition parties, especially those in Serbia, are even more chauvinistic than the governing party. And the Communist Republic of Serbia, which has recently absorbed its two formerly autonomous provinces, the Vojvodina and Kosovo, is intent on annexing parts of the Republic of Croatia and the Republic of Bosnia and Herzegovina, in order to realize, in association with the allied Republic of Montenegro, the old nationalist dream of a "Greater Serbia."

The worst danger to the future of Yugoslavia, however, lies not in the political crises of the present, but in the general atmosphere of fear and pessimism that feeds on the recollection of worse historical horrors. If Serbs and Croats kill each other today, it is mainly because they fear a repetition of the massive killings of the last World War.

What can explain the inability of the country's Serbs, Croats, Slovenes, Macedonians, Montenegrins, Muslims, Albanians, and Hungarians to come to a peaceful settlement of their differences? Why are things so much worse here than they were in that other great multinational state, Habsburg Austria-Hungary, from which over half of present-day Yugoslavia has emerged? Aleksa Djilas has set himself the task of explaining all this and more; and he has done so with verve, intelligence, and a superb mastery of facts.

Many of his readers may be astonished to learn from his account that one of the major causes for the continuous trouble in Yugoslavia is language: not the country's linguistic diversity, but its linguistic affinities. Aside from the Albanians and the Hungarians, who together represent less than 10 percent of the population, most other Yugoslavs speak closely related Slavic languages. Moreover, while Slovene and Macedonian are distinct languages, three-quarters of the population—Serbs, Croats, Muslims, most Montenegrins, and

---

This essay is a review of Aleksa Djilas, *The Contested Country: Yugoslav Unity and Communist Revolution, 1919–1953* (Cambridge, Mass.: Harvard University Press, 1991).

"Yugoslavs" (in the 1981 census, 5.4 percent of the population, or 1,216,000 persons, declared themselves Yugoslavs by nationality)—speaks the same language, which is Serbo-Croatian.

This fact has again and again given rise to an illusion of unity. In Yugoslavia, however, linguistic uniformity has tended to separate more than to unite. The old joke about the Americans and the British being divided by a common language is a cruel reality in Yugoslavia, where millions are in a position to savor fully the refinements of the nationalist insults hurled across ethnic boundaries, and where, precisely because of the vagueness of national identity, people wildly exaggerate the importance of nationality. It does not help matters any that one often needs, as in Northern Ireland or in Lebanon, a well-tuned ear and a keen eye to detect another's nationality.

Those of us accustomed to defining nationality primarily by language can never fully appreciate the trouble sown by Serbo-Croatian linguistic uniformity. To be precise, Serbo-Croatian is a literary language created by nineteenth-century Serbian and Croatian intellectuals. Popular speech is divided into several dialects and subdialects, but that is little help in separating Serbs and Croats. The boundaries between the various dialects do not run along ethnic lines. The Stokavski dialect, for instance, which served as a basis for the creation of literary Serbo-Croatian, is spoken by most Serbs, but also by millions of Croats and others. Some Croats, however, especially those around Zagreb, the Croatian capital, use the Kajkavski dialect, while those along the Adriatic coast speak Cakavski, both dialects being quite far removed from the Stokavski dialect. There is no such language, in other words, as Croatian or Serbian, but there is a Serbo-Croatian language and a number of "ethnically blind" dialects.

Nor is territory of much use in distinguishing one nationality from another. As the press reminds us daily, nearly every one of Yugoslavia's six republics (Serbia, Croatia, Slovenia, Bosnia and Herzegovina, Macedonia, and Montenegro) and two autonomous territories harbors several nationalities. According to Djilas, 22 percent of the entire Croatian population and 24 percent of the entire Serbian population live outside Croatia and Serbia (and the latter's two provinces). As for the Muslims, a recently recognized nationality of 2 million, the great majority live in Bosnia and Herzegovina, which they share with a lesser number of Croats and Serbs. Because all three nationalities in that republic speak Serbo-Croatian, it is obvious that the Muslims there are defined neither by language nor by territory, but by a religion that many of them no longer practice.

Paradoxically, only the Montenegrins can be said to be defined by the territory they inhabit. These Serbo-Croatian speakers of the Eastern Orthodox tradition (let us forget, for the moment, the Albanians and the Muslims in

their midst) differ from other Serbo-Croatian speakers of the Eastern Orthodox tradition only in that they live in what was once a fiercely independent
mountain principality.

If, in Yugoslavia, everything runs into everything else, if neither language nor
territory explains nationality, then what does? The answer, offered resound-
ingly by Djilas, is that nationality in Yugoslavia is defined by tradition and history. As he puts it: "Croats and Serbs are ethnically almost homogeneous, but
are heterogeneous from the standpoint of national consciousness and loyalties."

Croats, Serbs, and other Yugoslavs cultivate, or rather idolize, their vastly
differing historical memories: Byzantine Christianity in the case of the Serbs,
Roman Catholicism in the case of the Croats. The differences do not end
there. There is the Serbs' use of the Cyrillic alphabet as against the Croats' use
of the Latin alphabet; the great medieval Serbian kingdom as distinguished
from the great medieval Croatian kingdom; Serbia's long occupation by the
Ottoman empire as opposed to Croatia's avoidance of such enslavement at the
price of submission to the Habsburg dynasty; Serbia's self-liberation from
Ottoman rule in the nineteenth century as contrasted with Croatia's remaining in Austria-Hungary until the latter's dissolution in 1918.

Consider, moreover, the divergent social developments in Serbia and Croatia. In the former, the old native nobility did not survive the many centuries of
Ottoman rule. This meant that in the aftermath of liberation a new elite had
to be created. Independent Serbia and thus Serbian-dominated interwar
Yugoslavia were largely governed by the descendants of the small Serbian
merchant class, and even more by the descendants of peasants. In Croatia, by
contrast, the great landowning nobility survived until after the land reforms of
the post–World War I era, its foremost members being closely intertwined
with the nobility of Hungary, Croatia's historical suzerain. As large landowners, as officials in the Habsburg and Hungarian administrations, and as officers in the Habsburg army, the Croatian elites had had long experience in
local government.

And consider, finally, the events of World War I, when the kingdoms of
Serbia and Montenegro went to war against the Central Powers and were
subsequently occupied by the German, Austro-Hungarian, and Bulgarian
armies, while the Croats, Slovenes, Bosnian Muslims, and well over 100,000
Serbian soldiers from Croatia, southern Hungary, and Bosnia and Herzegovina went to war as part of the Austro-Hungarian army and navy. During and
after the war, pro-Yugoslav propaganda spread the myth of the unwilling

Croatian, Slovene, Serbian, and Bosnian soldier crushed under the heel of the Austro-Hungarian high command, but in reality the South Slavs numbered among the Habsburg monarchy's bravest and most loyal soldiers. Neither Croats, Slovenes, Bosnian Muslims, nor even the Serbs of Hungary, Croatia, and Bosnia and Herzegovina showed much hesitation in cracking the skulls of their Serbian opponents. When in 1917–18 South Slav soldiers finally began massively to desert the Austro-Hungarian forces, it was only because all the peoples of the monarchy, including German-Austrians and Hungarians, had begun massively to abandon the Habsburg cause.

II

It is worth considering just whom writers have in mind when they speak of the past history of Serbs, Croats, Slovenes, or Macedonians. Do they mean every member of the group, or only the relatively small number of educated elites within each society? In other words, when did Orthodox and Roman Catholic peasants (who amounted to as much as 90 percent of the population as late as a century ago) turn into self-conscious Serbs, Croats, Macedonians, and so on? And when did at least some of them become Yugoslav patriots? After all, the existence of medieval monarchies cannot be equated with the presence of popular nationalisms.

According to Djilas, Croatian and Serbian nationalisms were born at the end of the eighteenth century, at about the same time as their ideological and political opposite, the notion of a great South Slav unity transcending narrow ethnic boundaries. Both ideas, ironically, were largely the product of the Enlightenment, as it was imported into those parts by Napoleon's troops.

Following their victories over the Habsburgs and the capture of the Republic of Venice (which had ruled over the Adriatic coast of present-day Yugoslavia), the French armies conquered the region between 1805 and 1809. They quickly concluded that all South Slavs were descendants of the ancient Illyrians, and that they all spoke Illyrian. It was only a short step to the French generals' creation of *les provinces illyriennes,* attached to the French empire. It was also only logical to extend the blessings of the Enlightenment and the Revolution to the Illyrian people. All citizens were made equal before the law; the peasants were freed from their feudal obligations; the nobles were deprived of all their political and legal privileges; the monopoly of craftsmen's guilds was abolished; and schools were set up to teach French as well as *la langue du pays.*

The French were defeated in 1814–15, so all this lasted only a few years. Still, as Djilas explains, the idea of Illyrianism, of a united South Slav nation, has continued to thrive—and so has the idea of Croatian, Serbian, and other ethnic nationalisms. The French taught the intelligentsia to think in national terms, yet it was also the French who created a state that was the precursor of today's Yugoslav federation, and the dilemma of ethnic nationalism versus South Slav unity has haunted the region's intellectuals and politicians ever since.

Depending on the extent of their commitment to conservative nationalism or progressive Yugoslav "internationalism," intellectuals and politicians have tended to see the peasants as living either "inside" or "outside" of history: "inside" meaning that even the most wretched of Serbs or Croats can identify, on the basis of a shared historical memory, with the elite of the nation, and "outside" meaning that the lower classes, retaining nothing but memories of exploitation and oppression, could well be guided toward social progress and South Slav unification. And yet, as Djilas writes, to the bitter surprise of Communists and other utopian dreamers:

> Croatian and Serbian national consciousnesses were largely based on exactly those things that the Enlightenment was unable to see: history, tradition, religion. Moreover, the Enlightenment underestimated the propensity of the lower classes to identify with the ruling class and see its history as their own. The peasantry simply was not ahistorical to the degree that the Enlightenment and, especially, the Enlightenment's latter-day partial heirs, the socialists and Communists, believed.

It is impossible, of course, to measure precisely the extent and the depth of national consciousness in any social stratum, especially among peasants whose condition varied enormously from one place to another. Slovene peasants were generally serfs until their step-by-step emancipation by the Habsburg Emperor Joseph II in the 1780s and then by the revolutions of 1848. Croatian peasants were often free, enjoying the rank of lesser nobility; but more frequently they were serfs or, after their final emancipation in 1848, hired hands on the estates of large landowners. But just as often Croatian peasants doubled as soldiers. Dalmatian Croats were fishermen and sailors on the ships of Venice and the Habsburg monarchy. The Serbs in Hungary were merchants, soldiers, or farmers. The Serbs of Serbia, as well as the Bosnians and the Montenegrins, were either poor farmers or near-slaves on the estates of Ottoman and "Muslimized" South Slav landlords. Others were shepherds, and still others bandits who preyed on all but preferred Muslim officials and landowners. Hence the romantic term "patriotic bandits," made popular by the British historian Eric Hobsbawm and used by some progressive Western historians to designate the people who made travel and economic development nearly impossible in the Balkans for many centuries.

Even today it is difficult to know whether the Montenegrin mountaineer brandishing his Kalashnikov is brandishing it as a Yugoslav patriot determined to protect the unity of the country, or as a Communist, or as a Serbian patriot, or as a Montenegrin patriot, or as a defender of Eastern Orthodoxy, or as a peasant-farmer representing the interests of his class, or as a "patriotic bandit," or, perish the thought, as a plain old bandit.

I agree with Djilas that nationalism in Yugoslavia is a terrifically confusing affair. Still, I would add that nationalism is not so frequently the real cause of conflict as it would appear from the press. Consider, for instance, the present bloody struggle between Croats and the Serbian minority in southern parts of the Croatian republic. No doubt the conflict is being systematically promoted by the government of Serbia, but there can be no doubt about a certain degree of local involvement. Yet these villagers, "Serbs" or "Croats," speak the same dialect, have been neighbors for several generations, were in the practice of marrying each other, went to the same schools, and often worked in the same place. True, they could be distinguished by religious tradition (Eastern Orthodox versus Roman Catholic), but many of them, and certainly their Communist or ex-Communist leaders, are non-believers today. (To complicate matters further, there are, or there used to be, a good number of Catholic Serbs and Orthodox Croats in the region.) The killing today may be carried out in the name of nationality, but the real causes of the conflict must be sought elsewhere.

The antagonisms in southern Croatia began in the late seventeenth century with the massive arrival of Orthodox Christian refugees from Ottoman territory. Incorporated by Habsburg power into the famous Croatian-Slavonian Border Guard system, the refugees were trained to become militarized peasants, something akin to the Cossacks in the Ukraine and southern Russia. From earliest times, the Militärgrenze, as the Border Guard region was known, included not only Orthodox peasants, but a great number of local Roman Catholic peasants as well. In return for their services, the Border Guards were granted important privileges by the Vienna Court War Council: they were not considered serfs, that is, they belonged to no landowner; their children were taught how to read and write—in both German and the local South Slav dialect—by army sergeants, and their talented sons could rise through the ranks of the Habsburg army.

Many peasant offspring, Catholic or Orthodox, became commanding generals, and every Border Guard officer with a clean service record had a legal right to elevation into the hereditary Habsburg nobility. The Military Border was divided into regimental districts and detached from the rest of Croatia, the latter now being somewhat derisively fashioned "Civil Croatia." Meanwhile the peasants in Civil Croatia remained unfree, and as serfs they continued to toil away for the Hungaro-Croatian great landowners.

The Military Border was finally dissolved in the 1870s, and the regimental districts were reattached to Civil Croatia. The latter, of course, remained a part of Austria-Hungary until 1918. After World War I, all these lands became part of Yugoslavia, but the internal boundary continued to follow the historic line separating Habsburgs from Ottomans. People in the former Border Guard region therefore continued to live in Croatia.

During World War II, the fascist Croatian state, abetted by members of the Croatian Catholic clergy, attempted finally to assimilate the former Military Border—and, incidentally, also Bosnia and Herzegovina, which had been incorporated into the Croatian state—by forced conversions and mass murder. The primary target was the Orthodox population of the region, but many local Catholics were killed as well. For this, Catholics (or Croats) were soon repaid in kind by the Serbian Cetnik guerrillas and the Communist Partisans.

After World War II, as Djilas explains, one of the major dilemmas facing the Tito regime was how to deal with the massive presence of Serbs in the southern parts of the Croatian republic. Trusting in the wartime alliance of anti-fascist Serbs and Croats, the new Communist regime allowed the disputed lands to be left in Croatian possession. Today the Serbian government is attempting to reverse this decision and to incorporate these lands by force into a Great Serbian republic. This is, then, *not* a purely national struggle, for it reflects also the historic enmity between proud peasant soldiers and unarmed serfs.

Unfortunately, there is no fair solution to this problem. The Serbian minority's demand for separation from the Republic of Croatia has some historical foundation in the tradition of a separate Habsburg Military Border, but that Border was attached to Vienna, not to Belgrade. Moreover, none of the disputed territory ever belonged to Serbia. On the contrary, the southern border of the present Republic of Croatia has always marked the historic boundary between the Habsburg-Hungarian-Croatian lands and the Byzantine-Serbian-Ottoman dominions.

III

Few things are better known than that World War I erupted over the question of South Slav unity. In two earlier "Balkan Wars" in 1912–13, the Ottoman Turks were driven out of the Balkans and Serbia was vastly aggrandized—but not sufficiently to satisfy the radical Serbian nationalists. It was denied access to the sea, and millions of Serbs and other South Slavs continued to languish in what Eduard Benes, later the president of Czechoslovakia, effectively termed the "Prison of the Peoples," referring to the Habsburg monarchy or Austria-Hungary. (Never mind that the Croats, Serbs, and

Slovenes of the monarchy enjoyed the highest living standards among all South Slavs, and that generally they also enjoyed greater political freedom.)

The assassination of Archduke Francis Ferdinand on June 28, 1914, was preceded, and in fact caused, by a farrago of misunderstandings and misconceptions, many of which have survived to our time. There was the widespread idea in Serbia that Francis Ferdinand was an imperialist, a warmonger, and an enemy of the Slavs, when exactly the opposite was the case. There was the belief of Gavrilo Princip and his fellow terrorists that by murdering the archduke they would pave the way to the creation of a progressive, anarcho-socialist South Slav state and eventually a similar world. In reality, these youngsters were manipulated by a handful of Serbian army officers assembled in the "Black Hand," a radical nationalist secret society that was as threatening to the elected Serbian government as it was to Austria-Hungary. There was, of course, also the Austrian misconception that Serbia should be crushed at the first opportunity, that such a step could be taken without precipitating a major war. And there was, finally, the German notion that a great war, if it had to come, might as well come immediately, since Germany was bound to win it and, as a consequence, to assume its rightful position as one of the world powers.

Again, South Slavs in both camps did their duty, at least during the first three years of the war. By then Serbia and Montenegro had long been occupied by the Central Powers, but Austria-Hungary had also been totally exhausted. In the last year of the war, few people in the Habsburg monarchy could believe that the multinational empire would survive. And throughout the conflict some exiled politicians from the Habsburg monarchy—Slovenes, Serbs, Croats, Poles, Slovaks, but especially Czechs—successfully propagated the notion that the West was duty-bound to liberate all peoples from the Habsburg yoke and to allow all peoples and the South Slavs and Czecho-Slovaks in particular to set up progressive and democratic nation-states.

In 1918 the South Slav state was created. It was pieced together from parts of the Austrian Alpine provinces of Styria and Carinthia, the entire Austrian Alpine province of Carniola (the core of today's Slovenia), much of the so-called Austrian Adriatic littoral, the Austrian Kingdom of Dalmatia, Hungary's subordinate kingdom Croatia-Slavonia, large parts of southern Hungary, Bosnia and Herzegovina (a province that had been jointly administered by Austria and Hungary), the formerly independent Kingdom of Montenegro, the Kingdom of Serbia, and small parts of Bulgaria. Paradoxically, although the external frontiers of the new South Slav state attempted, or at least pretended, to run along ethnic lines and thus cut across many historical boundaries, the internal frontiers of the new state scrupulously respected the old historical boundaries, thus creating a number of multinational provinces within the multinational South Slav state.

In what way did the so-called successor states differ from the defunct Habsburg state? Mainly in this: the old monarchy had never pretended to be anything but a messy multiethnic mosaic, but Czechoslovakia and Yugoslavia claimed to be model nation-states. Along with this claim came the assertion that the "state-constituting nations," such as the Czechs and Slovaks, or the Serbs, Croats, and Slovenes, were of one will and one mind, and that in the face of these united fronts the grumblings of ethnic minorities lost all significance. Inevitably, interwar Czechoslovakia came to be dominated by a Czech elite, while the Kingdom of Serbs, Croats, and Slovenes (later to be renamed Yugoslavia) became, for all practical purposes, an expanded version of its strongest member, the Serbian kingdom.

Still, there were efforts made by some Serb politicians to live up to the founders' utopian expectations. One of the most significant, Djilas argues, was the attempt of King-Dictator Alexander I to divide Yugoslavia into a number of territorially equal, politically and ethnically neutral administrative units. Alexander I, a member of the Karageorgevich family, became regent of Serbia in place of his deranged father just before the Sarajevo assassination in 1914. In 1915 he led his army into exile on the Greek island of Corfu, and in 1918 he returned in triumph to Belgrade. Following the death of his father in 1921, Alexander became king of the Serbs, Croats, and Slovenes.

But his was a heavy inheritance. His family had come to power, in 1903, by means of the appallingly brutal massacre of Serbia's last Obrenovich king and his queen by army officers belonging to the Black Hand. This inauspicious beginning threatened to turn Alexander into a tool of nationalist Serbian officers, but soon he asserted his independence. In 1917, for instance, he inspired a military court to order the execution of Dragutin Dimitrijevic, a colonel of the Serbian General Staff and head of the Black Hand, as well as a number of other General Staff officers, not because they had organized the assassination of Francis Ferdinand and thereby precipitated the World War, but because they had allegedly conspired against him as regent and against the Serbian government in exile.

Alexander sought to become the ruler of all South Slavs. The failure of Yugoslav parliamentarianism in the late 1920s led him to set up a royal dictatorship in 1929 and to change the name of the country to Yugoslavia, in an attempt to wipe out the old historic divisions. Shortly thereafter, he divided the country into a number of new administrative units that were named after rivers, again in order to wipe out the memory of ethnic divisions. As Djilas puts it: "The king hoped to solve the national question by simply abolishing it." This was the high-water mark of both governmental fairness and extreme centralization; but it failed, as all such schemes have failed. The king himself was murdered in 1934 by the combined efforts of Macedonian and Croatian terrorists.

When the South Slav state was formed, a dynamic and militant socialist movement already existed in most of its territorial units. A large part of Djilas's book is dedicated to the history of the Yugoslav Communists. As communism is proving itself to be an ephemeral phenomenon in that country, however, whereas regional conflict appears to be eternal, Djilas's valuable discussion of the Communist movement is somewhat less exciting than his fine sections on the origins and the development of ethnic nationalism.

Transformed at an early date into a Communist Party, Yugoslavia's far left was never really able to resolve the dilemma of local nationalism versus South Slav unification. The first order of the Communist International to the Yugoslav comrades was to exploit the national conflicts so as better to fight the "expansionism" and the "hegemonism" of the Serbian bourgeoisie. This meant support for the bourgeois parties in oppressed Croatia and elsewhere. By the end of the 1920s, however, the differentiation between "reactionary" and "progressive" bourgeois nationalist movements had become a simple matter of Soviet foreign policy. In other words, the Yugoslav Communists had lost all right to decide who were their enemies and who their friends. (This was the period when the Comintern branded the German Social Democrats "social fascists" and praised even ultraconservative, anti-Western Muslim groups as eminently progressive.)

The Communist Party of Yugoslavia emerged from the parliamentary elections of 1920 as the fourth-largest party, but less than a year later it was driven underground, where it would remain until the final triumph of Tito at the end of World War II. By 1924 there were no more than 1,000 active members, who clung precariously to the Party's triune program of anti-Serbian struggle, Yugoslav nationalism, and proletarian internationalism. Although the Communists combatted Yugoslavia as an imperialist creation, they never abandoned hope for a unified South Slav proletarian state.

The 1930s brought the anti-fascist Popular Front policy, and with it Moscow's temporary acceptance of the Yugoslav state and monarchy. Those years also brought the near extermination of Yugoslav Communist émigrés in the Soviet Union and the appointment of Tito as general secretary of what remained of the Party. From 1937 on, Tito and his closest collaborators were to shape the history of Yugoslav communism.

IV

In March 1941 a British-engineered military coup overthrew a reluctantly pro-German Yugoslav government, and a few days later German armies invaded and quickly overran the country. As Djilas shows, military resistance was greatly weakened by the hostility to the state of many Croats and others. Defeated Yugoslavia was thereafter dissolved by the combined decision of the occupiers and a great number of Yugoslav citizens. Thus, the tragic fate of the multinational Habsburg monarchy now befell one of its major multinational successors. The old regime was rent asunder, writes Djilas, mainly because of its inability to create a Yugoslav political elite, which had forced it to operate with the Serbian political elite as a substitute.

German (and Italian) victory in 1941 gave the Croats what the Entente victory had given the Serbs in 1918. A Greater Croatia was created through the fusion of Croatia and Bosnia and Herzegovina. This new state was led by a group of military officers and politicians of the Ustasha movement. The Ustasha, or Croatian Revolutionary Organization, could look back to the tradition of some nineteenth-century Croatian nationalist parties, but it was in reality a uniquely brutal terrorist group that represented a small sector of the Croatian public.

It is worth noting that not only the Croats but the Albanians, too, benefitted, if only nominally, from the temporary Axis triumph. The province of Kosovo, today so hotly contested between Serbs and Albanians, was incorporated, in 1941, into the Albanian state. True, Albania was only an Italian colony at that time, but this act created one more precedent for later territorial claims and counterclaims. No doubt the eventual unification of the province with Albania will prove a difficult affair, if for no other reason than because the Serbs' original homeland lay partly in today's Kosovo province, and Serbia's greatest historical defeat, at the hands of the Ottomans in 1389, took place on the Plains of Kosovo. In a region where military debacles have been more common than victories—where resounding defeats have become cherished historical memories—the Plains of Kosovo constitute a sacred Serbian land. (As legend has it, when the defeated Serbian troops withdrew across the snow-covered Kosovo battlefield in 1915, they held their boots in hand so as not to disturb the sleep of their fallen heroes.)

Curiously, the Yugoslav Communists at first sympathized and even collaborated with the Ustashas in the common struggle against the Serbian "bourgeoisie," but the Popular Front policy of the late 1930s put an end to such collaboration. In any case, as Djilas excellently explains, for the Ustashas anti-communism amounted to a religion. Arguing that the Ustashas were not genuine fascists, Djilas writes that the movement's ideology was primarily a pseudo-romantic, populist, terrorist nationalism. In southeastern Europe it was perhaps most similar to Corneliu Codreanu's Legion of the Archangel Michael in Romania. The Legion was also extremely nationalist, mystically attached to certain events in distant national history, oriented to the peasantry, which it romanticized, and influential in poor peasant regions with mixed population. However, for the Ustashas genocide was a central element in their program.

There followed, after 1941, the most terrible bloodbath in all of Balkan history. Djilas emphasizes a point that is well known to Western historians but that was diligently suppressed in Communist Yugoslavia: that the Italian occupation forces actively opposed the Ustasha program of exterminating one-half of the Serbian-Orthodox population in Croatia and Bosnia and Herzegovina, and that even the Germans condemned the genocide of Serbs (but not, of course, the Ustasha massacre of Jews and Gypsies, or the German army's massacre of Serbian hostages). The truth is that much of the Yugoslav bloodshed in World War II was suicidally self-inflicted.

The story of Tito's rise to power and his unchallenged leadership for nearly four decades is well known. No doubt, at the end of World War II, the Yugoslav Communists were in a hurry to establish themselves. Skipping the first stage of a Communist takeover, that is, a genuine coalition with anti-fascist democratic parties, they proceeded immediately to the second stage of a bogus coalition, and then very quickly to the third stage of a monopoly of power. Because all this and more was done without consulting Stalin, an eventual break between Moscow and Belgrade was unavoidable. In fact, the break came as a godsend to Tito. It allowed him to annihilate all potential rivals in the Party, to rally even anti-Communists to the flag of national resistance, and to ask for (and to receive) American economic and military assistance.

Djilas freely admits that Tito's transformation of Yugoslavia into a centralized party state that was respectful of some provincial rights was initially a great success. After World War II, the Communist Party of Yugoslavia aimed to create a united Yugoslav political consciousness on a threefold basis: ethnic and linguistic similarities and common traditions, the wartime "national-liberation struggle," and the "building of socialism." This worked for several decades, but once the charismatic leader was dead, and the Soviet threat had passed, and the Communist economic and social system had proved to be as oppressive as it was inefficient, the old problems began to emerge. The dream of a brotherhood of progressive South Slav peoples evaporated.

As Djilas explains, the instability of the Croatian and Serbian medieval states, followed by the Ottoman conquest, prevented the development either of two clearly separate identities or of a homogeneous proto-Yugoslav one. As a result, in the nineteenth century the Croats and Serbs found themselves lacking the strong state tradition that had allowed such old, continuous nations as the French or the Swedes to emerge as modern nation-states. One cannot but agree with his conclusion:

> [As] soon as social, economic, and other realities showed that a [Yugoslav-ist and internationalist] society was unrealizable, traditional national ide-ologies reappeared, sometimes allied with the party bureaucracy of the republics, sometimes with the anti-Communist intelligentsia. Based on an ideology that proved utopian and on a power structure that was both undemocratic and bound to be inefficient . . . , the Communist solution of the national question in Yugoslavia was destined to be only transient.

Whatever possessed Slovenes and Croats in 1918 to prefer the Balkans to Central Europe, it is clear that such foolishness no longer prevails among them. And so, what next? Djilas does not discuss the subject. I would note that there may have been a chance, until quite recently, for the only surviving Yugoslav institution, which is the federal army, to hold the state together. After all, the Habsburg monarchy, too, was kept together by the mostly peace-ful and always splendid presence of the multinational Habsburg army. The absolute majority of its officers were German-speakers (though not necessar-ily ethnic Germans), yet the loyalty of these officers was not to the German nation but to Emperor Francis Joseph. In fact, the officers were most hated by German nationalist students and by much of the German-Austrian middle class.

Unfortunately for South Slav unity, however, the Yugoslav federal army is neither splendid nor truly multinational. We are now told that 70 percent of its officer corps is of Serbian nationality. This would be no tragedy, if there were something to bind the Serbian officers to the others, but nothing that binds is left: no father figure, no dynastic loyalty, no supranational political ideology.

The Habsburg army was recruited territorially: soldiers from the same province found themselves in the same regiments. This system threatened to collapse in the summer of 1848 when His Imperial and Apostolic Royal Majesty's loyal Croatian and Serbian regiments clashed with the same ruler's loyal Hungarian regiments, but it functioned afterward until the collapse of the monarchy in 1918. The Yugoslav army (like the Soviet army) does not rec-ognize territoriality, and recruits are thrown in pell-mell with soldiers from all over the country. Moreover, whereas in the Habsburg army, officers and NCOs were obliged to instruct, discipline, and curse their troops in the languages prevailing among the rank and file, the Yugoslav army speaks only one language, Serbo-Croatian. Recent experience seems to show that the Habsburg army's careful balancing act between supranationality and respect for the provincial and linguistic peculiarities of the troops was more successful than the Yugoslav army's hypocritical insistence on absolute supranationality, and this in a state constitutionally divided into separate units.

If the Habsburg army was able to hold together an empire made up of eleven major nationalities and scores of minor ones, and practically without any bloodshed between 1848–49 and 1917–18, it was only because the majority of these peoples and their leaders, their nationalistic slogans to the contrary, did not really desire the breakup of the monarchy. In Yugoslavia, by contrast, it appears less and less likely that the population wishes to maintain the state in its present form. And even if it does, it would not want to entrust the federal army with this task. As for the army, it seems to have abandoned its original reason for being. If it is true that the Yugoslav army is now fully siding with one nationality against another, then there is not, at this late date in the failing attempt to make one out of the many, any reason to expect or to desire the continued survival of Yugoslavia.

(OCTOBER 7, 1991)

The Nation That Wasn't

ALEKSA DJILAS

Beneath the Bosnians' passion, thirst for justice, faithfulness, and strength of character, Ivo Andric wrote in 1920, "the storms of hatred lie hidden in opaque depths." Andric noted that although hatred was endemic to Bosnia, Bosnians were rarely conscious of it. Andric won the Nobel Prize in 1961 for his novel *The Bridge on the Drina,* and his work was internationally acclaimed as a humanistic attempt to span Bosnia's three close and yet distant "shores": Sunni Muslims, Eastern Orthodox Serbs, and Roman Catholic Croats.

Though he came from a Croatian family in Bosnia, Andric considered himself a Yugoslav—a nationality that encompassed identities of all the different Yugoslav groups. Like many distinguished Croatian and Serbian intellectuals of the nineteenth and early twentieth centuries, he believed only a general acceptance of such a Yugoslav identity within a common state could put an end to the ancient conflicts among various Yugoslav groups. Andric knew Bosnia could not survive the collapse of Yugoslavia. Its political and historical traditions were too weak for the formidable task of state-building.

Many commentators on today's war in Bosnia seem unaware of Andric's warning. The common contemporary belief is that Bosnian sovereignty and indivisibility is a prerequisite for peace. Such thinking represents a misunderstanding of the nature of the region's long history of interethnic strife. While the West's refusal to accept Serbia's and Croatia's land grab in Bosnia is commendable, its recognition of Bosnia in April, just a month after it had proclaimed independence, will be remembered as one of the most irresponsible Western decisions in postwar history. It plunged Bosnia into the civil war.

Indeed, it is difficult to imagine how Bosnian Serbs and Croats could ever identify with Bosnia rather than with Serbia and Croatia. In a referendum held earlier this year, Muslims and Croats (43.7 percent and 17.3 percent of Bosnia's 4.4 million inhabitants, respectively) voted to separate Bosnia from Yugoslavia. (Slovenia, Croatia, and Macedonia had already seceded.) This was wrongly interpreted in the West as a declaration of independence. Bosnian Croats, however, were not in favor of independence, only for secession from Yugoslavia. Like the Serbs (31.3 percent of the population) who opposed the secession and boycotted the referendum, Croats do not want to be a part of Bosnia. They want to unite with Croatia. Likewise, the Serbs now want to unite with Serbia. This leaves the Muslims as the only possible supporters of the new state. And Muslims are far outnumbered by Serbs and Croats.

The subordination of Muslim identity to Serbian and Croatian nationalism is not new. Since the early nineteenth century, Serbian nationalists have claimed that Bosnian Muslims were Serbs of Islamic faith, while their Croatian counterparts professed with equal zeal that Bosnian Muslims were actually Croats of Islamic faith. Most Bosnian Muslims, however, have never identified themselves as either. Bosnian Muslims have distinct customs, dress, and architecture, as well as political traditions and historical memories.

But then, the notion of Bosnia as a state is something of a misnomer. Although for convenience many writers use "Bosnia" to denote both Bosnia and Herzegovina, the two are hardly interchangeable. Herzegovina has a distinct history: a Herzegovinian, whether Serb, Croat, or Muslim, would never call himself a Bosnian. Indeed, there has not been a Bosnian state since the medieval period, and even then its borders often changed, each time further obscuring ethnic and national identities. Whereas the historical memory of the medieval state is essential to the national identities of the Serbs and Croats, Bosnian Serbs and Croats are largely indifferent to Bosnian history. When they show interest, it is to highlight facts or myths that "prove" Bosnia should belong to them.

Muslims, too, are uneasy with the memory of medieval Bosnia. The Ottoman Turks completed the conquest of Bosnia in 1463 and then converted the nobility to Islam. Forced conversions were generally rare in Islam, but because it faced a Christian frontier, Bosnian Islam was unusually harsh. In the case of Bosnia's nobility, the Turks applied pressure, along with economic and political advantages. As a result, the nobility collectively apostatized.

From then on, Christians labeled all converts to Islam "Turks." Converts themselves sometimes used that appellation. Of course, Bosnian Muslims had nothing in common with real Turks. But they were politically Turks—loyal to the Turkish Ottoman Empire and the Sultan. (The name "Turk" can be heard even now in embattled Bosnia. It is used by Serbs and sometimes by Croats as a derogatory term for Muslims.)

Yet Bosnia's Muslim nobility preserved through the centuries a sense of Bosnia's separateness from the rest of the Turkish empire. Several times in the nineteenth century they rebelled against Ottoman rule, preaching a "holy war" against the Sultan. They did not, however, develop a sense of modern nationality or a desire to create a Bosnian state.

At the Berlin Conference of 1878 in the aftermath of the war between the Orthodox Serbian and Catholic Croatian peasantry and Ottoman Turkey, Bosnia was given over to Austria-Hungary. Austria-Hungary modernized Bosnia with roads and industry. Yet it left agriculture largely untouched, hoping to win the allegiance of Muslim landowners, whom it considered the most loyal of the three groups. Muslims were indeed untouched by modern national sentiments that were so strong among Serbs and Croats. But while Muslims refrained from challenging Austria-Hungary, they did not trust it. On the one hand, they perceived it as primarily a Catholic country with proselytizing tendencies, and on the other, as a promoter of threatening secularism. Many Muslims left Bosnia for Turkey.

Fearing the establishment of a strong South Slav state on its southern flank as much as it feared a large South Slav unit within its own borders, Austria-Hungary prevented Bosnia from ever joining either Serbia or Croatia—even though the latter was part of Austria-Hungary. In doing so, Vienna and Budapest also hoped to put an end to all plans for the unification of Croatia and Serbia. To satisfy the need for an ideological underpinning to its Bosnian policy, Austria-Hungary promoted "Bosnian" nationality. While allowing the Bosnian Serbs economic development, it defined them simply as people of Orthodox faith. Croats, in turn, were simply Catholics. Bosnia was to become a land with one nation and three religions.

In order to combat feared political and cultural influences from Serbia and Croatia from promoting the growth of national consciousness within Bosnia, Austria-Hungary transformed Bosnia into a police state. Serbia was considered particularly dangerous after it became a parliamentary democracy in 1903 and its nationalism allied itself with liberalism. But Serbs and Croats in Bosnia retained their loyalty to their respective nations, and no amount of propaganda could convince them that "Bosnian" was anything more than a regional appellation.

In 1918, however, when Yugoslavia was created from the kingdoms of Serbia and Montenegro and the South Slav parts of Austria-Hungary, it was obvious that Bosnian Muslims were something more than just a regional appellation, and more than just a religious group. But the Serbs, especially after their struggle on the side of the Allies in the Great War, tended to regard the new kingdom as an extension of Serbia and organized it in a centralist manner. Non-Serbs, including Bosnian Muslims, were rightly dissatisfied.

Croatian resistance forced Belgrade in 1939 to give autonomy to Croatia, and Slovenia would most likely have been granted the same status had the Second World War not engulfed Yugoslavia. No autonomy, however, was envisaged for Bosnia. Serbs considered it simply a Serbian land. They pointed out that in May 1915, the Allies had offered the whole of Bosnia to Serbia, and that Serbs were the largest group there (an indisputable fact at that time). But they also based their demands on the fallacious and immoral claim that Muslims were simply Serbs who had not yet been awakened to the fact.

Serbs thought the case of Bosnia was closed. But the majority of Muslims felt no allegiance to the Serbian-dominated Yugoslav state. Although there was no official state religion, and Islam was respected, they felt the Serbian Orthodox Church was much closer to the authorities than their religious leaders could ever be. Muslims therefore tried to improve their lot by making deals with different royal Cabinets in Belgrade. In addition, they supported Belgrade policies detrimental to other non-Serb groups, in particular to Croats.

When Yugoslavia was occupied by Germany, Italy, and their allies in 1941, Bosnia became a part of the newly formed fascist Croatia. Ustashas, a kind of Croatian S.S., began massacres of Serbs, Jews, and Gypsies. Although their crimes were horrendous, Ustashas were a minority movement in Croatia. Many Croats also volunteered for the Partisans, the Communist-led resistance movement, and fought in it together with Serbs, who responded to the massacres with a mass uprising.

In Bosnia, however, where the tradition of Catholic-Orthodox conflict was centuries old, Croats joined the Ustashas in much larger numbers than in Croatia proper, and only a few supported the Partisans. The Croatian fascist government proclaimed the Bosnian Muslims "the flower of the Croatian nation" and tried to recruit them into its units. Indeed, at the beginning of the war Muslims in some regions joined the Ustashas in pogroms of Serbs. But in general they did not identify with the Croatian state. The majority remained passive through most of the war.

The creation of a Bosnian Muslim S.S. division is a favorite theme of Serbian propaganda, however. Indeed, there was such a unit. The Nazis asked the Grand Mufti of Jerusalem, el Husseini, to lend his support to the project. He accepted, visited Bosnia, and convinced some important Muslim leaders that a Muslim S.S. division would be in the interest of Islam. In spite of these and other propaganda efforts, only half of the expected 20,000 to 25,000 Muslims volunteered. The S.S. unit was nonetheless formed, named the "Handzar" (scimitar) division, and was brutal in the "cleansing" of Serbian regions in eastern Bosnia. But it never achieved the reputation of a good fighting unit, and failed to sell the idea of a Muslim Bosnia under a Nazi protectorate.

During the Second World War, the Communist leadership of the Partisan movement decided postwar Yugoslavia should be a federation. Initially, it did not envisage Bosnia as being, together with Serbia, Croatia, Slovenia, Macedonia, and Montenegro, one of the component republics. But Croats and Serbs were so intermixed in Bosnia that it could not be divided between Croatia and Serbia. The Communists therefore planned to make Bosnia into an autonomous unit, but to link it closely to Serbia, since Serbs were its largest group. The Muslims were expected in the future to develop freely their national identity—some Serbian, others Croatian.

But the extremely bloody wartime struggle between Croatian and Serbian nationalists in Bosnia influenced the Communists to change their minds and proclaim toward the end of the war that Bosnia should be the sixth republic of Yugoslavia. This decision promised to put an end to the rivalry between Serbia and Croatia over Bosnia and provided Muslims with a federal unit with which they could easily identify. The Communists intended for all six republics to stay forever in Yugoslavia and severely punished secessionists. The separation of Bosnia was considered unthinkable, since Bosnia was in the center of Yugoslavia, its population was the most intermixed, and it had no state traditions.

Serbia's losses in the Second World War and the Croatian fascist genocide are the central theme of contemporary Serbian nationalism. One million Yugoslavs lost their lives. Bosnia suffered most. Of its 2.8 million people, 400,000 perished—every sixth Serb, eighth Croat, and twelfth Muslim. The much larger Serbian losses contributed to making Muslims the most numerous group in Bosnia.

Like all nationalists of former Yugoslavia, the Serbians exaggerate their losses, sometimes claiming that more than 1 million Serbs were murdered in concentration camps of fascist Croatia alone. (Realistic estimates put the total of Serbian casualties between 500,000 and 600,000. Probably half were civilian victims of Croatian fascism.) Serbian nationalists are, however, right when they point out that Serbian casualties were both absolutely and relatively larger than those of any other Yugoslav group, and that only Serbs, Jews, and Gypsies were the victims of systematic and planned extermination. But Croatian and Muslim casualties were extremely high as well, and a considerable number of them were civilians who fell victim to Serbian extremists.

After 1945 Yugoslavia became a Communist dictatorship. Communist rule in backward and war-ravaged Bosnia was harsher than in the rest of Yugoslavia: the police were more brutal, prison sentences longer, the economy more "planned," intolerance in public life and culture greater. But Bosnian Communists, closely supervised by Belgrade, also prevented the domination of one group over others and kept education and economic resources accessible to all groups. And like Communists elsewhere in Yugoslavia, they encouraged individual national cultural traditions as long as these did not challenge Communist dogma.

Reports from today's war-torn Bosnia often say different nationalities have peacefully co-existed there for centuries. But Bosnia's history shows that although all three main groups have traditions of tolerance, extremists dominated in unstable periods. Tolerance, such as there was, was often the result of rule by a foreign power, which forcefully prevented groups from fighting each other.

And Bosnia, of course, was ruled by a foreign power from the fifteenth century until its secession from Yugoslavia in March of this year [1992]. Even Communist rule was in a sense foreign, since the Bosnian Party was merely a subordinate section of the larger Yugoslav Party. So Bosnia's own internal resources for finding solutions to religious and ethnic diversity never had a chance to develop fully.

Communist repression was sufficient to overcome separatism and nationalist extremism. But the Communists failed to achieve lasting results in propagating Yugoslav unity. The memory of the Partisan struggle, "the building of socialism," workers' self-management, the cult of Tito, even Tito's non-aligned foreign policy—all these were propagated at some time by Yugoslav Communists as common rallying points for all national groups. But the groups remained unconvinced.

And because under communism the spirit of critical, rational inquiry could not develop, the nations of Yugoslavia failed to free themselves from pseudoromantic images of themselves and negative stereotypes of each other. The dominant form of political consciousness beneath the veneer of Yugoslav Marxism remained mythologizing ethnocentrism that could envisage full rights only for members of one's own group.

In 1990 all six republics of Yugoslavia held free multiparty elections. Bosnia voted in November. For the first time in history the destiny of Bosnia was in Bosnian hands. All those in Yugoslavia who still desired a peaceful solution to the crisis hoped the majority would vote for political parties that included members of all three groups and addressed themselves to all Bosnians. But they were painfully disappointed. Loyalty to one's nation proved stronger than all other loyalties. The large majority of Muslims voted for the Muslim party, the large majority of Serbs for the Serbian party, and the large majority of Croats for the Croatian party.

Alija Izetbegovic, the Muslim leader, won the most votes, since the Muslims are the most numerous group. He then became president. A coalition government was formed, but it was soon obvious that the three national parties not only had mutually exclusive programs, but that they actually represented incompatible national ideologies that could not be modified through political compromises. It was only a matter of time before irreconcilable differences in the government would be transformed into civil war.

Muslims imagined Bosnia as an independent state in which they should predominate. Although it was only Muslim extremists who thought non-Muslims should be expelled from Bosnia, most Muslim leaders believed only a Muslim should be allowed full citizenship. Religious Muslims based their demand for supremacy on the traditional belief that the rule of non-Muslims over Muslims was blasphemous. But most Muslims were typical nationalists. They wanted more for their group because, like Serbs and Croats, they believed the history and culture of their group were superior.

The Serbs, for their part, wanted Bosnia to stay inside Yugoslavia and increasingly demanded a Yugoslavia dominated by Serbs. When Slovenia and Croatia seceded in June 1991, the rump resembled greater Serbia, and the threat of Serbian predominance over Bosnia became real. When the Muslims demanded Bosnia's independence, the Serbs demanded "cantonization" of Bosnia. But their views about the size of this Serbian canton, and its degree of independence in relation to the Sarajevo government, were megalomaniacal.

The Croats for a while worked hand in hand with Muslims, both in the government in Sarajevo and at the local level. But no one was surprised when this anti-Serbian coalition turned out to be temporary. It ultimately played into Serbian hands, helping their propagandistic claim that a wartime Ustasha-Muslim cooperation had re-emerged. The coalition did not increase Croatian loyalty to Bosnia.

The Croatian maximal fantasy was to incorporate the whole of Bosnia. There were also more modest hopes that fear of the Serbs would move Muslims to demand a federal arrangement between Bosnia and Croatia. More realistically, Croats planned to take those territories of Bosnia with a Croatian majority and integrate them into Croatia. They secretly, and not-so-secretly, held talks with Serbs about dividing up Bosnia. Both Franjo Tudjman, the president of Croatia, and Slobodan Milosevic, the president of Serbia, supported such plans. And so did many other influential political and intellectual figures in Croatia and Serbia.

For all their divisiveness, Bosnian Serbs and Croats should not be blamed for their refusal to adopt "Bosnian" nationality either under Austria-Hungary or today. But they must be censured for denying the individuality of Bosnian Muslims. Since the war started, Croatian military units from Bosnia and military units from Croatia proper (including the regular troops of the Croatian army) have conquered a third of Bosnian territory. On this territory they have engaged in "ethnic cleansing." Serbs were forced to leave and Muslims either left or were reduced to second-class citizens. Although the Western press mentions Croatian misdeeds, it is much more vocal about the Serbian ones. Indeed, these are greater. Better-armed Bosnian Serbs have captured almost two-thirds of Bosnia. They have also expelled and imprisoned more people than the Croats, and many more than the Muslims.

What, then, can be done? The most attractive idea is that all refugees should return to the places they came from. But in Bosnia the return would mean mixing the three groups again. The intensity of present hatred among them is such that remixing could be achieved only if a foreign power sent several hundred thousand soldiers to police every village and valley in perpetuity.

Although refugees from all three groups deserve equal sympathy, the Muslim situation is particularly tragic. Serbian and Croatian refugees have Serbia and Croatia as well as parts of Bosnia under their control, where they can be safe. But where can Muslims go? Their forces control perhaps as little as 5 percent of Bosnia. The macabre joke from a few years ago that the Muslims would be the losers in the war between Serbs and Croats has turned out to have been a prophecy.

Izetbegovic still hopes to solve the Muslim problem by dragging the West into a war against the Serbs (and perhaps also Croats), and placing the whole of Bosnia under Muslim rule. This is unrealistic. If it really wants to help, the West should focus its energies on creating a large area in central Bosnia, where Muslim concentration has always been the greatest, and make it a safe haven for Muslim refugees. This territory should be under the Muslim government in Sarajevo. It could then become a separate state, or join with the Serbian and Croatian parts to create a Bosnian federation.

A new Berlin Congress is needed. Its main task should be to put pressure on Bosnian Serbs and Croats to give Muslims some of the territories they now control. The governments of Serbia and Croatia should also be pressured, because they have considerable influence over their Bosnian counterparts. The West has sufficient diplomatic and economic means at its disposal to make this happen. And it is much more likely that the Serbs and Croats will give some territory to Muslims than that they will ever be coerced—as the West seems to be attempting to do at the moment—into laying down their arms and accepting the restoration of a unified Bosnia. For them this would mean subjugation under Muslim rule.

The creation of a Muslim unit as a solution for Bosnia's crisis means the acceptance that Bosnia's exotic mixture of cultures and religions will not be restored. This severely challenges some of the basic notions of modern humanism. But given Bosnia's tragic history, it might be the only way toward stable peace.

(SEPTEMBER 21, 1992)

A House Divided

ALEKSA DJILAS

In the late 1980s, just before the disintegration of Yugoslavia began, the country's international position was unprecedentedly good. Never since its creation in 1918 from the kingdoms of Serbia and Montenegro and the South

Slav provinces of Austria-Hungary had it had fewer enemies and more friends. Separatists within its national groups had no significant support from abroad, and the major powers—the United States, the Soviet Union, Western Europe, China—as well as the overwhelming majority of Third World countries, wanted Yugoslavia to continue as one country. It was generally expected to be the first Eastern European country admitted into the European Community.

In 1990 the six republics of Yugoslavia held free elections in which Yugoslav communism was completely defeated. Although the Communist parties (with suitably altered names) won the elections in Serbia and Montenegro, the political system that they were fashioning was, for better or worse, as different from Titoist communism as the systems that the victorious anti-Communists were set to create in Slovenia, Croatia, Bosnia-Herzegovina, and Macedonia.

The Communists, led by Josip Broz Tito, a Croat, had come to power in Yugoslavia at the end of the Second World War, after fighting valiantly against the Nazi German and Fascist Italian occupiers of Yugoslavia. After the war they succeeded in reuniting the various national groups, and they defied Stalin's attempt in 1948 to subjugate Yugoslavia. They also created a political and economic system that was more open and moderate than the Eastern European ones. By 1990, however, the majority of Yugoslavs correctly regarded the system as oppressive, corrupt and incapable of solving any of the country's problems: economic decline and rising unemployment, crises in the relations among national groups, discontentment among intellectuals.

The rejection of communism in the elections was accompanied by a reaffirmation of nationalism. Nationalist parties won the elections in all the republics, and nationalism had been the central political platform of almost all the losing parties as well. The prevalence of nationalism inevitably led to tensions and violent clashes, in particular between the Croats and Serbs, the two largest groups. (In the summer of 1990 there had already been exchanges of fire between Croatian forces and Serbian irregulars, who were struggling for control of Serbian regions of Croatia.) Croats and Serbs had a long and bitter tradition of conflict, but they had also often cooperated in the past; for centuries they had lived mixed together in many parts of Croatia, Bosnia-Herzegovina and Serbia's northern province of Vojvodina. But the coexistence of the past was soon forgotten in the nationalist fervor that overwhelmed the country.

This essay is a review of the following books: Mark Thompson, *A Paper House: The Ending of Yugoslavia* (New York: Pantheon, 1992); Misha Glenny, *The Fall of Yugoslavia: The Third Balkan War* (New York: Penguin, 1992); and Alex N. Dragnich, *Serbs and Croats: The Struggle in Yugoslavia* (New York: Harcourt Brace Jovanovich, 1992).

• • •

Under Communist rule, and frequently in opposition to it, a powerful common culture that was genuinely Yugoslav had developed. Still, many inside and outside the country were not surprised by the electoral triumph of nationalism. Yugoslav communism had not persecuted any one national group, and it had repressed all open expressions of nationalism, but it could not truly enlighten people and teach them to think rationally and critically about their past. There was little to counteract the tendency of the Yugoslav groups to forget their ethnic and linguistic similarities, to say nothing of the much more dangerous tendency to overemphasize differences in their religious and their historical traditions, drawing on pseudoromantic, self-aggrandizing myths about themselves and negative stereotypes about the others.

After the elections in 1990, it became obvious that the Slovene nation wanted to split from Yugoslavia. So did the Croats, who hoped to take at least a part of Bosnia-Herzegovina with them. Separatist sentiments also ruled the hearts of Macedonians and Bosnian Muslims, but for a while they felt too weak to make any open demands. Serbs (along with Montenegrins, who regard themselves as closely related to Serbs) wanted to keep Yugoslavia united, but only if the others would accept Serbian predominance; and if not, then the Serbs wanted to secede as well, but not without taking with them the parts of Croatia and Bosnia-Herzegovina containing substantial numbers of Serbs. Under Communist rule no independent institutions—no assemblies or judicial bodies—had been created that could mediate between the national groups once disagreements among them arose. Thus the stage was set for a civil war.

The cover of Mark Thompson's book shows a large building on fire, presumably somewhere in war-torn former Yugoslavia, but his account will disappoint those looking for reportage or analysis of the civil war. Thompson seems to have left the country before serious fighting had started: the main characters of the Yugoslav tragedy never appear in his account. Instead he offers antebellum conversations with mostly marginal intellectual and political figures, and his ruminations about the history and the character of the various Yugoslav groups are based exclusively on well-known books in English. Occasionally he makes an astute remark—"I watched Serbia destroy Yugoslavia in the name of Yugoslavia, while storing up disaster for itself, in the name of its own future"—but most of what he says is not new.

For an account of what has actually happened during the Yugoslav conflict, Misha Glenny's book so far stands unparalleled. Between the spring of 1991 and the spring of 1992, Glenny, who speaks Serbo-Croatian, made a number of journeys through what used to be Yugoslavia for the BBC. He talked to important political leaders and visited all the major battlefields, often at great risk. His courage (which he modestly downplays) was well rewarded: his book is vigorous, passionate, humane, and extremely readable. It is also fair and objective, a rare virtue in Western writing about this war.

In June 1991 the Slovenes announced that they had seceded and took control of Slovenia's borders with Italy, Austria, and Hungary, which were also Yugoslavia's internationally recognized borders. The Yugoslav army (acting on orders from the federal government, which in turn seems to have had the approval of the United States) made a feeble attempt to regain control but was attacked by the units of Slovenian territorial defense. No major conflict ensued. Slovenes won easily, and the army withdrew quickly. The army, increasingly dominated by Serbian nationalists, was simply not very interested in Slovenia, which did not have a Serbian minority.

Croatia was a different story. Since the ascent to power in May 1990 of an intransigent nationalist party led by the former Communist general Franjo Tudjman, Croatia's Serbian minority had been severely persecuted. Glenny is one of the rare Western journalists who has shown an interest in the predicament of the Serbs in Croatia:

> Even before the war began, the government [of Croatia] was concerned to hush up nationalist-motivated crimes against its Serb population while when applying for [international] recognition, its police and soldiers were involved in the slaughter of innocent Serbs in Gospić, Ogulin, Sisak, Karlovac, Daruvar, Virovitice, Zagreb and elsewhere. . . . These urban Serbs were among the greatest victims of the war, whose plight, however, is one of the least well known. Tens of thousands were hounded from their homes in the big cities either through direct intimidation, expulsion or through the pervasive climate of fear.

This treatment of Croatia's Serbian minority played perfectly into the aggressive plans of Serbian nationalists led by Slobodan Milosevic, the president of Serbia. They could portray contemporary Croatia as a reincarnation of the fascist state of the Second World War that massacred between 200,000 and 300,000 Serbian civilians, as well as many thousands of Jews and Gypsies. (Actually Serbian nationalists characteristically exaggerate the number of Serbs killed, claiming 1 million or more.) The Serbs' own expansionist ambitions could thus be portrayed as a noble struggle to help their persecuted brethren.

•   •   •

After many months of sporadic fighting, the war proper began in Croatia in the summer of 1991, soon after Croatia's formal secession, and reached its greatest intensity that autumn. By the beginning of 1992, fighting had almost completely halted, leaving some 10,000 dead (two-thirds of them Serbian) and many towns destroyed (most of them with Croatian majorities). The Serbs had captured one-quarter of the Croatian territories, mostly those regions in which they were a majority before the fighting had started. Although these territories are formally still part of Croatia, and the United Nations troops are now keeping the peace there, the local administration and police are completely in Serbian hands. The horrors of war and Serbian pressure forced perhaps as many as 200,000 Croats to leave. Similar numbers of Serbs left parts of Croatia under Croatian control.

The Serbian authorities in the Serbian-controlled territories of Croatia are successfully obstructing the efforts of the U.N. peacekeepers to allow the return of the Croats who have left. In their place, they are, in cooperation with the Milosevic government of Serbia, bringing in Serbs who had left other parts of Croatia. Once these Serbs are settled, it is unlikely that they will ever give the land back to the Croats, since they themselves cannot return to those parts of Croatia that they had to flee. But even if the Croatian government were to encourage the Serbs to return, the majority would be reluctant to go back unless the anti-Serbian atmosphere in Croatia were to change, which is an unlikely prospect anytime soon.

After failing to achieve unity in a common Yugoslav state, or tolerance toward each other in separate national states, Croats and Serbs seem determined to separate once and for all. Since the second half of the nineteenth century, Croatian nationalists have considered acquiring independence ("sovereignty") their first priority, and national homogeneity (that is, the suppression or the expulsion of minorities, in particular the Serbs) their second. Territorial demands have come only third. Croatia is now an independent country, internationally recognized, and since May 1991 it has been a member of the U.N. It has only an insignificant number of Serbs still within its frontiers, so only the reconquest of Croatia's territories controlled by Serbs remains to be accomplished.

The Croatian government may not be ready to risk very much for the completion of this traditionally less important task. Of course Tudjman will never formally recognize Serbian rule over any part of Croatia: if he did, the opposition would instantly accuse him of treason. But fearing the censure of the West and a boycott (which has already been threatened), he may abstain from starting a military offensive against Serbian-controlled territories. Moreover, Croatia is economically exhausted, and if the war drew in Serbia and Montenegro, it would be outgunned and outnumbered, too.

The sensible and fair solution to the problem of the Serbian-held territories of Croatia would be for Serbs to allow these regions to be reincorporated into Croatia, and for Croats to grant the Serbs considerable autonomy in them. But the mood of intransigent nationalism that now rules both groups makes such a settlement very unlikely. Even if it were reached, as a result of Western pressure on both sides, it is still unlikely that the Croatian and Serbian populations would mix again. There has been too much hatred, too much mistrust.

In Bosnia-Herzegovina the separation of Croats and Serbs is almost complete. This was not some unintended consequence of the war that is being fought in this former republic of Yugoslavia; it was one of the main reasons the Croats and the Serbs started the war in the first place. In the referendum of February 29–March 1, 1992, the Croats voted together with the Muslims for the secession of Bosnia-Herzegovina from Yugoslavia (from which Slovenia and Croatia had already seceded), while the Serbs, who were opposed to secession, boycotted the referendum. The Croats shared with the Muslims only the desire to separate from Yugoslavia. They did not wish to stay inside Bosnia-Herzegovina once it became independent, but, like the Serbs, wanted out of it. Their aspirations enjoyed the full support of Tudjman's government, which long before the referendum had openly declared the borders between Croatia and Bosnia-Herzegovina to be invalid. Croats from western Herzegovina, a region that during the Second World War contributed some of the most fervent fighters and leaders to the fascist Croatian state, were particularly determined to secede.

In April 1992, just a month after the Bosnian referendum, the European Community and the United States recognized Bosnia-Herzegovina's independence. (The United States also recognized Croatia and Slovenia, both of which had already been recognized by the European Community in January.) By means of such recognition, the Europeans and the Americans intended to give an international guarantee to the borders of Bosnia-Herzegovina, and in this way to prevent the Croats and the Serbs within them from seceding. They failed to understand that, in the absence of a constitutional reorganization of Bosnia-Herzegovina that would be acceptable to Croats and Serbs, and in the absence of a broad-minded policy on the part of the predominately Muslim government of Bosnia-Herzegovina, recognition would inevitably produce war.

The fighting started immediately, and from the beginning the main strategy of the paramilitary formations of each of the three groups was the mass expulsion ("ethnic cleansing") of the members of the other two groups. Much has been made in the Western media of the multiethnic character of Sarajevo's defenders, but they have always consisted mostly of Muslims, and as the fighting has continued the number of Croats and Serbs among them has dwindled to insignificance. Although Sarajevo had some tradition of tolerance, it could not succeed where both Yugoslavia and Bosnia-Herzegovina had previously failed; it could not preserve its multinational unity against that seemingly irresistible historical force that makes one's national group the primary focus of loyalty. The greatest victims of "ethnic cleansing" have been the Muslims, who by now have perhaps as many as 1 million refugees, and the greatest victimizers were the Serbs, whose conduct encountered particularly strong condemnation from the international community. (Glenny rightly devotes considerable attention to the "barbaric behavior of the Serb paramilitary organizations who committed crime after crime against civilians.") Serbs now control almost two-thirds, and Croats one-third, of Bosnia-Herzegovina. The remainder is still under the control of the Muslim government in Sarajevo.

Croats and Serbs continue to fight fiercely with each other in some regions of Bosnia-Herzegovina, but they have not engaged in large battles for quite some time. There is clearly a general agreement between them about the lines along which Bosnia-Herzegovina should be partitioned. And the majority of ordinary Croats and Serbs in Bosnia-Herzegovina seem to have accepted with fatalism that they will be expelled from the territories that the other group controls. The Muslims are left with hardly any territory by the present Croatian-Serbian division. If territories conquered by Croats and Serbs are not returned to Muslims, and a sizable Muslim political unit is not created, the Muslims will be a people without a homeland.

The inability of Yugoslavs, particularly of Croats and Serbs, to find a peaceful and civilized way to live together or to separate has puzzled Western politicians, journalists, and scholars since the creation of Yugoslavia in 1918. In his new book, Alex N. Dragnich, an American scholar of Serbian origin, sets himself the task of correcting "errors of fact" and "highly misleading interpretations" about Yugoslavia's past that have in his view influenced the reporting by the American press of the 1991–92 civil war. His other goal, this one less explicit, is to defend the Serbian side in past and present conflicts.

Dragnich is not a belligerent Serb. By the standard of the many books, journals, and newspapers published in Belgrade during the last few years, his book is moderate. Yet he is far from fair in his distribution of blame for the nationalist conflicts. His version of history, though it purports to portray a workable path toward unity that was misguidedly abandoned, in fact reveals just how heavily the past weighs on any efforts to chart a course for the future. Dragnich focuses on King Aleksandar of Yugoslavia as the great reconciler, but his portrait is too simple and generous. Aleksandar was not, as Dragnich claims, a constitutional monarch even during the 1918–29 period of parliamentary rule. He had many prerogatives, and the Serbs, the most numerous Yugoslav group and the one from which Aleksandar's Karadjordjevic dynasty came, never trusted a fully sovereign Parliament. The soldier-king's suspension of Parliament in 1929, and his introduction of a new constitution in 1931 (which made him the center of political power), represented the completion of his long struggle to enlarge and to consolidate his authority; they were not temporary aberrations forced onto this supposedly democratically-minded Serb and "sincere Yugoslav."

Many Serbs shared Aleksandar's contempt for Yugoslav parliamentary politics and supported his 1929–34 personal rule, believing that it would achieve the national unity that had been endangered by the incessant quarrels and fights between Serbian and Croatian deputies. Aleksandar embraced the ideology of Yugoslav unity known as "Yugoslavism": he was the one who in 1929 had changed the country's name from the "Kingdom of the Serbs, Croats and Slovenes" to Yugoslavia. But he robbed Yugoslavism of its liberal democratic essence.

As envisioned by the leading Croatian and Serbian intellectual and political figures in the nineteenth and early twentieth centuries, Yugoslavism was an enlightened and voluntary agreement to transcend the narrow confines of individual South Slav religious and historical traditions (in particular Catholic Croatian, Orthodox Serbian and Muslim) in the name of a larger Yugoslav unity upheld by free political institutions. This Yugoslavism was not only the most noble and high-minded solution to the South Slav national question, it was also the most sensible solution, given that the different groups were mixed together and that Croatian and Serbian national ideologies often demanded the same territories (for example, Bosnia-Herzegovina), which inevitably led to conflict.

It is true that Aleksandar's rule was not particularly harsh by the standards of interwar Europe, where all the countries in the south, center, and east (except Switzerland and Czechoslovakia) were either dictatorships or on their way to dictatorship. Mussolini called the king "a disgrace to all us dictators." But this does not alter the fact that in promoting Yugoslavism through personal rule, increased centralism, arrests of political leaders, special courts for political offenses, censorship, and much police brutality (including regular torture for Communists and militant nationalists), Aleksandar was alienating the non-Serbian groups. They might have resented Aleksandar's dictatorship less had he not relied so much on Serbian political, military, diplomatic, and administrative elites. Croats in particular saw dictatorial royal Yugoslavism as promoting Serbian interests, and reacted with separatist demands.

• • •

The failure of interwar Yugoslavism to create genuine unity caused deep divisions among the Serbs about what course the Serbian nation should take. Some important figures were inclined toward compromises with non-Serbs and the transformation of the country into a federation. Many more came to believe in a Serbian state, encompassing all those lands in which Serbs were the majority or which they considered historically theirs. This was a resurrection of the idea of Greater Serbia that had arisen among the Serbs in the nineteenth century, at a time when similar ideas were thriving in most other parts of Europe: Germans wanted an enlarged Reich, Poles dreamed of Poland stretching all the way to the Black Sea, the Greeks had their "Megali [great] idea," Hungarians, Bulgarians, and Croats wanted respectively Greater Hungary, Greater Bulgaria, and Greater Croatia.

Such ambitions for territorial expansion, megalomaniacal though they were, usually did not entail demands for the expulsion of minorities. But the more these states expanded, the more precarious the position of minorities became. The establishment of federalism would have assured equality of minority groups, and it might have made them loyal to the states in which they had suddenly found themselves. But national ideologies in central, eastern, and southern Europe (again aside from the Swiss) never accepted this principle. Nationalists were too distrustful of neighbors to allow the devolution of central power. Federalism was therefore regarded as weakening the state structure, and demands for it were often treated as treason.

In Yugoslavia, federalism was imposed after the Second World War by the victorious Communists, and it became an efficient barrier to the hegemony of any nation over others, as well as a framework in which particular national traditions could be preserved. But national ideologies, in particular the Croatian and Serbian ones, never accepted federalism. Many Serbs dreamed of a centralized, Serbian-dominated Yugoslavia or of a centralized Greater Serbia, while many Croats hoped for an independent, enlarged, and centralized Croatia. Since Communist power would not allow the realization of such ambitions, national ideologies moderated themselves for tactical reasons, and demanded only greater autonomy from the federal center in Belgrade.

In the late 1960s and early 1970s, the Communists adapted themselves to the demands of national ideologies and gave more and more power to the six republics and the two autonomous provinces that composed Yugoslavia. This process, which became known as the "confederalization" of Yugoslavia, accelerated with Tito's death in 1980. But no state structure was loose enough for the nationalists who became dominant both inside and outside the Communist Party. They increasingly insisted on completely independent national

states. As Yugoslav unity began to crumble, Croats and Serbs went even further and demanded Greater Croatia and Greater Serbia. Immediately, the
specter of ethnic cleansing arose.

As Daniel Patrick Moynihan recently and rightly observed, "Of the next
fifty states which will come into being in the next fifty years, ethnic conflict will be almost the defining characteristic by which that process will take
place." Thus international organizations and the United States are confronted
with an immense task: the preparation of a blueprint for dealing with ethnic-
ity in Yugoslavia and elsewhere in the world. That will involve the establishment of new procedures regarding international law, and a new role for the
U.N., NATO, and the United States.

Above all, it will require a sober awareness of what cannot be achieved. In
our century more often than at any other time in history, ethnic groups have
been forced by other groups with which they once lived to flee their territories. They have hardly ever returned; and when they have, it is most often as
pitiless victors expelling those who once expelled them. A powerful external
force (for example, the United States) may prevent, by means of condemnation, embargoes, or the threat of air strikes, the most extreme forms of "ethnic cleansing," that is, those organized on a large scale and in a centralized
way. But there are many other ways in which a stronger group can "cleanse,"
and force a weaker one to leave: terror through unofficial paramilitary units;
discrimination at work and in school; hostile propaganda and incitement in
the media. All this can happen, and for the most part does happen, without
any overall plan or central control, so there is no government or central
authority that can be pressured to stop it.

Only direct and permanent military occupation can ensure that hostile
populations will peacefully coexist on the same territory. Until not so long ago,
most of the world was ruled by empires that forcefully prevented ethnic
groups from fighting with each other. Of course, no country in today's world
wants to create an empire. Too many soldiers' lives would have to be sacrificed
and too much money spent. And the idea of empire itself is now alien to most
people.

That leaves only the "solution" of partition, as equitable a partition as possible, once it becomes obvious that certain ethnic groups cannot coexist
peacefully any longer. Formulating such arrangements—a task that is likely to
fall to the U.N., NATO, and the United States—will not be easy. Determining
which part of the territory a particular group should get, and how large it
should be, requires taking into account not only the size of the population but

also economic, historical, strategic, and many other factors as well. As soon as the new borders are established, they should be internationally recognized, and any attempt to change them should be severely discouraged. In the coming decades, the formation of new states by means of ethnic conflict cannot be prevented, but at least it may be controlled and regulated. A house divided against itself cannot stand, and only rarely can it be reunited, but it can be transformed into separate and livable homes.

(JANUARY 25, 1993)

In Europe's Shadows

FOUAD AJAMI

I

The writer Ivo Andric, a Bosnian Croat born in 1892 in the town of Travnik and raised in the Latin Quarter of Sarajevo, knew success and fame. A beneficiary of Yugoslavia's special position during the years of the cold war, he was awarded the Nobel Prize for literature in 1961. All the requisite things were said about the man and his artistry and his vision. But one great theme that ran through so much of Andric's work went unmeditated upon: his great dread of Islam in the Balkans, his allergy to the four centuries of Ottoman rule in Bosnia.

The hostility was difficult to miss; it was everywhere in his fiction. And it had been directly taken up in a work of his youth, *The Development of Spiritual Life in Bosnia Under the Influence of Turkish Rule.* There, in full force, were so many of the great charges that Serb and Croat intellectuals would hurl against Ottoman rule and Slav converts to Islam:

The effect of Turkish rule in Bosnia was absolutely negative. The Turks could not even bring a cultural content or a higher economic mission to those southern Slavs who converted to Islam; for their Christian subjects their rule meant a coarsening of customs and a step back in all respects.

Bosnia lay at the crossroads of empires, Andric writes of the remote, backward territory, but Turkish rule robbed it of its place in the life of Europe, and brought about its cruel isolation:

> According to its geographical position, Bosnia should have been the connection between the countries along the Danube and the Adriatic Sea, i.e., Bosnia should at one time have connected two peripheries of the Serbo-Croatian elements with two zones of European culture. Having fallen to Islam it lost the possibility of fulfilling this, its natural, role and of participating in the cultural development of Christian Europe (to which it belonged through ethnographic and geographic features). Instead, Bosnia became a mighty fortress against the Christian West. Bosnia was to remain in this unnatural position for the remainder of Turkish rule.

A religion born in "a foreign climate and social order," a religion "resistant to change of any kind" had disfigured the life of Bosnia, Andric maintained. A native elite of southern Slavs acquiesced in this tale of ruin, and they did it to preserve their large estates: "Everybody who wanted to retain his property, the position associated with it, and all his privileges, had no choice but to convert to Islam." In this spectacle of endless desolation there stood out only the Franciscan monks, who kept alive an intellectual tradition, and broke the "fateful isolation of Bosnia" and worked with a "self-denial that bordered on martyrdom." The Franciscans managed to "preserve a lively literary activity which even though chiefly serving religious purposes, nonetheless represents the fruit of noble effort."

Sarajevo, a city of Ottoman Islam, had been home to Andric, but he saw only degradation and backwardness. And in a selective rendering of history so typical of nationalist tracts, the old pre-Ottoman past of Bosnia was made

---

This essay is a review of the following books: Noel Malcolm, *Bosnia: A Short History* (New York: New York University Press, 1994); Robert J. Donia and John V. A. Fine, Jr., *Bosnia and Hercegovina: A Tradition Betrayed* (New York: Columbia University Press, 1994); H. T. Norris, *Islam in the Balkans* (Columbia: University of South Carolina Press, 1994); Mark Pinson, ed., *The Muslims of Bosnia-Herzegovina* (Cambridge, Mass.: Harvard Center for Middle Eastern Studies, 1994); Alija A. Izetbegovic, *Islam Between East and West* (American Trust Publications, 1994); Dzevad Karahasan, *Sarajevo: Exodus of a City* (New York: Kodansha International, 1994); and Brian Hall, *The Impossible Country: A Journey Through the Last Days of Yugoslavia* (Boston: David Godine Publishers, 1994).

pretty and grand, a veritable Eden before the coming of the Turkish plague. Andric, of course, was a careful man. He was anxious to cover up his tracks. For, before the literary career and the Nobel Prize, he had been ambassador of (Royal) Yugoslavia to the Third Reich at the time of the signing of the Tripartite Pact; and he was there in Vienna in March 1941, when Yugoslavia capitulated and joined the Axis powers. As Ivo Banac, the noted historian of the Balkans, has observed, one can see, in the photographs of the signing, the "silhouette of Ivo Andric" alongside Ribbentrop and Cincar Markovic, the foreign minister of Yugoslavia.

Andric was allowed to put that past behind him. A reinvented Yugoslavia led by Tito (the last Habsburg, as A. J. P. Taylor called him) gave the South Slavs a reprieve, at a terrible price, from the wild calls of nationalism. Yet the phobias expressed by Andric went deep, and they survived the change of political regimes. The tide had long gone out on Islam in the Balkans. Muslims had remained in the lands of Yugoslavia, but they were marked men and women, caught in the cross-currents of Serbian and Croat nationalism.

In the eyes of their detractors, the survival of the Muslims was proof of cunning, yet another trick on history. "Muslims change their cap as the wind changes," a Croat tells Brian Hall in *The Impossible Country,* a fine book of reportage. It is the old stereotype, "the Yid with the thousand faces," as Hall writes. "The wily trader whose state was elsewhere and nowhere, whose God was Mammon, and who would melt away during dangerous times but would be right back after the war, owning the store when the famine struck." From the time that doctrines of nationalism and ideas of chosenness hit the Serbs (and, to a lesser extent, the Croats), Islam's people had seemed only like a lingering aftermath of the Ottoman incursion.

The Serb and Croat integralists could not concede the legitimacy of the Muslims. Whatever the Muslims were, they were not a national community. The Serbs were certain that the Muslims were "Serbs of the Muslim faith," whereas the Croats were equally sure that the Muslims were people of a "Croat coloration." After a mighty storm, a change of fortunes, a long campaign of terror, those lapsed Slavs would return to the faith, casting aside the religion of the Turks for their ancestral faith.

II

There is a Serb way of telling history. At its heart, of course, is the apocalypse at Kosovo, the great divide of 1389. There is only grandeur before it, there is only usurpation after it. In this history, the Serbs suffer earthly defeat, but they acquire a heavenly kingdom; the Turks are kept at bay and the Serbs keep themselves intact, put themselves beyond the conqueror's reach and the conqueror's embrace, refrain from collaborating with their infidel oppressors and wait for historical redemption. Fate had been cruel to Serbia: the capital city of Belgrade, the chroniclers say, was destroyed forty times; its holy lands in Kosovo were lost to the infidels, overwhelmed by the Albanians. Serbia had done sentry duty for Christendom, but its neighbors showed no appreciation. Devoted and pure and noble, the Serbs would win great campaigns after heart-breaking sacrifices only to be tricked and swindled by the Magyars and the Austrians and the Croats. Brian Hall, traveling among the Serbs in 1991, is exceptionally good at capturing this Serb sense of pride and betrayal at the hands of outside powers.

This history is an invention, spun out of vanity and a need for consolation. For fate meandered in the Balkans. And its meanderings can now be more clearly understood, and measured against some of the region's deadly myths, thanks to the appearance of outstanding works of research by the impassioned British journalist Noel Malcolm, the exacting American historians Robert Donia and John Fine, and the painstaking British historian H. T. Norris, and thanks to a splendid collection of essays edited by Mark Pinson. The real history of Bosnia can now be retrieved and told.

The old order that the Turks overran in the Balkans had all but collapsed of its own weight, and the region had been brought to ruin by peasant revolts. The peninsula was divided among Greeks, Bulgars, Serbs, Albanians, Venetians, Genoese, all people at odds with one another. The Turkish conquests were swift: Athens in 1456, Bosnia in 1462–66, Hercegovina 1481. The Pax Turcica created "structures of collaboration," in the words of Fernand Braudel. In return for tribute and obedience, the subject peoples were left to lead the lives they had known. There was no great missionary impulse in the Turkish incursions, no overwhelming urge akin to the spirit that Spain brought with it to the new world, to extirpate old ways. On the margins, life improved for the peasantry, for they were given a break from forced labor. The Serbs, like others around them, made their accommodation with the new order of things.

The Serbs love the legend of themselves standing at the ramparts defending Christendom. But the truth is much less simple. After Kosovo, Serbs fought Hungarians, and they fought on behalf of the Turks as their vassals and allies in intermittent campaigns that stretched nearly two centuries. Serbs made their way into the Ottoman court and imperial army, and found a niche for themselves in the polyglot Ottoman world. A report from the final years of the sixteenth century, cited by Malcolm, tells us that Slavonic was the third language of the empire after Turkish and Arabic, that the Sultan's court was full of renegade Slavs.

The Ottoman order, after all, was remarkably decentralized. Its basic social unit was the *millet,* or community, which was defined along religious lines. The *millets* were self-governing entities left to their own laws and their own leaders. In this scheme of things, the Orthodox Church thrived. The Papacy had been the great enemy of the Ottoman; the Ottomans thus showed favor toward Orthodoxy. As John Fine puts it, "the Patriarch lived in the Ottoman capital where he was easily controlled. The Pope lived in Rome, outside the empire, and was the main source of crusades against the Ottomans." Catholicism was the faith of Austria, and Austria was the Ottoman Empire's great enemy. Orthodoxy, by contrast, was easy to co-opt, and to work with. Where Franciscan monasteries suffered, and the Catholics were denied permission to repair old churches or to build new ones, Orthodoxy prospered.

Indeed, the demographic edge that the Serbs today enjoy in Bosnia relative to the Catholic Croats (Bosnia entered its current troubles with a population that was 43 percent Muslim, 31 percent Serb and 17 percent Croat) was a gift of the Ottoman conquest. Malcolm tells us that a Metropolitan (Orthodox) bishop in Bosnia is first mentioned in 1532, that the first Orthodox Church in Sarajevo was built in the mid-sixteenth century. There had been a scant Orthodox presence in Bosnia before the Turks, for the Franciscans had the upper hand. Orthodoxy had been present only in Hercegovina, among the nobility and the landholders; and even there the Franciscans had been making inroads and gaining converts from among the Orthodox. But the balance was to change with the advent of the Turks in Bosnia. It was the Orthodox Church that now gained new converts.

There was high religion and low religion. The world of the Balkans was a peasant world of superstition and folk belief. There was little, if any, literacy in the scripture. There was no priestly class of any status. Conversion was easy, and believers were often chameleons. Onto their new faith the converts grafted their old ways. What emerged, according to the historian Peter Sugar, was a "variety of European or rather Balkan folk-Islam, which tended to include baptism, icons to prevent mental illness and many other basically non-Muslim features." There were mountaineers who called themselves Constantin in front of Christians and Sulayman in front of Muslims. The dead would be given a service by the Orthodox Church and a subsequent burial in a Muslim cemetery. The religious boundaries were easily, and frequently, transgressed. And the guardians of the differing faiths knew the fickle ways of their flocks. "There was unspoken agreement," H. T. Norris writes in his superb book, "dictated by a common interest among priests, rabbis, educated imams and others to seek some common religious ground." A church favored by the authorities—as the Orthodox Church was favored by Ottoman rule—could prosper in such a fluid environment.

Bosnia in particular lacked a strong national church of its own. The Bosnian Church, an independent Catholic Church in schism with Rome, had no bishops of its own who lived within its territory. The Bishop of Bosnia lived in Slavonia. As Donia and Fine write, "many peasants probably rarely or never saw a priest, and peasants tend to be indifferent to formal religion if it is not pressed on them." Catholicism and Orthodoxy fared no better than the local Bosnian church. Thus Islam had little competition here. The Bosnians had never been fervent Christians.

Conversion, though, was only one explanation for the demographic growth of the Orthodox under Ottoman rule. Settlement, the migration of Serbs into Bosnia, was the other part of the story. With the Ottoman conquest there was large-scale migration of Catholics from Bosnia into Croatia and Dalmatia. Their vacant land, the research of Fine and Malcolm confirms, was settled by Muslim newcomers and by the Orthodox. Some of the Orthodox came into Bosnia proper from the poorer Hercegovina, others from the lands of Serbia. Good conquerors who were out for taxation and income, the Ottomans wanted the vacated land settled. The Orthodox were given their deal—the independent *millet,* a more advantageous taxation system than that of the Catholics—and they took it.

This, then, was the setting within which the Slavs who converted to Islam made their choice. They did it over a long period of time; and they did it while leaving much of their social life unaltered. In the towns of Bosnia, Islam found particularly fertile ground.

From its rise in Mecca and Medina in the seventh century, Islam had been a religion of towns and cities, a thoroughly urban culture of mosques and bazaars and *madrasahs* (religious schools). Bosnia was to be no exception. It was here, in the principal towns of Bosnia and Hercegovina, that Ottoman Islam spread its own brand of culture. Sarajevo was the child of this development. From a frontier mining town it grew into a major city of the empire, equal in rank and in size to Thessalonica and Edrine, eclipsed only by Istanbul itself. An enterprising governor named Isa Bey, a nearly legendary figure who came into Bosnia with the beginnings of the conquest and was governor from 1464 to 1468, gave Sarajevo its most precious monuments. It was to him that the city owed its governor's residence, its Emperor Mosque (*careva dzamija*), its public bath. A governor of a later period (1521–1541), Ghazi Husrev Bey, laid out its streets of crafts and trades, and its great mosque on the grounds of which he was buried. A folksong celebrated the generosity of the man:

> I built the seminary and the minaret.
> I built the clocktower and near it a mosque.

I built Taslihan and the cloth market.
I built three bridges in Sarajevo.
I turned a village into the town of Sarajevo.

Sarajevo was far away from the center of the Ottoman Empire in Istanbul. It was twice as far from Istanbul as from Vienna, four times further from Istanbul than from Belgrade. The Ottomans ruled, to be sure; but geography dictated that their rule would be indirect. Islam anchored the political life of the province, but this was not a Muslim state. The local urban elite of Sarajevo and the landed elite of smaller towns governed the mountainous territory. In the words of Ivo Banac, the Bosnian Muslims "identified with the Ottoman state but were always fully aware that they were not Anatolians." A class of local *kapetans* (force and garrison commanders) kept the peace, and also kept the Habsburgs at bay. It is true that Islam was accepted as the religion of the conquering state, but this was a rather cosmopolitan faith, and it gave a cosmopolitan cast to Bosnia's culture and to its institutions. Landlords converted and kept their prerogatives, merging their interests, as they were bound to, with those of the dominant faith.

The world of Ottoman Bosnia was a fragile world. Since it was relatively tolerant, it was relatively easy to bring down. Bandits, or *haiduks,* stalked this territory of impossible mountains through much of its history, their ballads alternating between expressions of anarchism and expressions of revenge against the rapacious infidels. The old *haiduks* were lambs compared with the breeds that modern nationalism would bring to the fore. When Balkan nationalism grew enraged in the nineteenth century, and the Pan-movements assaulted the ancien regime in that belt of mixed populations from the Baltic to the Adriatic, the half-hearted reforms that the Ottoman rulers were tinkering with in the 1850s and 1860s were overwhelmed. The Ottoman Empire had entered the "Concert of Europe" after Britain and France had come to her aid against Russia in the Crimean War in 1853. Europe now gained access to the Ottoman domain. The Christians of the Ottoman Empire came to enjoy the protection of the European powers. The juridical inequalities between Muslims and Christians were struck down, and political life grew increasingly secular. But the westernizing reforms did not work. They triggered a backlash among the conservative populations of the empire; what began as an effort to save the feeble realm speeded its demise. There is no need to prettify the old Ottoman world; it was pretty and vindictive, it had its countless cruelties and slights. But it was nothing like what was to come, nothing like the hell that ethnic hysteria would make out of the Balkans in the age of nationalism.

For the old live-and-let-live pluralism of the ancien regime, the purveyors of the new nationalisms substituted a more militant idea of the self. Where lines once meandered and broke down, the world was tidied up and made pure and whole. The new world and its emerging outline could be seen, and its shrillness could be heard, in the poetry of the new nationalism. Here is a Montenegrin monk and poet, the Prince of Montenegro, Petar II, Petrovic-Njegos, in bloodthirsty doggerel written as the nationalisms of the Balkans were gathering force (the reference to Milos Oblilic is to the Serbian knight who is said to have assassinated the Ottoman Sultan Murad I at Kosovo; the 'Id, literally a festival, refers to the principal Muslim holidays—the feast of sacrifice and the feast following the month of Ramadan).

> So tear down minarets and mosques,
> and kindle the Serbian yule logs,
> and let us paint our Easter eggs.
> Observe the two fasts honestly,
> and as for the remainder, do as you like.
> I swear to you by the creed of Milos Oblilic
> and by the trusty weapons that I carry,
> our faiths will be submerged in blood.
> The better of the two will rise redeemed.
> The 'Id can never live in peace
> with Christmas Day.

III

The old order came crashing down in the 1870s. The Ottomans were overextended and on the run; their ramshackle empire had declared its bankruptcy and gone into a kind of receivership, existing at the sufferance of the European balance of power. Peasant revolts in Bosnia and Bulgaria in 1875, revolts that began as class rebellions and turned into rampant slaughter and a religious fight between Muslim rulers and Christian serfs, blew up the feeble Ottoman system of control.

A quarter of a century earlier, in the Crimean War, Britain and France had gone to war on the side of Turkey against Russia. This time around, when the Balkan troubles sparked a Turko-Russian War, Britain had taken a more detached view of things. The conscience of Europe had been stirred by the slaughter. In Britain, a "human rights campaign" pitted the furious moralism of Gladstone against the cool realpolitik of Disraeli. Gladstone argued that the balance of power ought to be shredded and pushed aside: "We have been involved in moral complicity with the basest and blackest outrages upon record within the present century, if not within the memory of man." He had accepted the logic of empire in the Crimean War, but now he railed against the Turks for their "elaborate and refined cruelty," their "relentless fatalism," their "abominable and bestial lust," their "utter and violent lawlessness."

Many of Turkey's European possessions were severed in the diplomacy that followed the Russo-Turkish War. At the Congress of Berlin in 1878, Serbia, Romania, and Montenegro were granted full independence. Bulgaria was enlarged, and a part of it set up as a Russian satellite. Bosnia-Hercegovina, the poorest of the lot, was handed over to the Habsburgs. The Dual Monarchy had not wanted Bosnia, which meant more Slavs. Austria only wanted Bosnia denied to Serbia, the would-be Piedmont of the South Slavs. And so the move into Bosnia in 1878 was a defensive one.

The Muslims of Bosnia were now faced with the great wrenching question of living under alien rule. A debate unfolded about the permissibility of life under a Christian power. Thousands left, landholders and peasants. Perhaps as many as 150,000 Bosnian Muslims emigrated between 1878 and the end of Austrian rule in 1918. The majority ended up in Turkey. Thanks to the scholarship of Robert Donia and Mark Pinson, among others, it is easier to reconstruct that Austrian interlude. The Austrian rulers were to disappoint Bosnia's Christians. More than anything else, the Austrians were interested in order, in keeping the new nationalist ambitions in check. And so the prerogatives of the Muslim landlords were left largely intact, the communal life of the Muslims was undisturbed.

Benjamin Kallay, the shrewd Hungarian-born Finance Minister from 1882 to 1903, and the architect of Austria's Bosnia policy, set out to promote the notion of *bosnjostvo,* or Bosnianism, as a counter to the doctrines of Croat and Serb nationalism. A historian who knew the southern Slavs, a diplomat who had served as Austrian consul in Belgrade, Kallay was well acquainted with Serbia, with its grievances and its ambitions. His *Bosnjak* project, however, was doomed. It was an old, eighteenth-century answer, and it could not stand against the furies of nationalism. Malcolm has it right: "Had Kallay somehow been able to isolate Bosnia's Orthodox and Catholics utterly from the religious, cultural, and political developments in neighboring lands, his policy might have stood a chance, but such total isolation would have been quite impossible."

The Dual Monarchy introduced some industrialization into Bosnia, and a higher measure of literacy. The Bosnians were given, that is, the means of rebellion against their rulers. Austria formally annexed Bosnia in 1908, after the Young Turk rebellion in Istanbul, but it had no way of coping with its troubles: student unrest, peasant revolt, growing militancy among the Serbs. Some political liberalization was permitted, and political parties based in the three religious communities, networks of prosperous elites, made their appearance. But it was too late for this kind of benign politics of restriction. Secret societies seized with the romance of Pan-Serb unification (the Black Hand, Unification or Death), radical groups committed to Yugoslav (South Slav) unity, were a better reflection of what was to come. From this crucible emerged Gavrilo Princip, the Bosnian Serb assassin of Archduke Francis Ferdinand in Sarajevo on June 28, 1914. That date was the anniversary of the battle of Kosovo. At his trial Princip proclaimed, "I am a Yugoslav nationalist, aiming for the unification of all Yugoslavs, and I don't care what form of state, but it must be free from Austria." Princip had been educated and trained in Belgrade; it was there that he and his fellow conspirators acquired their bombs.

In the beginning, in Bosnia, there had been the great question of land ownership. It would never go away. It was more important than the deeds of young assassins. It was the land that had, presumably, led Muslim converts astray: for vines and apple trees they had forsaken the ways of their ancestors, and delivered themselves to the dreaded Turks. The land question was not only a material issue, it was also a great metaphor: the large Muslim estates versus the Serb *kmets* ("sharecroppers" is a better translation than "serfs"), the wily people who had given themselves over to the devil on one side versus the burdened peasants who clung to their ways, the parasitic towns living off the fat of the land (Sarajevo's image in Serb folklore) versus God's chosen but tormented people tilling the fields. It was easy work turning the land question into a hurricane of resentments.

The landowning class was a small one. On the eve of the First World War, as Donia and Fine tell us, the large Muslim landlords made up only 2 percent of the more than 600,000 Muslims of Bosnia, less than 1 percent of the total population. The great mass of the Muslims were "free peasants." Still, there was an intersection between land ownership and religious affiliation. Of the nearly 80,000 *kmets,* the overwhelming majority (about 75 percent) were Serbs, the rest were divided between the Croats (20 percent) and the Muslims. The *kmets* may not have been the serfs of medieval times, but they were a burdened lot. The courts of the land invariably preferred the propertied class. The religious separation, in sum, deepened the customary chasm between the landed class and the tillers of the land. Though peasant revolts had brought the Ottoman regime to an end, the peasantry was to be denied its revenge and its fulfillment. The first great disappointment had been handed down by the Dual Monarchy. Land reform and the breakup of large estates were anathema to the Magyar gentry of the empire, and that powerful class, with a disgruntled Slav peasantry of its own, was to prove a natural ally of the Muslim landholders.

• • •

The Muslim elites took the burden of the land question—the defense of property rights—into the successor state created in the aftermath of the war. The landed interests knew that such a narrow defense of prerogatives would not do: they would have to offer a broader appeal on behalf of all Muslims. But their politics was, inevitably, conservative, a rearguard action against grander causes. To the Kingdom of Serbs, Croats, and Slovenes—in 1919, it was renamed Yugoslavia—the Serbs and the Croats had brought far greater ambitions than the Muslims.

The Serbs in particular came with a heady sense of triumphalism. In their eyes, Yugoslavia was really "Serboslavia." And there was a handy legend to sustain them: defeated in 1915 by a joint German-Austrian-Bulgarian operation, the Serbian army had marched through Montenegro and Albania to the Adriatic, and crossed to Corfu to return at the end of the war. The retreat became an epic: the chosen nation overcoming adversity yet again. The new state was their gift and their redemption. "In Serbian eyes," Donia and Fine note, "Yugoslavia was the embodiment of Serbian centralism, ruled by the Serbian dynasty and led by Serbian army officers, bureaucrats, and parliamentarians." In the Serb fantasy, they would remake the others. The Croats and the Slovenes, "corrupted" by contact with the Habsburgs, would be rehabilitated, and the Bosnians, really lapsed Serbs, would be forced back into the fold. And one thing the Serbs were sure of was the disposition of the land. The estates of the Muslims, they promised, would be destroyed. In 1917, the Serbian government in exile had pledged five hectares of land to each combatant who would join their cause.

It is no wonder the Muslims of Bosnia viewed the collapse of the Dual Monarchy with ambivalence. Much as they would have wanted to identify with the new freedom—and many of them were devoted to the cause of South Slav unity—they knew that the new order would not be fully theirs. The unbridled enthusiasm of the Serbs for the new dispensation, and the attacks by Bosnian Serbs against Muslim estates and property, sobered the Muslims. In November 1918, Serb and Montenegrin soldiers entered Bosnia, and mayhem was the result. The leading Muslim cleric reported that 1,000 Muslim men were killed, 76 women were put to the torch, and some 270 villages were pillaged. The worst offenders, Noel Malcolm writes, were from Serbia proper, men who had not known Muslims or lived with them.

It was a nervous Muslim community that went into the Serb-dominated Kingdom of Serbs and Croats and Slovenes. But the Muslims were to become a swing force between Belgrade and Zagreb, the people in the middle between Serb centralism and the Croat project of a decentralized country. Led by astute politicians, they made the best of their situation. Luck threw on the scene a shrewd political leader named Mehmed Spaho, who dominated the politics of the Muslims' principal political instrument, the Yugoslav Muslim Organization. A son of the merchant class, Spaho identified himself as a Yugoslav. (One of his brothers identified himself as a Serb, and the other as a Croat.) He found a role for himself in the fractured parliamentary life of the inter-war years. He secured an alliance with the Croats as a balance to the power of the Serbs. He used the power of his political bloc to ease the burden of the land reforms on the Muslims. He obtained some financial compensation for lands that were distributed to the *kmets*. More important perhaps, Spaho and his Yugoslav Muslim Organization were able to retain the geographical and administrative identity of Bosnia in the new federal polity. The center of Muslim life held.

An interlude of royal dictatorship imposed in 1929 redrew the map of Yugoslavia, cutting across the old ethnic and national lines, strengthening Serb hegemony and denying Bosnia its old boundaries. This was a triumph for Serb extremists, who were tired, they said, of indulging "the Turks." But this administrative change did not stick. The Muslim community had become conscious of its own identity and weight, and the Croats were in full rebellion. The Serbs had the centralized polity they had wanted, but they could not hold it or reconcile the other communities to it. Ante Pavelic, a Croat zealot with ties to Mussolini's Italy, soon quit the country for its fascist neighbor to agitate for Croatian independence. He returned to head the notorious Ustasha regime in Croatia, which was set up under the protection of the Axis Powers after the Germans overran the country. Yugoslavia had tried to appease the Reich, and signed the pact in Vienna that Ivo Andric witnessed on March 25, 1941. But a rebellion in Belgrade against the accord had brought down on Yugoslavia the Führer's wrath. A campaign of massive bombing, and a swift ground attack of German, Italian, Bulgarian, and Hungarian forces, put an end to the old Yugoslav monarchy.

The Ustasha ideologists who ran the collaborationist Independent State of Croatia knew what to make of Bosnia's Muslims: they were Croats of the Islamic faith. As Ante Pavelic put it, the "Croat national consciousness never was extinguished in the Muslim element of Bosnia, and after the departure of the Turks has resurfaced." Croatian integralism borrowed a page from the book of its Serbian counterpart: the autonomy of Bosnia-Hercegovina was denied, its boundaries redrawn to subordinate it to the Croat project. Inflamed after years of frustration, Croatian chauvinism grew genocidal.

Nearly one-third of the population of the Croat regime (1.9 million out of

6.3 million) was Serb. It was time for the Yugoslav calamity to begin in earnest. The Ustasha would show the Serbs, the Jews, and the Gypsies no mercy. As for the Muslims: "for their part," writes Banac, "the Ustasha sought to implicate the Muslims in their anti-Serb violence." No group covered itself with glory in those years. The great terror of the Ustasha begat the terror of the Chetniks—the Serb irregulars named after the brigands who had defied Ottoman power in Serbia, Bosnia, and Macedonia. Some upper-class Muslims in Hercegovina and southeastern Bosnia were drawn into the ranks of the Ustasha and committed their share of the terror.

In the struggle of those years between Zagreb and Belgrade, the general tilt among the Bosnian Muslims was in favor of Zagreb; but the worldview of the Ustasha did not accommodate fine distinctions. It had no room for a Muslim role in the great Croatian undertaking. As early as the summer and autumn of 1941, the Muslim *ulama* of Sarajevo, Mostar, Banja Luka, and Tuzla issued resolutions condemning the theft of property, the forced conversion of Serbs to Catholicism, the rampant illegality. Of course, these resolutions would not stay the hands of the Chetniks. A Serb fury, particularly in Hercegovina, was let loose on the Muslims. Malcolm writes, summing up those terrible years:

> Altogether 75,000 Bosnian Muslims are thought to have died in the war: at 8.1 percent of their total population, this was a higher proportion than that suffered by the Serbs (7.3 percent), or by any other people except the Jews and the Gypsies. Muslims had fought on all sides—Ustasha, German, Chetnik, Partisan—and had been killed by all sides.

The program of the anti-fascist Partisans, led by Josip Broz (Tito), was perhaps the best outcome the Muslims could have hoped for. True enough, the former Austro-Hungarian corporal and labor organizer had attracted a disproportionate number of Serbs into his guerrilla bands. But this son of a Croat father and a Slovene mother, born in Kumrovec, a village on the Croat-Slovene border, had to restrain the passions of the Serbs if his own dictatorship was to prevail. For Tito, the multinational option was a practical necessity. The Communist labor organizer was not especially fond of Islam and Muslims. And he had no sympathy for Muslim landlords in Bosnia; the prerogatives of that class would be liquidated in no time. Still, the marginal man in Tito made him a natural ally of the Muslims and of Bosnia's mixed identity.

Tito knew that the Muslims needed protection, and he offered it. He had provided Muslims protection during the war, when he reined in sectarian revenge with strict rules on how captured Muslim (and Croat) villages were to be treated. His slogan "Brotherhood and Unity" succeeded because it gave the South Slavs a way out of the murderous fight between Croats and Serbs. There was violence aplenty, in Tito's way of doing things; the Partisans hunted down and murdered thousands of their opponents or drove them into exile. There are estimates that 250,000 may have been killed by Tito's new regime. But Tito's political success was owed to more than violence. The lands of Yugoslavia had seen enough killing, and Tito prevailed because he made the traumatized population an offer that was hard to refuse: order and a suspension of nationalist strife.

In a parody of another multinational state, the Soviet Union, Tito both acknowledged and denied the contending nationalities. They were given their republics, but hemmed in by a ruling party, and by personal autocracy at the top. Yugoslavs were given liberties unknown in the Communist world, such as the freedom to travel and to work abroad. Bosnia was given its own independence and identity, a microcosm of the larger multinational state. It was a juggling act, merciful in retrospect. Islamic courts were suppressed, and the *mektebs,* or primary religious schools, were shut down, as was the Muslim printing house in Sarajevo; but the Muslims were given in return the gift of ambiguity. The murderous issue of their identity was deferred.

In the census of 1948, some 72,000 Muslim Bosnians declared themselves Serbs, 25,000 declared themselves Croats, and 778,000 chose to register as undeclared. Yugoslavism may have been an artificial identity, manufactured for the convenience of a dictatorship, but it was an identity that the Bosnian Muslims received with relief. And they were to be aided by Tito's grandiose international ambitions. In the 1950s, his bid for leadership in the "non-aligned" world went hand in hand with a general improvement in the treatment of Islam at home. By 1968 the regime and its ideology granted the Muslims their identity as a distinct nation; and the Muslims of Bosnia came to revere the vain man at the helm. He did not put an end to the poverty of their republic—in 1965 the per capita income of Bosnia was 69 percent of the Yugoslav average—but he gave them a rough measure of equality; and he extended them the protection of his court against the mob. But Tito was an improviser, and his skill went with him to his grave.

IV

It was in 1983, in the brief interlude between Tito's death and the deluge, that a Sarajevo court sentenced a lawyer by the name of Alija Izetbegovic and a dozen other Bosnian Muslim leaders to long prison terms for plotting to transform Bosnia into Islamistan, an Islamic state. The remnants of the old apparatus charged Izetbegovic also with another sin: he sought, they said, to transform Bosnia into a parliamentary democracy. In those days the Pan-Islamic millennium in Iran was in full swing, and the fear of Islam was an uncontrollable obsession on both sides of the Atlantic. The Islamic bogeyman invoked in the Sarajevo district court would be there for the Serbs and the Croats to use in the imminent scramble for Bosnia. Between the Louvre and the Quran, there stood only Christendom's soldiers—the Croat inheritors of Latin Christendom, the Serb children of Byzantium. The old victories of the Turks would be avenged.

Izetbegovic's book, *Islam Between East and West,* published in 1980, should have been a defense lawyer's dream. An amateurish work, an intellectual hodgepodge, it is the product of an anxious *assimilé,* a child of the Western tradition reassuring himself that all the sources of his mind add up to a coherent whole, a man of our messy world born at the crossroads of cultures. The index alone is sufficient proof of the man's eclecticism. This must be the only book on Islam with nine references to Dostoevski, seven to Albert Camus, eleven to Engels, nine to Hegel, three to Malraux, two to Rembrandt, ten to Bertrand Russell, eight to Kenneth Clark, and so on. This is not the work of a Muslim fundamentalist, or a traditional apologist.

A fundamentalist or an apologist would not heap praise on the Anglo-Saxon world, on the "Anglo-Saxon spirit in history," seeing in the "Anglo-Saxon way" and its blend of church and state a method akin to that of Islam. The Anglo-Saxons, Izetbegovic observes, broke with continental Europe, because they had been influenced by the Arabs and Islam: Roger Bacon, the "founder and forerunner of England's later spiritual progress," had been a student of Arabic "strongly influenced by Ibn Sina, whom he considered to be the greatest philosopher since Aristotle." And everything about Bacon and the Anglo-Saxon legacy "might by explained by this fact." Like the culture of the Anglo-Saxons, the culture of the Muslims knew no inquisition.

It is a strange but affecting sight, this man of modern Sarajevo cutting a deal between Anglo-Saxon pragmatism and his ancestral faith. It is no wonder that zealous Muslim volunteers from "the East" who went recently to Bosnia found the Muslims of Bosnia a peculiar lot, secularists through and through, children of Europe lightly touched by the faith. And a Bosnian from the town of Zenica issued the definitive verdict on the volunteers and on Bosnian Islam: the volunteers from "the East," he said, had tried to grow palm trees in Bosnia, but they failed, because "only apple trees grow here."

The terrible work of Franjo Tudjman in Croatia and Slobodan Milosevic in Serbia has been made easier by the Islamic bogeyman stalking Europe, but there is a great pathos in the nervous Izetbegovic clinging to the pluralist myth of Europe to ward off the dangers all around. For the pluralism of Europe *is* a myth. In their insistence that their own tolerance and their own multiethnic city of Sarajevo are the true expressions of Europe, Izetbegovic and his brave people have misread European history. It is much more likely that the genuine sons of Europe, the perfect embodiments of its cruel history and dark nationalism and populist frenzy, are Milosevic and Tudjman—and not Izetbegovic. Europe has not been kind to the outsider. It cast out and destroyed its Jews. There is no evidence that it will gladly make a place for its Muslims.

I do not know Sarajevo, but the elegies for the city are familiar to me. I grew up in Beirut, and the echo is unmistakable. The mourners for Sarajevo have been saying the sort of things that the mourners for Beirut once said: it was a place of many cultures, a city where diverse faiths met and mated. In the laments for the Balkan city that was created by Islam and Rome and Byzantium, I recall the bitter features of Beirut's fate: the fragile civility stalked by its nemesis in the hills above, the ethnic neighborhoods bringing communities together while keeping them apart, the unexpected volatility and the sudden call to arms, the terrifying magnitude of the hatred and the ease with which civilization slips away. Sarajevo's Latin Quarter had formed Ivo Andric and given him its culture, but all its culture had not stilled in him his primeval fear of "the Turk." Years later Radovan Karadzic, a Bosnian Serb of Montenegrin origin and a Sarajevo psychiatrist, would take up arms against his own city. Serbs and "Turks," he said, were like cats and dogs: they could not live together. And so it was fine to kill.

The Sarajevan way, we now know, was one of the few and the finest moments of cosmopolitanism. It is delicately depicted by Dzevad Karahasan, a former dean of the Academy of Theatrical Arts at the University of Sarajevo, now in exile in Salzburg, in *Sarajevo: Exodus of a City*. It is a book of lamentations. It shows an exile's grief, and an exile's love of detail. A Muslim with a Serb wife, Karahasan has little to say about politics, which he treats with an almost willful contempt. He prefers to behold Sarajevo as it was before its fall, and so he writes about the cuisine of the city and its architecture.

An Ottoman city in a river valley, Sarajevo is made up of *mahalas,* or residential quarters, on the inner hillsides, and a *charshiya,* the city center. "The *mahalas,*" he writes,

> are like rays spread around a focal point. Hence, looking from the city center, on one side stands the Muslim *mahala* called Vratnik; on the other side the Catholic *mahala* called Latinluk; on the third side the Eastern Orthodox *mahala* called Tashlihan; on the fourth side the Jewish *mahala* called Byelave. There are also some lesser *mahalas* (Bistrik, Myetash, Kovachi), each of them determined—just like the bigger ones—by one faith, one language, one system of customs.

This kind of city survives on sufferance. The communities must want it, they must be willing to live with the saving pleasantries and juggling of identities. The communal self is never erased in such a setting. "Discovering the other I discover myself," Karahasan says, "recognizing the other I recognize myself." Men do not have to "rejoice in differences," in Karahasan's sentimental words; they need only tolerate them. And tolerate them Sarajevo did. Austrian *sevdalinkas,* or folk love dirges, composed in Vienna to the verses of Germanic poets, were adopted by the Sarajevans as their own long after they were forgotten in Austria itself. The architecture of the city, too, reflected its tangled paternity: the "pseudo-Oriental" style that Austria brought, to make the Habsburgs feel at home in the old Turkish domains, alongside the "traditional" architecture of old.

Karahasan picks a fitting metaphor for the passing of the city's old way: the destruction, in the summer of 1992, of the Hotel Europa, "the physical and semantic center" of Sarajevo. Hotel Europa lay at the border between the Turkish and Austro-Hungarian parts of the city. Middle Eastern and Central European elements were jumbled together in a hybrid establishment. It was a place, the nostalgist writes, "where Sarajevo can be felt with one's fingertips, where it can be smelled and sensed." By the time the hotel was set ablaze by an artillery barrage, the Sarajevo of old belonged to memory. For Sarajevo had to be laid low, if the new conquests were to have a chance. The Serbs seduced by Sarajevo's ways—"the apartment-building Serbs," the Serb ultras call them—had to be summoned back to the tribe. The example of a place that erased lines had to be obliterated.

"The Turks are going to be like walnuts in a Serbo-Croat nutcracker," said a Serb in Radovan Karadzic's gang. The dilemma of Bosnia was all its own. It took precious little time for the vulnerabilities of Bosnia to be put on cruel display. No sooner had Slovenia and Croatia declared their independence in June 1991, than the stage was set for the cruel scramble for Bosnia. Bosnia lacked Slovenia's homogeneity, and its distance from Serbia; and it lacked Croatia's power. Slovenia, of course, was the easiest case: there were few Serbs in Slovenia and it was granted a quick and easy divorce. Croatia was a messier affair. Its destiny clashed with that of Serbia. Ten percent of the population of the proposed Croat entity were Serbs; a grim fight was inevitable, and it was fought in 1992. But the Serb-Croat war was a war of borders, a limited war. The Serbs reasoned that Western Europe and Germany and the Vatican would not permit an outright conquest of Croatia and the consequent slaughter.

The fight for Bosnia was different. Here Serbian nationalism was vengeful, a campaign of "politicide." The very idea of Bosnia was at issue. There was no Serbian restraint. The Yugoslav army had become a Serb instrument of war. In prosecuting the war against Croatia, the army of rump Yugoslavia had built protected turfs in Bosnia, and they came in handy in the campaigns of "ethnic cleansing" and in the uneven struggle between Bosnia's Muslims and the Serbs. The abandon with which the Serbs fought this war was owed not least to their definitions of their victims. Those were "Turks" and "Muslim fundamentalists" that the Serbs were cutting down.

The Serbs concluded also that nobody would come to the rescue of Bosnia. An old legend about the martial virtues of the Serbs (a legend like the one that was circulating about Iraq's Republican Guard before that particular bluff was called) served as an excuse for Western abdication. It was the passivity of the United States in the period of its global primacy that put the Bosnians and their cause in great peril. And so it was that the city that lived on sufferance became the city that lived on suffering.

The American abdication never even paid the Bosnians the compliment of candor. The truth about our inaction had to be covered up; and so our cavalry was always a day or a provocation away. We picked our way through the colorful history of the Balkans in search of exculpations, and they were not hard to find. Where ordinary bullies and tacky brigands with expensive sunglasses ran protection rackets and a former Belgrade banker and Communist Party hack tested the limits of what he could get away with, we saw implacable ghosts and ancient furies, irresistible and primeval forces rising from the land itself, from a romantic and unchanging history. The president of the United States backed away from military action after reading a book called *Balkan Ghosts*. This preference for ghosts is understandable. Whatever else they are, ghosts are not policy problems. Statesmen are powerless against haunted places. You cannot launch an air strike against the fourteenth century. And so the Serbs have been busy spinning their stories. They have a need for them, so great have been their crimes. But we, too, have a need for the old-wives' tales. They have made it easier for us to avert our gaze.

(NOVEMBER 21, 1994)

War Crimes

ANTHONY LEWIS

At the commemoration of the liberation of Auschwitz some weeks ago, the old questions came back. How could ordinary people in what was thought to be a civilized society have taken part in a monstrous crime? How could the world have allowed it to go on? David Rieff's great achievement is to shed light on those mysteries. He gives us hard evidence on how the process of genocide works, and is allowed to work.

Bosnia is not Auschwitz, and the Serbian leaders are not Hitler. It is necessary to make that disclaimer. The scale of the crime is much smaller. But the principle is the same. A people was picked out for destruction because it was different. The difference was religion: only religion. The Muslims of Bosnia and the Serbs and the Croats are all of the same ethnic origin, South Slav, and they speak the same language. But centuries ago, when the Ottoman Turks ruled the area, some were converted to Islam, as other historical episodes made the Serbs Eastern Orthodox Christians and the Croats Roman Catholics.

Before the disaster, Bosnia was an example of multiculturalism in the fine sense, an instance of different cultures finding common ground, rather than the separatism that some American multiculturalists want the word to mean. In the towns, intermarriage was common. Most Muslims were secular in outlook. Assimilated, one might say—like German Jews before 1933, and like them, complacent. "We worried about our kids listening to too much rock and roll," Rieff was told by a man whom he identifies as a Muslim notable in Banja Luka, Bosnia's once-beautiful second city. "We really did not worry about ourselves. Our troubles were going to be personal—divorce, aging, mortality. But we did not think our society was mortal."

That vision ended when Bosnian Serb irregulars and Serbian soldiers of the Yugoslav Federal Army attacked Bosnian villages and cities in the spring of

1992. The siege of Sarajevo began on April 6, and it continues to this day. Banja Luka and much of the rest of northern Bosnia fell to the Serbian forces at the end of April. There was little military opposition; at that stage Bosnia had no army. Then began what a linguistically creative Serb called "ethnic cleansing."

To some in the outside world, ethnic cleansing evokes the image of a Serbian soldier shooting people at random. That happened, especially in remote villages; but the cleansing was not casual or accidental. It was deliberate, comprehensive, designed with clear aims in view. And it had a military purpose: it is much easier to hold territory seized in the name of Serbian nationalism if all the non-Serbs there are killed or terrorized. As Rieff observes, you do not have to worry about a restive subject population. Another purpose was to deprive any future Bosnian state of a trained leadership. In the northern part of the country, which the Serbs occupied most easily and quickly in 1992, educated men were systematically killed, so that, as Rieff reports, the professional classes of the region all but disappeared. Pol Pot redux.

In Banja Luka and other towns where foreign journalists or relief workers might turn up, the process of ethnic cleansing was legalistic and incremental. First the occupation authorities made it a rule that non-Serbs could not be company managers. Then non-Serbs were barred from senior positions in any line of work in which they might make independent decisions, even as accountants or shop foremen. Muslim men received military draft notices, and when they failed to appear for duty with the Serb forces they were automatically dismissed from their jobs. In a holdover from the days of Tito, housing often went with jobs, so the families lost their homes as well. By means of killings and economic pressures, the Muslim population was methodically terrorized into flight, if that was still possible. Often Muslim families had to bribe Serbian paramilitaries for permission to become refugees, another action reminiscent of Nazi ingenuity.

Not only Muslim human beings, but also Muslim history and culture, were cleansed—which is to say, eradicated. Serbian gunners targeted and destroyed the great National Library in Sarajevo and many of the city's mosques. There had been about 1,000 mosques in the northern part of the country before 1992, many of historical interest. Rieff estimates that no more than 100, and probably fewer, still stand. Radovan Karadzic took pride in pointing out to Cyrus Vance and David Owen, when they visited Banja Luka in September 1992, that the city's famous sixteenth-century mosque was still there. "We all live in peace here and all over the parts of Bosnia where we control and where the Muslims do not attack us," he said. "We will not harm them, and we will

---

This essay is a review of David Rieff, *Slaughterhouse: Bosnia and the Failure of the West* (New York: Simon & Schuster, 1995).

respect their religion." A year later the Serbs dynamited the great mosque of Banja Luka.

Serbs are not monsters. What could lead Serbian engineers and factory workers and doctors—yes, doctors—to take part in the extermination of a people and a culture? There is the old question. Rieff's main answer is: propaganda. In Serbia itself, Belgrade television and radio broadcast unending invented horror stories about the massacre of Serbs. Bosnian Serb broadcasts told viewers and listeners that Serbian fighters were being roasted alive on spits. For many, this was the only source of news, and they believed. "Serb minds as well as Muslim bodies have been cleansed in Bosnia," Rieff writes.

"Live Serbian babies are being fed to the zoo animals in Sarajevo," Biljana Plavcic, a Bosnian Serb official, once complained to a U.N. refugee officer. This at a time when the zookeepers were risking their lives to try to get to the zoo; and in the end the animals all starved to death. Can people really believe such things? Yes, they can. Karadzic, a former psychiatrist, believes his lies only in the sense that his former schizophrenic patients believed their ravings. But many Serbs, in Bosnia and Serbia, certainly do believe that their soldiers only began fighting when attacked by Muslim terrorists—mujahedin, they call them—and they believe also that the Muslims have carried out massacres. Rieff describes a schoolteacher in a Serbian area near Sarajevo telling him, with tears in her eyes, that the things written about Serbian atrocities were all lies. He asked her why, if Serbs were the victims of the war, Serbian snipers killed children in Sarajevo. "If we shell the city," she replied, "it is only because the Muslims shoot at us first. Don't we have the right to defend ourselves?" And the sniping? "Serbs are incapable of behaving in this dishonorable way. . . . They would not kill children. If kids are being killed, it must be the Muslims who are doing this to blame the Serbian people." At the time 3,500 children had been killed in Sarajevo by Serbian shelling and sniping.

The Bosnian tragedy reminds us, then, what a powerful weapon the fear of The Other can be. Herbert Okun, who was Cyrus Vance's deputy in the Yugoslav negotiations, told Karadzic at the start: "If you continue to talk about the mortal danger that Serbs are under in Bosnia, you will end up committing preemptive genocide." A memorable phrase, "preemptive genocide." But Karadzic did not care. He and his colleagues, Rieff concludes, "won because they knew how to take old fears and old complaints, repackage them and cause otherwise decent Serbs, people from a national community with no more of an innate predilection for murder than any other national community, to commit genocide."

Fear was used also more directly than in propaganda. Serbian fighters would go to a Serb's house in some village, take the man to a Muslim neighbor's home, hand him a knife or gun and order him to kill the neighbor. If he refused, he was shot. When this happened a few times, Serb householders stopped refusing to be killers, whatever their feelings about the war. Thus were they made accomplices to genocide. When it was all over, 200,000 people had been killed in Bosnia and 2 million forced to flee the country as refugees. And it is not yet all over. Within the past few months, there has been more ethnic cleansing in the areas of northern Bosnia, where the worst tortures took place, where the worst Serbian concentration camps were established.

The world has done nothing to stop the genocide in Bosnia, offering as excuses for its inaction a number of myths. One is that the Balkans are just hopeless, a collection of tribes impervious to reason, whose ancient hatred for each other is bound to break out from time to time in mass murder. It is true that Serb and Croat nationalism has produced much bloodshed in the past, that there is a bitter historical memory of the Ottoman years, that neither the royal Yugoslavia before World War II nor Tito's Yugoslavia afterward erased the smaller national loyalties and created a true sense of Yugoslav citizenship; but the recent wars that have savaged Croatia and destroyed Bosnia were not the product of historical inevitability. They were the product of politicians.

They arose fundamentally from the ambition of Slobodan Milosevic, the former Communist who leads Serbia. He destroyed the balance of communities that Tito had arranged in the Yugoslav government, taking more and more power for himself and the Serbs. Resistance by the Slovenes (in northern Yugoslavia) and the Croats made the breakup of Yugoslavia inevitable. Then Milosevic let loose the propaganda that transformed the thinking of many Serbs and enabled them to kill without troubling their consciences. Victimology was the crucial tactic. Serbs were made to feel victims of an unfair history going back to their defeat by the Ottomans at Kosovo in 1389: a defeat that Serbian soldiers would actually say they were avenging as they sniped at Muslim women and children.

It took a lot of work, Rieff says, for power-hungry Serbian politicians, soldiers, and intellectuals to create the necessary fear and hatred in a place where the rate of intermarriage was so high and the consciousness of division had faded. But Radovan Karadzic and Ratko Mladic, the general who commands Serbian forces in Bosnia and Croatia, are masters of the trade: so good at it, in fact, that Milosevic has sometimes seen them as threats to his power in Serbia. In *Yugoslavia's Ethnic Nightmare,* a collection of essays edited by Jasminka Udovicki and James Ridgeway, the editors make the point about the myth of the hopeless Balkans: "The hatred that astounded the world [in Bosnia] was engineered, not innate."

Another myth is that President Alija Izetbegovic and other leaders of the Bosnian government brought disaster upon themselves by seceding from

Yugoslavia and declaring Bosnia an independent country in 1992. That step was indeed the signal for the Serbian assault, but the choice was forced on a Bosnian government that knew the danger but had no good alternative. Izetbegovic preferred Bosnia to remain in a Yugoslavia that was a genuine federation, and he had worked for such a solution through 1991. But Milosevic was intent on centralizing power in his own, and Serbia's, hands. After the European Community's recognition of Croatia as an independent state in January 1992, Bosnia was left with a choice of independence or submersion in a Yugoslavia that amounted to a Greater Serbia. The E.C. promised recognition if a referendum in Bosnia approved independence. The referendum was held and won, but Bosnian Serbs boycotted it. Foreseeing the onslaught, Izetbegovic asked for U.N. peacekeepers to be stationed in Bosnia, but none were sent. The E.C. recognized Bosnia on April 6, 1992, the day that Serbian forces began the siege of Sarajevo.

Then there is the argument that Germany brought on the disaster by insisting on early recognition of an independent Croatia. History—that is, the Nazi creation of a Fascist Croatia during World War II—did make the German role in 1991–92 a provocation to the Serbs, even a spark for paranoia. (A Yugoslav television commentator, visiting the United States last year, told me solemnly that everything had resulted from "the German conspiracy.") The Croatian government of Franjo Tudjman was greatly at fault for not guaranteeing the large Serbian minority a special constitutional status, and the E.C.—having made that guarantee a condition of recognition—was mistaken in going ahead and recognizing Croatia without it. But it is impossible to say that any of this actually caused the Serbian aggression in Croatia and Bosnia. In November and December 1991, before recognition of Croatia, the Serbs shelled Dubrovnik on the west and laid siege to Vukovar on the eastern side of Croatia, hideously leveling Vukovar. Serbian forces took control of the Krajina, the southern third of Croatia. I see no reason to think that they would not have done those things if recognition had been delayed or handled more carefully.

Europe's role in the Bosnian genocide has been scandalous. After the victory over Nazi savagery and the great, successful effort to keep Western Europe free during the cold war, one might have expected the leaders of Britain and France especially to be sensitive to the rise of extreme nationalism and murderous aggression in Europe. Instead the record reeks of Munich. The best analysis that I have seen of the European performance is by Stanley Hoffmann, in an essay written for *The World and Yugoslavia's Wars* [Council on Foreign Relations, 1995].

From the start, Hoffmann notes, Britain and France insisted on limiting international action on the ground in Bosnia to a relief effort assisted by the United Nations Protection Force, UNPROFOR. The British and French governments then argued that the presence of their soldiers in UNPROFOR made military action to defend the victims of Serbian aggression impossible, because the Serbs would attack the U.N. forces. British and French troops were thus made Serbian hostages, an excuse to let the Serbs break successive promises without response. "The British and French preference for 'sustained negotiations' without deterrence or the use of force," Hoffmann writes, "and without even the lifting of an unfair arms embargo that mainly helped the aggressor, was both a political and a moral mistake." He concludes that Britain's policy has been "sadly reminiscent of the 1930s" and that, "as in the 1930s, France in effect followed Britain into spinelessness."

American leadership has been no better. George Bush, fresh from his triumph in the Persian Gulf war under the banner of "a new world order," flinched from acting to stop Serbian aggression when it was easiest to stop: at the beginning, in 1991, in the attacks on Dubrovnik and Vukovar. General John Galvin, the American who was NATO's supreme commander at the time, later testified to Congress that NATO air strikes could have stopped the Serbs there and then—and thus could have prevented the subsequent tragedy in Bosnia.

Why did Bush avert his eyes from Yugoslavia? His explanation, insofar as he offered one, was that it was primarily a European problem and the Europeans should handle it. True; but long experience has shown that the Europeans cannot act effectively on security matters without American leadership. NATO, which had the force to take any military action, was led by the United States. We had invested hundreds of billions of dollars over four decades to keep the peace in Europe, on the premise that the United States had a vital interest in maintaining that peace and the principle that bars acquisition of territory by force.

The excuse of Europe's responsibility was, and is, unpersuasive. And there was a personal reason that may have been crucial: the fall of Margaret Thatcher. When Iraq invaded Kuwait, it was Thatcher, at an Aspen conference that day with Bush, who stiffened the American president's backbone. "Don't go all wobbly on us, George," she told him, as Bush himself later disclosed. But suddenly the British prime minister was the weak John Major, who together with Foreign Secretary Douglas Hurd put one in mind of Chamberlain and Halifax.

If Thatcher had stayed in office, I believe, she would again have stiffened Bush's spine. I think that she and Bush—and possibly François Mitterrand—would have issued an ultimatum to the Serbs in something like these terms: "At the end of the twentieth century, we who fought and won the war in Europe—with the gallant help of the Yugoslav resistance—will not allow the peace to begin unraveling. We understand that the Serbs feel threatened by political change in Croatia, but the place to work out those concerns is at the conference table. If military aggression continues for one more day, our aircraft will strike at the guns shelling Dubrovnik and Vukovar and at other Serbian military targets in Croatia and in Serbia." The phrase "our aircraft" would have meant NATO planes if NATO had agreed, as I think it would. And if NATO did not agree, the aircraft would have been American, British, and perhaps French. Like General Galvin, I am confident that Milosevic and Mladic would have stopped at once.

The Bush administration bears a responsibility beyond inaction. Early in 1991 the CIA had told the administration that Yugoslavia would not survive as a single state and that the breakup had effectively started. On June 21, 1991, however, Secretary of State James Baker chose to go to Belgrade and declare that the United States was committed to a unified Yugoslavia. His words were taken by Milosevic as a green light for the use of force to maintain the state. Four days later, when Croatia and Slovenia declared their independence, Milosevic immediately sent his troops into action. Why Baker chose to make that trip and those remarks has never been explained.

When Bill Clinton took office in 1993, the obstacles to effective international action in Bosnia were high. Serbian aggression and genocide had changed realities in ways that were hard to undo. But Clinton made things worse. By condemning Bush's policy as weak and promising firm action, he led the Bosnian government to expect intervention of a kind that would help. With that expectation, the Bosnians went on fighting and dying, only to find that Clinton's words were hollow. The president called for a policy of "lift and strike": lifting the arms embargo and making air strikes on Serbian military targets. But when Britain and France objected, Clinton abandoned that policy without even a whimper.

Clinton led Vance and Owen to believe that the United States would support their plan for a Bosnia of cantons, loosely connected but still preserving Bosnia as an internationally recognized state. Then he rejected the Vance-Owen plan as not good enough, with the result that Bosnia was in due course offered diplomatic plans more demeaning than Vance-Owen, whatever its problems. Throughout 1994 Clinton pushed the Europeans to agree to firm NATO responses, meaning serious air strikes, when the Serbs violated their agreements and resumed their killing. Then he dropped that idea. Today the Clinton administration has nothing that can be called a policy on Bosnia.

"The story of Bosnian defeat," Rieff says, is

the story of Western European and North American disgrace. What has taken place in Bosnia has revealed the bankruptcy of every European security institution, from the North Atlantic Treaty Organization to the Conference on Security and Cooperation in Europe, exposed the fact that nowhere in these great structures was there either intellectual preparedness or moral fortitude for dealing with the crises of the post–cold war world.

One other actor in the Bosnian tragedy remains to be discussed: the United Nations. On the subject of the U.N. operation in Bosnia, Rieff is brilliant and chilling. It is possible to mention only a few of the examples that he reports of shameful behavior on the part of UNPROFOR officers and Yasushi Akashi, the U.N. special representative in the former Yugoslavia. As part of arrangements that it has made with the Serbian aggressors, UNPRO-FOR effectively polices the siege of Sarajevo. It patrols the airport and uses lights to pick out people trying to flee at night, many of whom have then been shot by Serbian snipers. UNPROFOR armored personnel carriers actually ran over Bosnians cowering near the runway in 1993; officers explained that pre-venting people from leaving was part of the deal with the Serbs. When Ser-bian rape camps were discovered by journalists that same year, UNPROFOR explained that helping the captive Muslim women was not part of its mandate. It also declined to investigate repeated charges that UNPROFOR soldiers had been taken to the camps for sex.

The U.N. published a pamphlet for children in Bosnia. Called "What the United Nations Does for Peace," it says: "UNPROFOR is a big group of peo-ple from a lot of different countries who have come to the former Yugoslavia to try to stop the war. . . . It tries to protect people from getting hurt in the fighting, just like a teacher who stops bullies from hitting you at school." Those statements are lies. UNPROFOR insists that it has no mandate to stop the war or to keep people from getting hurt in the fighting. Indeed, Akashi and Sir Michael Rose, the British general who was until January the UNPRO-FOR commander, consistently veoted proposals for air strikes against Serbian guns and tanks that were killing Bosnian civilians in Sarajevo, Bihac, Gorazde, and other places. Rose himself said, in a BBC interview, that "we are not here to protect or defend anything other than ourselves or our convoys." The latter is a dubious claim, since UNPROFOR has almost always backed off when the Serbs invented a reason to forbid convoys going through. For that reason, some of the besieged towns have been without relief supplies for months at a time.

So narrowly does UNPROFOR view its function that Bosnians have come to call it the Self-Protection Force. When the Serbs attacked the Gorazde "safe area" in 1994, capturing all of it except the small area of the town and thereby depriving it of food resources, Rose said that the magnitude of the attacks was exaggerated. But the terrible low point of UNPROFOR's record occurred on January 8, 1993, when French officers taking the Bosnian vice president, Dr. Hakija Turaljic, back to Sarajevo from a meeting at the airport allowed Serbian soldiers to stop the convoy and kill Turaljic in cold blood.

The French colonel in charge went home and was awarded the Legion of Honor. A U.N. inquiry concluded that it was the Bosnians' fault for creating "an atmosphere of anxiety" among the Serbs. Rieff affectingly dedicates his book to the memory of Turaljic. He concludes what he has amply proved: "UNPROFOR and the [U.N.] Department of Peacekeeping Operations became accomplices to genocide."

The last argument to justify the West's indifference to genocide in Bosnia was that military intervention on a scale that would have been bearable by the American or European publics would not have worked: the Serbs were too strong, the terrain was too difficult. To be sure, a massive Western involvement in a ground war would have been mistaken; and the Serbian aggression could not have been stopped by a few "surgical air strikes." That phrase is as misleading when used with reference to the Balkans as it was when Henry Kissinger used it in the Southeast Asian setting. But air power could just as surely have been used in a meaningful way. NATO aircraft could have lifted the siege of Sarajevo or maintained the safety and integrity of such "safe areas" as Gorazde and, more recently, Bihac.

What really mattered, however, was not bombing, but belief: the belief of General Mladic and his colleagues that they would feel the force of NATO if they went on killing. Force and the threat of force are the only things that have moved the Serbs in this war of aggression. Every time there was a credible threat of NATO strikes, they gave way—as in their agreement to the heavy weapons exclusion zone around Sarajevo after the marketplace massacre there briefly roused the Clinton administration to demand action.

There were, and there still are, many obvious targets. The bridges over the Drina, which have borne supplies of weapons and ammunition from Serbia to the Bosnian Serb forces, are one. Another is the Bosnian Serbs' military headquarters in Pale, the mountain town that is their self-styled capital. It is one of the many curious inequalities of this war (along with the gross injustice of the arms embargo) that the Bosnian capital of Sarajevo has been starved and shelled, its electricity and gas cut off, and its people murdered by snipers while the Serbian "capital" of Pale is a privileged sanctuary. NATO aircraft could obliterate Pale in a few hours. If a credible threat had been made to attack Pale, as it should have been made long ago, Mladic would have listened. But the Serbs have known for years that there was no will in the West to resist their aggression. While gloomy Western experts talked of the difficulty of spotting Serb weapons in the mountains, they left their guns and tanks in plain view because they knew nothing would happen. Rieff says: "The West's refusal to act while Vukovar was being destroyed and Dubrovnik shelled had shown them . . . all they needed to know."

Rieff's important book is not easily categorized. It is not a work of history, or a scholarly analysis of Yugoslav politics, or a military chronicle. It is not an orderly book neatly listing names and dates. It is an impressionistic work. Unlike those of us who have condemned this genocide from a distance, Rieff went to see it. He spent months in Bosnia during the period from mid-1992 until the end of 1994. He reports what he saw, condemns what he came to detest, vents the frustration that an American or European ought to feel at the culpability of Washington and London and the rest. He has written an epitaph for Bosnia, or for us. I do not think that anyone should be able to read this book without pain and anger.

"The systematic attempt on the part of the Serbs to exterminate the Bosnian Muslims," in Rieff's words, will have consequences not yet calculable. Two hundred thousand Bosnians have been killed, a cultural and architectural history has been ravaged, a rare symbol of tolerance and pluralism has been destroyed. For the West to have saved all that, Rieff rightly says, would have been "self-defense, not charity." But the reckoning for us, in other nationalist and religious savageries, is still to come. Stanley Hoffmann sums it up well: "The precedent set by the treatment of the Yugoslav crisis—the massive brutalization of international relations and the destruction through ethnic cleansing of a multinational state—is as shocking as it is disastrous."

(MARCH 20, 1995)

PART II

A People Destroyed

Love Story

SLAVENKA DRAKULIĆ

I have seen their picture in newspapers. It was not clear, obviously taken from a distance: two bodies lying on the Sarajevo ground, two sports bags next to them. Admira is wearing a dark skirt covering the soft curves of her body. Bosko is in jeans—what else?—and they both wear sneakers. But one can tell, even looking at that blurred photo, that Admira is embracing Bosko as they are lying there, dead. This is how it happened: On Wednesday afternoon, May 19, around 4 P.M., they walked along the Miljacka river in no-man's-land, visible to both sides, the Serbian and the Bosnian. Their escape from the besieged city onto the Serbian side was prearranged; both sides had agreed to let them pass. They had to walk about 1,000 yards, but just before the Vrbana bridge—some fifty yards before safety—they fell to the ground, hit by a sudden burst of a sniper's fire.

I can almost hear that distinctive, short, yelping sound in the afternoon air. Bosko died immediately, Admira lived long enough to crawl to him and embrace him. There they stayed for almost a week, rotting in the sun (unusually strong this May), the odor of their decaying bodies mixing with that of the young grass.

It is not known who killed them, and maybe it is not even important. There are people on both sides who saw them walking, then falling. Some of them say the fire came from the Serbian side, others claim just the opposite. However, for the next five days the two sides fought for possession of the bodies. On the sixth night, Serbian soldiers resolved the dispute by snatching the bodies.

Bosko's mother, who had left Sarajevo a year before and now lived in Belgrade, had given permission for her son to be buried in Sarajevo. Admira's parents said they would prefer to have them buried in Sarajevo in order to attend to their grave, but they also said that the place was of no importance as long as the two were buried together. And finally it happened: the Muslim girl and the Serbian boy who had loved each other for nine years were put in the same coffin and buried in the same grave at the Serbian army graveyard south of Sarajevo.

Their attempt to escape from the war that threatened to destroy their love as well as their very existence had failed—so had their naive belief that love could overcome all obstacles. But I wonder: What did being a Serb or a Muslim mean to them before the breakout of this war? And when exactly did they realize that belonging to one nation or the other might determine their future? Looking at a picture taken after their high school graduation in 1985—both of them handsome, smiling as they hold each other—I can hardly imagine that nationality had any important meaning for these kids, or for any of their peers in ex-Yugoslavia. I am not suggesting that they were not aware of such things. They probably were, as much as anyone else around them. But nationality did not matter much: it could not decide their destiny, or prevent them from falling in love.

They were born in the late 1960s. They watched Spielberg movies; they listened to Iggy Pop; they read John Le Carre; they went to a disco every Saturday night and fantasized about traveling to Paris or London. They had friends in Croatia and Serbia whom they would meet in the summer to go camping somewhere along the Adriatic coast. And then the war broke out, and it was as if someone had opened an old history book: Chetniks against Ustashe, although this time Tito's Partisans were not around. It was the absurd, monstrous war of their grandfathers' stories. And now this war descended on them, crushing a whole generation that had been brought up under the illusion that they belonged to Europe, that they had a better, different future in store.

Bosko and Admira decided to save themselves. After all, it was not their war. When Bosko's mother asked Admira if this war could separate them, she answered, "No, only bullets could separate us"—as if she knew. This happened only a year ago. The moment Bosko decided to stay behind when his mother left for Serbia, Admira and her parents understood it was only love that kept him in Sarajevo. But I imagine that he also decided to stay because neither he nor Admira believed that a war in Bosnia would be possible at all, not really. How could you divide people living on the same floor of an apartment building just because they are of different nationalities? (This is what people from Sarajevo would tell you as late as last spring.) How can you split up a mixed family?

•   •   •

Of course, the power of politics proved stronger than their belief in tolerance and togetherness. After tens of thousands of civilians—their neighbors, friends, and relatives—had been killed for no other reason than being of the "wrong" nationality, Bosko and Admira realized that they had no chance. The rest of the world had given up on Sarajevo. And while one can perhaps stand lack of electricity and water, even bitter cold and no food, one cannot stand a state of hopelessness for too long. So, when Bosko and Admira decided to leave, it made it easier for them to go knowing that the city they once knew did not exist any longer. Perhaps Admira's friends thought she was crazy to leave for Serbia, being a Muslim. What would happen to her once she arrived there? But how could Admira explain to them that in the war she was nothing—only part of a nation, doomed to be "cleansed"? She was confident that Bosko and his mother would protect her and that in Belgrade there would be at least a chance for survival.

I can almost see her on that evening of Tuesday, May 18, as she takes out her old Adidas sports bag and begins to pack. "Don't take too many things with you,"—Bosko warns, as he leaves the house to make sure everything is ready—"just imagine we are going to visit my mother for a week." But this time Admira lacks imagination. If she would go for a week's visit, she would not take a photo of her parents, her high school diary, her diploma. She would not take her favorite winter dress (not now, it is spring), her golden bracelet and an old rubber doll that brings her luck.

And she would not sit down to write a letter.

When she finishes packing, it is late at night. The city is strangely quiet as if everyone is sound asleep, tired from this endless war. Admira takes a piece of lined paper out of her notebook. There is only the dim light of a candle in her room, but her eyes are used to it by now. "Dear mother and father," she writes. Then she pauses. What can she tell them? that she has to go because Sarajevo is not safe for Bosko any longer, that he could be drafted by the Bosnian army at any moment? that they could be separated or killed because they are of different nationalities? or that it is only a matter of time before they *will* be killed by shells in the middle of one of Sarajevo's streets, for no reason other than that they live there? Mama and Papa know it all, thinks Admira, as she sits alone in her room. There is nothing to tell them, nothing to explain. They only need to be sure that we managed to escape the death sentence.

Admira sits for a while, then decides to write about her cat. "Please, take care of my cat. He is looking at me and meowing as I am crying and writing this. Sleep with him at least once a month and talk to him all the time." Then she puts out the candle (candles are precious) and goes to bed, staring into the darkness for a while.

The next day it all happened, and this is how I imagine it: On Wednesday afternoon, after briefly hugging her parents, she leaves the house. She must have been very brave not to have shed tears, not to have looked back. As she approaches the river, she can see Bosko waiting. It is easy to recognize his tall figure, his nervous gestures. Suddenly she feels that her palms are wet with sweat, but as she rushes to him, she fears no longer. Everything is going to be all right—she thinks—as long as we are together. Then they leave their shelter and get out into the open. They are on the north bank of the river. They do not run. They think there is no need to because they have been guaranteed safe passage. Holding hands, they walk briskly toward the bridge, and all that they hear is the creaking of sand under their feet and the murmur of the river.

The safety zone is not so far away now, and Bosko speeds up a little. Slow down please, I can't run, Admira wants to tell him, thinking about how foolish she was to pack so many things in her bag, so many unnecessary things that make it heavy now, too heavy to run. But just as she is about to utter those words, she feels something warm gushing out of her stomach. As she looks down in surprise, she sees that her hands are full of blood. Then pain takes over and she falls on the ground. She can see Bosko already lying there motionless, far from her, as if he had been pushed away by some unknown force. "How strange, I heard nothing," she thinks, crawling toward him with the bag in her hand, as if they might still have a chance. But before she sinks into emptiness, she lives long enough to come close to him, to raise her left hand and embrace him.

Bosko's mother, Radmila, is the only one from the two families to attend the funeral on May 27 on the barren hilltop south of Sarajevo. Admira's parents don't dare come, although the Serbian forces have guaranteed them safe passage. They can hardly trust guarantees from either side. What should we make, then, of the fact that the two families were never at odds? They tried together to help the young couple escape from what finally became their destiny. On the top of a plain wooden coffin Radmila drapes a pullover she has knitted for Admira. Then she throws a handful of dust into the open grave: "My children, you were blown here by the wind of war," she says. She has no more words, no more tears. I can imagine her there, her feet sinking into a greasy yellow clay. Even if she was not aware of it, her grief had become our grief. Bosko and Admira, two young people who represented the future, were driven into the past by a war from which neither generation could save itself.

(OCTOBER 25, 1993)

Dateline Sarajevo: Besieged

CHARLES LANE

In the midst of a recent Serb artillery barrage, Mersad Berber took shelter in the bathroom of his Sarajevo studio. Hunched and trembling, he reached for a paintbrush and began to work an oil-on-wood diptych. On the first panel a naked man slouches amid a fog of black and green; his hands are clenched, eyes closed, belly distended. On the second the man is joined by another, kneeling, his hands bound behind his back in the unmistakable pose of a hostage. Berber calls the images "Sarajevo Spring." After three months of savage street fighting and artillery bombardment, there are plenty of horrors in Sarajevo's streets: burned-out schools, dazed old men, headless corpses rotting in a stream. Yet these stark paintings are as chilling as any of them.

Last year, as Serb forces shelled the ancient Dalmatian city of Dubrovnik, Montenegrins fighting on the Serb side looted Berber's home there, carting off both his own work and his private collection of modern European art. Soon he will leave his native city for Western Europe. "We were always European," insists Berber, who is Bosnia's best-known artist. "This is a European culture; we Bosnians are Europeans." Berber, like so many of Sarajevo's essentially secular, modern Muslim population, cannot understand the failure of the West to intervene militarily on Bosnia's behalf. My introduction to him came through a young intellectual who works as an English translator for the Bosnian government. She asked if I thought the United States would send its planes to bomb the Serb artillery positions which ring Sarajevo. When I said no, she exploded. "Then you should go see those paintings tomorrow, because pretty soon they will all be blown up," she said, "and it will be your shame."

The West's policy is hard to explain. It brands the Serbs as military aggressors, yet limits its response to humanitarian relief, as if the people of Sarajevo were the victims of an earthquake or hurricane. Sarajevans see themselves

as waging resistance. To them, the Bosnian republic, which declared its independence last April, represents a unitary state in which power would be
shared more or less democratically among the republic's Muslims, Serbs, and
Croats. Granted, it's a vague, possibly unworkable, idea. But it's the closest
thing to a model of civic tolerance to emerge from the wreckage of the state
Tito built. I didn't meet a single citizen in Sarajevo who didn't think it was
worth holding out for. The Muslims, of course, have little choice because the
heart of the problem is in the capital of their republic; unlike the Croats, who
were bombed out of the city of Vukovar last year by the Serb nationalists and
the Yugoslav National Army, they have nowhere to retreat to. Yet many ethnic Serbs have also been bearing up under the bombardment of Sarajevo, or
even fighting in the Territorial Defense, alongside Muslims and Croats.

Nevertheless, Britain's Lord Carrington, representing the European Community, arrived in Sarajevo on July 3 pushing a peace plan that would divide
Bosnia into autonomous ethnic "cantons." It is a thoroughly undemocratic
idea, which plays into the hands of the Serb nationalist forces. They're bent
on the "ethnic cleansing" of the Bosnian countryside, a euphemism for burning Muslim and Croat villages, killing some of the residents, and herding the
survivors into refugee camps, or out of the former Yugoslavia altogether. Once
Muslim or Croat areas have been "cleansed," the Serbs declare them part of
the "Serb Republic of Bosnia and Hercegovina," an area which now encom-
passes about two-thirds of Bosnia's original territory. Should cantonization
ever come, the Serbs figure, they will be in a position to claim the lion's share.

I stumbled across ethnic cleansing in progress near the town of Zvornik,
about halfway between Belgrade and Sarajevo. Zvornik has been the scene of
numerous alleged atrocities against Muslims, perpetrated by paramilitary Serb
bands such as the one led by "Arkan," a former organized crime figure from
Serbia. Arkan's name was daubed in black paint on the walls of burned-out
homes and businesses in the town. When I arrived shortly after midday along
with about eight carloads of Sarajevo-bound journalists, the Serb gunmen
manning the local checkpoint were drunk, mad, and in a mood to poke us
with their automatic weapons.

A friendly Serb policeman intervened, informing us that a battle was going
on up ahead that made it too dangerous to continue. But, he said brightly, the
"battle" would be over in forty-five minutes. As we waited, a Serb paramilitary officer, dressed in a camouflage tunic and riding breeches, drove up in a
Mercedes and waved an AK–47 at me and a Spanish journalist. "If you take a
single picture between here and Sarajevo," he said in precise English, "I will
personally kill you." Moments later three buses went through the checkpoint.
Each bus was full of Muslim men, their heads bowed and touching the seats
in front of them, and their hands behind their necks. I caught a glimpse of one
man's fearful eyes through the window. That, apparently, was the scene we

weren't supposed to photograph. The "battle" concluded, the Serbs waved us through.

Ethnic cleansing is almost as absurd as it is repugnant. Everywhere you go in former Yugoslavia, you encounter ethnically mixed couples or their children—particularly in cities such as Sarajevo, whose long history of relative ethic tolerance was accentuated by further residential mixing in the high-rises built by communism. Such people face a somber future. In Sarajevo I helped Yazo, 29, tape new plastic sheet windows on his Volkswagen. A shell had crushed its roof and shrapnel had turned its hood into Swiss cheese, but somehow the car still runs. "This is my lucky car," he tells me. It is all that's left of Yazo's fish import business, which once included nine retail outlets and a refrigerated warehouse. His home was burned to the ground by Serb incendiary shells. He is a Muslim. His girlfriend Mariana is a Croat. "Lord Carrington is wrong about cantonization," he tells me. "Because if she lives with me in a Muslim canton she'll have a hard time, and if I live with her in a Croat canton, I'll have a hard time. We should live together like we always did." I had to disappoint Yazo, too, when he asked me if the United States would come to Bosnia's rescue. "Maybe we should discover oil," he says.

Toward the end of my stay in Sarajevo, Gordana Knezevic, a Serb journalist, and her husband Ivan, a Croat philosophy professor, loaned me their son, 13-year-old Boris, as a guide to their hillside neighborhood. Boris showed me the dank basement in his apartment building where some middle-class ladies were sweating over a wood stove, cooking pasta, which has become the staple food of the besieged. They seemed abashed that I had seen them in this unseemly station. We moved on to the concrete bomb shelter where Boris had spent dozens of nights recently. He showed me the apartment of Adil Gadic, a bank worker. It had been destroyed by a shell. A solitary goldfish, still swimming in a fish tank full of precious water, was the only living thing left in the flat. Two girls from the neighborhood hovered nearby, hectoring me with the one phrase in English they seemed to have mastered: "U.S. military forces, U.S. military forces."

Boris and I crunched across broken glass to the nearby Lav Cemetery, pressed into service recently after years of disuse. There were a hundred or so fresh graves on the sloping green ground. About two-thirds were marked with the crosses of the Roman Catholic Croats and Orthodox Serbs; another third bore the elongated quadrilateral markers favored by Muslims. Boris scampered through the narrow spaces between the dead, reading off their birth dates from the crosses and quadrilaterals. The death dates, he reported, were all the same: 1992. I warned Boris about sniper fire, but he pressed on, calling back, "Maybe there are some people here I know."

(JULY 27, 1992)

Dateline Banja Luka:
City of Fear

ANNA HUSARSKA

The tree trunks in the main street here are covered with a patchwork of death announcements, testimony to four months of bloodletting. "Ilic Drazenko, 24 years old; died in defense of his country," reads one of the fliers, which is adorned with an Orthodox Serb cross. "Skopljak (Muhamed) Sadik, age 21" also died defending *his* country. As it happens, it was the same country: Bosnia and Herzegovina. The two were likely fighting each other; the announcement of Muhamed's death is adorned with a crescent—he was a Muslim.

Posted among the death announcements are hand-lettered ads written by Serbs desperate to swap their houses in towns still held by Muslims for anything in Serb-controlled territory. An offer of a sixty-nine-square-meter flat in Sarajevo sounds surreal—a bit like an invitation to a beheading—and it is unlikely that anybody will jump at the offer. Instead, as Muslims flee the "ethnic cleansing" campaign, many Serbs have moved into Banja Luka's scores of freshly abandoned houses.

The Serbs, headed by Radovan Karadzic, now control 70 percent of the former republic of Bosnia and Herzegovina; Banja Luka is their main town in the north. At first they called this self-styled country "the Serbian Republic of Bosnia and Herzegovina"; now they have shortened it to the "Serbian Republic." The resemblance to the former Yugoslavian republic of Serbia is intentional. The composite area would be Greater Serbia.

After initially supporting the Bosnian Serbs, the Serb-led Yugoslav National Army, or JNA, theoretically withdrew from this territory in June. But some 80,000 uniformed Serb troops have stayed behind with weapons, ammunition, cars, helicopters, even MiG fighters. The badges on the soldiers' uniforms have changed slightly, but their belt buckles are still engraved with the old insignia. On army vehicles, the letters "JNA" are barely visible beneath a thin coat of white paint.

Despite extensive reports to the contrary, the defense minister of this "Serbian Republic," Lieutenant Bogdan Subotic, insists that his army does not engage in ethnic cleansing. After shocking TV images of skeletal figures behind barbed wire fences were broadcast around the world, Serbs became more cautious. Some of the detention camps have since been moved. Others are inaccessible to journalists or even the special U.N. rapporteur on human rights violations (who was refused entry because he did not ask for permission far enough in advance).

The Serbs have adopted other methods of ethnic cleansing, for instance pressuring Muslims into fleeing the region by enforcing harsh regulations that apply only to them. This is especially evident in the case of Celinac, a town of 4,500 people a few miles east of Banja Luka. A Serb dissident in Belgrade gave me a copy of a document issued in late July by the "war presidency" of Celinac that confirmed the worst stories later told to me by Banja Luka's Muslims. The decree imposes apartheid-like restrictions on Celinac's non-Serbs. "Due to military actions in Celinac," the document declares, all non-Serbs are given a "special status." In addition to a 4 P.M. to 6 A.M. curfew, non-Serbs are forbidden to:

- meet in cafés, restaurants, or other public places
- bathe or swim in the Vrbanija or Josavka rivers
- hunt or fish
- move to another town without authorization
- carry a weapon
- drive or travel by car
- gather in groups of more than three men
- contact relatives from outside Celinac (all household visits must be reported)
- use means of communication other than the post office phone
- wear uniforms: military, police, or forest guard
- sell real estate or exchange homes without approval

Also outlined are the obligations of non-Serbs in Celinac. They must fulfill the tasks assigned to them by the Serbs, behave in a disciplined way, and "mustn't show contempt for the struggle of the Serb population for its independence." They must also "accept and breed cattle if the military authorities demand it."

Journalists cannot move freely around Serb-controlled Bosnia. So, along with colleagues from Canada, Britain, and Spain, I went to the military press center in Banja Luka and asked its director, Major Milovan Milutinovic, for a permit to go to Celinac. At first he claimed not to know of such a town. I pointed it out on the map. Yes, he knew the town, he said, but we couldn't go there. Fundamentalist *mujaheddin* there are waging a jihad against the Serb population, and for our security it would be better if we did not go there. But, he said with a sly smile, he would be more than happy to give us a permit to go anywhere else.

While his assistant typed the travel permit, the major briefed us on what he said were atrocities committed by Muslims against the Serb population. The *mujaheddin* kill Muslims, Croats, and Serbs alike, he warned, and then roast them on a spit. The major showed us a long scroll of paper covered with Arabic script. It had been found on a jihad fighter, he said, explaining that it was a call to arms against the Serbs, promising salvation to anyone who died in defense of Islam.

At last we were handed the permit: it authorized us to tour Banja Luka, speak with citizens, and leave at 3:00 in the afternoon to go back to the border of Serb-controlled, U.N.–supervised Croatia.

In Banja Luka's Muslim office of humanitarian aid, Merhamet, I heard stories that explained why one-fifth of the city's Muslims—some 10,000—have left. In the last two weeks alone several Muslim-owned businesses have been destroyed. A shop across from the mosque was blown up with dynamite; a bomb was placed inside a restaurant. Families barricade themselves in their homes during the strict 10 P.M. to 5 A.M. curfew. Women are often attacked in the street and their jewelry stolen. Only old men now attend noon prayer at the mosque. The young are afraid that if they go into the street they will be drafted into the Serb army.

Everyone I met in Merhamet had been fired: lawyers, doctors, clerks, tailors. None would give his name. Their stories were similar: one said his neighbor, a 35-year-old taxi driver, had been killed in the night; one said his brother had been taken to the Manjaca detention camp; the aunt of another had her house taken away during her absence; one had his car confiscated and was given a receipt: "Taken for military use."

As I listened to the horror stories, I was struck by the memory of the monument I had seen earlier that morning in Jasenovac, a town forty miles north of Banja Luka. A huge concrete flower, it was erected in memory of the dozens, some say hundreds of thousands, of Serbs—today's bad guys—as well as Jews and Communists slaughtered there by the Croats during World War II. Meanwhile, on tree trunks across Banja Luka, the region's new monument to the dead is appended daily.

(SEPTEMBER 21, 1992)

Dateline Sarajevo: Deadline

ANNA HUSARSKA

In many places here one has to run for fear that the Serb snipers will shoot. In some, one has to run because one *knows* the snipers will shoot. The entrance to the local newspaper, *Oslobodenje* (Liberation), is one such place.

The Serbs who are besieging Sarajevo hate everything about this newspaper. *Oslobodenje* is the only staple produced here daily (even bread is sometimes missing). It maintains high spirits among the population and, more important, it gives the lie to Greater Serbian propaganda about the impossibility of the three ethnic groups—Serbs, Croats, and Muslims—living together in peace. Just as in Bosnia and Herzegovina as a whole, at the newspaper a third of the staff is Serb. The editor in chief, Kemal Kurspahic, is a Muslim, but when he was hospitalized after a car accident, the acting editor was Gordana Knezevic, a Serb.

Western Sarajevo, where the newspaper is located (on the way to the airport), is one of the city's fiercest combat zones. At the end of June, Serbian gunners fired incendiary shells at the twelve-story tower belonging to the publishing house Oslobodenje—which before this war produced sixty textbooks and twenty periodicals a year in addition to the newspaper—and gutted it almost entirely. Now journalists work in a two-story building adjacent to the tower, which is pretty much gutted itself. The printing is done in the basement. In late August five journalists were wounded when the building was hit by a dozen missiles.

Alas, both buildings are modern, glass-fronted edifices, so the snipers have an unobstructed view. The staff of *Oslobodenje* has hung posters and sheets over the windows and put upended desks against them to provide some protection, but the staff is far from secure. When I toured the offices with a photographer, Svetlana Anotic, she periodically warned me to duck, declaring

77

either "big *opasno*" or "little *opasno.*" (*Opasno* means "dangerous"—one of the first words I learned). I felt like a mouse scampering from one safe hole to another in a room full of nasty cats.

These journalists may sound like kamikazes, but they have some survival instinct. Those who can do so work from home and fax or dictate their texts. But most telephone lines inside the town are dead, so this can involve venturing out to a friend's home where the line still works. Some ten editors, the production personnel, and the printers work in shifts, and live in the building for a week at a time to minimize the risk of being shot at the entrance. Photographers have to appear daily with their film, and miraculously none has yet been killed by snipers (although one photojournalist died after being hit by a mortar shell as he took pictures for a story on the water shortages in town).

Avoiding enemy fire is psychologically exhausting, but it's not as bad as the work itself. Photographer Safet Gubelic told me: "I am a machine registering the dead people in the street, in the market, in the garden. After six months of this I am a wreck, I need a rest." But he cannot get out: only foreigners are allowed through the checkpoints by the Serbs who have circled Sarajevo.

The journalists' work is made particularly difficult by the lack of communication with the external world. They have only one fax line and two telephone lines. Ham-radio operators in Sarajevo, who have contact with those in Zagreb and other towns, serve as go-betweens for *Oslobodenje* and its correspondents in London, Moscow, Brussels, and New York. International news is also picked up from radio broadcasts by those who speak foreign languages. Safet speaks English, so when he is not taking photographs or attending press conferences given by the U.N. forces stationed here, he does some monitoring.

According to one of the editors, Branko Tomic, the biggest problem is the electricity needed for running the offset presses. The generator works on diesel, which is scarce now and will be even more so when it gets cold and the fuel is needed for heating. "In winter we will be ice people," he predicts matter-of-factly. In the basement, looking over the proofs of the next day's issue, the chief of this shift of printers, Sefket Terzic, was more concerned about newsprint: the paper has reduced its print run from 50,000 to 4,000 (the journalists themselves distribute the copies, which disappear from the makeshift stands in hours); the size was reduced from ten to twenty pages of broadsheet to four, with a weekly eight-page edition (the obituaries can take up three pages); the format of the pages is smaller too, since *Oslobodenje* now uses newsprint that was meant for children's books. But Tomic informed me that despite these measures, reserves will not last for more than a month.

Muhamed Hrlovic, who oversees the technical side of the printing, told me that a French organization (later I learned it was Reporters Sans Frontières) has donated forty tons of paper. It is said to be waiting in Split, on the Adriatic coast, but the Serbs will not let it go through, and the U.N. argues that it cannot transport it, since it is not, in the strictest sense, humanitarian aid.

Before the breakup, Yugoslavia was known for its high standard of typography, and Western countries often commissioned art books to be produced here. The computerized presses of *Oslobodenje* were among the most sophisticated in Europe. Terzic remembered an American cookbook printed here, but the orders were mostly for dictionaries and Bibles. Now they print *Oslobodenje* and *Věcernje Novine,* Sarajevo's afternoon tabloid. The only book I saw lying around, about to be bound, was a report on concentration and extermination camps in Bosnia and Herzegovina.

Although truncated, *Oslobodenje* still looks like the high-quality daily it once was: professional, objective, well designed. The big difference is that now it deals almost exclusively with war: the counting of mortars that landed and people who were killed, the threat of epidemics, the humanitarian aid, the drama of the orphans, the overcrowded cemeteries, the uncertain news about water of electricity. International news is consumed by the mission of "Sajrus Vans," by the activities of the U.N., and by the peace conferences. Even the weather forecast is war-related, since the dropping temperatures and the advent of snow mean death in unheated and windowless apartments.

Nine years ago, in the autumn of 1983, Sarajevans were hoping that there would be plenty of snow: their city was hosting the Winter Games. At that time, *Sports Illustrated* wrote: "Meanwhile, the Sarajevo newspaper *Oslobodenje* was conducting an 'Olympic smile' promotion in which just about everybody in town—taxi drivers, waiters, store clerks—was rated for courtesy and friendliness, with the widest smilers getting praised in print." Nowadays in Sarajevo there are no taxis, only foreign journalists are served by waiters, I have not seen a single open store, and those who get praised in print by *Oslobodenje* are not the widest smilers, but the best soldiers.

(OCTOBER 26, 1992)

Dateline Belgrade: Mob Rule

CHARLES LANE

The economic collapse of Serbia may be the best thing that ever happened to Jezdimir Vasiljevic. "Boss Jezda," as he styles himself, still looks like the small-time hustler he once was. His fireplug frame is draped in an off-the-rack pinstriped suit that flops over his shoe tops. A gigantic gold watch dangles from his wrist. A cheap cigar juts from a face framed by what looks like a five-dollar wig—but is in fact Boss Jezda's own hair. These days, however, Boss Jezda epitomizes capitalism, Belgrade-style. He controls Yugoskandic Bank, one of the fastest-growing private financial institutions in Serbia, as well as a chain of factories, retail shops, and gas stations where smuggled petrol goes for eight German marks a gallon. His company sponsored the chess match in Yugoslavia between Bobby Fischer and Boris Spassky. The latest tightening of international sanctions, designed to crack down on petroleum smuggling to Serbia, doesn't scare Boss Jezda. "The only effect was to raise prices," he scoffs, stubbing out another cigar.

But Boss Jezda's company is hardly a sign of capitalist renaissance in the Balkans. Rather, it is yet another measure of how deep the rot runs throughout the increasingly isolated Serbian republic ruled by hard-line President Slobodan Milosevic. Yugoskandic and other private banks make their millions by offering interest rates of up to 14 percent per month on hard currency deposits. A million Serbs now derive their only steady income from these monthly payments—about $100 to $200 on a typical account. But in Serbia's bankrupt economy, there's no way (at least no honest way) the banks can make enough money to sustain such astronomical interest payments. They are officially sanctioned Ponzi schemes that Milosevic is using to drum up hard currency for his government and to buy "social peace."

Boss Jezda denies it, but diplomats say the banks were started with profits from arms and petroleum smuggling, and continue to launder funds generated by such activities. One of the banks, Defiment, employs a well-known paramilitary leader implicated in ethnic cleansing as its "security chief," according to a Western European embassy here. Other paramilitary leaders also swagger about the capital, such as the Serbo-Australian known only as "Captain Dragan" (he has office space a few floors down from Boss Jezda) and Zeljko "Arkan" Raznjatovic, whose "Tiger Brigade" was responsible for savage atrocities against Muslims during the ethnic cleansing of eastern Bosnia.

Arkan operates out of an ice cream parlor in a wealthy neighborhood of Belgrade. There's no sign over the door, but you can tell the place is his by the gigantic socialist realist painting of Serbs marching under their tricolor banner—and the two muscular young men in trench coats pacing the sidewalk just outside. Arkan is a candidate for Parliament in the elections on December 20. He's running in Pristina, the capital of the heavily Albanian province of Kosovo. Arkan's campaign posters show him in a vintage Serbian chetnik military uniform, steely eyes gazing benignly, his hand resting on the shoulder of a little girl. "This is holy Serbian land," the poster says. Since the Albanians are going to boycott the vote in Kosovo, he'll probably win. Given the path-breaking role Arkan's men played in the ethnic cleansing of Bosnia, and the ever present threat that Milosevic is preparing to do the same in Kosovo, Arkan's appearance on the scene in Pristina is an ominous development. He's already opened a station for selling smuggled gas in the town; and he's getting into banking.

Everyone in Serbia knows that the banks are a scam. Yet most Serbs are too broke, too resigned, or too opportunistic to do anything but grab an attaché case and join the cash queue stretching for a hundred yards outside Yugoskandic's branch office on Marshal Tito Street. "The one thing I can't forgive Milosevic for is how he's legitimized organized crime here," a young medical student grumbles. "It's gotten so bad that if I see someone who has nice clothes and drives a pretty car, I don't even want to know them, you know?" In the next breath, she asks whether I think the banks can survive until March, when her $125,000 six-month certificate of deposit is supposed to mature.

The atmosphere in Belgrade is so saturated by intimidation, ethnic hatred, absurd hopes, and outright lies that the public can almost be forgiven for being sucked in by the false promise of the private banks. The news on Belgrade Television, the only channel that reaches the entire republic (as well as Serb-held areas of Bosnia), is a nightly compendium of conspiracy theories, turgid speeches, and lurid rumors—all conveying the view that Serbia and its leader, Milosevic, stand alone against a vast, genocidal German-American-Croat-Muslim plan. Scenes of shells blasting houses in Sarajevo are accompanied by a narrative telling viewers that Serb troops once again were forced to respond to Muslim aggression. My favorite outrageous Belgrade TV report concerned the Serb babies whom Muslims fed to the lions at the Sarajevo zoo. I was amused, until I heard the story repeated verbatim by a 55-year-old woman standing in line outside the Yugoskandic bank. "That's why the Serbs had to kill the animals," she explained.

Belgrade's Museum of Applied Art currently features "The Genocide Museum," an exhibition of graphic photos of Serbs who have been hacked, stabbed, shot, and mutilated by Croats. A section downstairs is devoted to butchery by the fascist Croatian independent state during World War II. It displays black-and-white shots of bloated bodies washed up on the banks of the Sava River, as well as lovingly exhumed bits of skin, teeth, and bone. Upstairs, contemporary horrors are presented in living color. The curators have included a picture of Pope John Paul II above a photo of Croatian President Franjo Tudjman. Croat atrocities, a sign says, "are backed up by the organized force of state, church, and party." Nearly every high school student in Belgrade has been brought to absorb the message that, as Svetlana Isakovic, the museum's director, puts it, "what's happening now is just a continuation of World War II."

Milan Panic, the 62-year-old prime minister of what's left of Yugoslavia, is the only remotely credible political force standing between Milosevic and uncontested power. Panic, who parlayed $200 and a U.S. immigration visa into a vast pharmaceutical manufacturing fortune, returned to his native land at Milosevic's invitation last July. At the time, Milosevic thought Panic might help him clean up Serbia's image abroad. Instead, he got off the reservation. Waving his arms and expostulating in Serbian-accented English and American-accented Serbo-Croatian, Panic warns that only he can democratize Serbia and get the sanctions lifted. A good many Serbians, at least those in Belgrade who have access to independent TV and radio, have been listening.

The Panic-Milosevic showdown pits a quixotic, American-style liberal against a former Communist steeped in the sinuous political culture of the Balkans. Milosevic seems to be toying with his opponent. A month ago the Serbian president sent his goons to seize the Federal Interior Ministry, the one agency with any muscle that Panic conceivably could have used against him. Last week Milosevic cast the Panic campaign into limbo by arranging for the electoral commission to rule Panic ineligible for the presidency because he hasn't been a resident of Serbia for at least a year, as required by a law Milosevic quietly pushed through Parliament on November 3. Ever the democrat, Panic appealed to the Supreme Court, which happens to be headed by the same member of Milosevic's Socialist Party as the electoral commission. The court threw the matter back to the commission, which promptly ruled against Panic again. Panic appealed again, and this time Milosevic let him win.

There's little chance that Milosevic and his paramilitary minions will go quietly even in the unlikely event that they do lose the election. Milosevic still enjoys considerable popular support, particularly among the older generation who depend on his government for pensions and on Belgrade TV for information. But voters do have an alternative to both Milosevic and Panic. Boss Jezda is a candidate for president too. "I decided to run as a private referendum, to find out how many of my clients are ready to protect their income and myself," he explains. It's the kind of information a man needs when his business activities depend so heavily on the trust of his customers. "Besides," he adds, "I didn't want any of the other candidates hitting me up for contributions."

(DECEMBER 28, 1992)

Dateline Croatia: Survivors

CHARLES LANE

A stale mist of frozen breath and cigarette smoke hangs over the town square of Karlovac, Croatia. Hundreds of haggard men clad incongruously in bright blue, red, or green ski jackets shuffle about on the chilly gray pavement. Every now and then someone spots an old friend, or a long-lost child or his mother—and a cry of recognition punctuates the collective murmur. But mostly the men converse quietly among themselves, or gaze at nothing in particular. They have recently been released from the Serb-run concentration camps in northern Bosnia.

The catastrophe of Bosnia's Muslims may not be, as some have analogized, the Holocaust. But it is a holocaust. And the men of Karlovac are holocaust survivors. Their faces, puffy and scarred like the mugs of welter-weights, testify to savage beatings. Their blank eyes reflect psychological wounds. Months after the outside world first became aware of the camps' existence, international relief agencies are still working to get all the men out of the camps, to bring them to the barracks in Karlovac, to give them medical care and ski jackets—

and to begin the laborious process of finding asylum for them in the West. Countries that chorused denunciation of the camps when confronted with television images of emaciated prisoners last August have been slow to offer refuge for the men and their families.

The stories the men tell are all more or less the same, but that heightens rather than diminishes their impact. Schefik, a square-jawed 38-year-old construction worker, lived in a Muslim village near Klucj. Serb forces surrounded his village with artillery sometime last spring but assured the people they would be safe if they didn't move. On June 26, Schefik says, the Serbs broke their promise. They arrested all the men in the village, packed them in buses, and took them to a school building in Klucj. Local Serbs—children included—formed a gauntlet and beat the Muslims with clubs as they went in. Inside, each man was stripped to the waist, interrogated and savagely beaten by Serb police demanding to know where nonexistent weapons were kept. Schefik says he saw four men die from repeated beatings. He himself passed out three times from the rain of blows.

After two days in the school, Schefik was loaded onto another bus bound for the infamous Manjaca camp. A tape deck blared a song about how the Serbs would "butcher" Muslims there, while Serb police shook prisoners down for money and watches. The bus stopped en route, and local Serb women and children boarded to beat the prisoners. At the camp, a doctor measured the bruises on the men's backs; those whose bruises were considered minor based on this "medical examination" were taken out for additional punishment. The men were herded into cattle barns. "There was no light, no heating. They said, 'Find a place' but there was just sand and cement," Schefik recalls. "Every night they would call people out to take them to solitary confinement. Whoever was on the list to be killed would be killed." The list included all wealthy or prominent citizens, intellectuals, and leaders of the Muslim Party of Democratic Action.

Prisoners who weren't killed were fed a diet of bread and water and forced to chop wood and pull large fields of weeds. As I learned from Schefik and other former Manjaca prisoners now at Karlovac, a team of forty Muslim craftsmen was ordered to rebuild an old Serbian Orthodox church that had fallen into disrepair near the site of the concentration camp. Guards taunted the men as "Turks" as they worked. For roofing material, the Serbs ordered them to use the copper roof of a nearby mosque that the Serbs had demolished. Schefik thought he would die in Manjaca; if international condemnation of the camps last August had not scared the Serb nationalist authorities into permitting the International Red Cross to visit and feed the prisoners, he might have.

The Karlovac survivors are trying to come to terms with the fact that so many of their former neighbors in Bosnia's small towns and villages were so readily recruited to the cause of ethnic cleansing. "My brother is married to a Serb. They live in Sarajevo," Schefik says. "I was friends with them. I drank coffee in their cafés. I went hunting with them. I cannot believe there could be that much hate in a person." Another survivor from Sanski Most told me he was accosted at Manjaca by a Serb who used to play soccer with him on a hometown team. "This is for that time you kicked me in practice," the guard told him—and proceeded to administer a fierce beating.

The men of Karlovac want asylum, but they also want guns. "I feel like a different person now," 22-year-old Edin, a Muslim from Prijedor, told me. His face reddened as he spoke about his time in the Omarska and Manjaca camps. "Now I would do some things I never would have done before. I don't know if it would make a difference to fight now, but I would." This widespread attitude is yet another measure of how toxic the political culture of Bosnia has become as a consequence of so many unchecked war crimes—of how late it is for the United States and other Western powers to be discussing military intervention. Intervention to create a safe haven for Muslim refugees may yet save thousands of lives, or force the Serbs to talk seriously at the bargaining table in Geneva. Yet Karlovac is just one of many places where the fresh rage of horribly wronged individuals is hardening into a permanent collective political grievance. It is a grievance that could haunt Europe for generations.

After all, this process has occurred repeatedly in the history of the Balkans, as ethnic groups have transformed remembered trauma into a contemporary rationale for violence. Many Serbs rationalize today's ethnic cleansing as a payback for the wrongs committed against their people by the Ottoman Turks. Now the Serbs' own horrible crimes could turn their propaganda about the threat of "Muslim fundamentalism" into a kind of self-fulfilling prophecy. Even if the survivors of today's savagery don't fulfill their vows to retake their homes, or even if they don't get a chance to try, some of their children will.

Perhaps the cycle might have been interrupted if outside powers had shown the Serbs that aggression in Bosnia would be met with punishing force, or if the West had attempted to shore up the Muslim-led government in Sarajevo before the war, when it was still pursuing relatively democratic, moderate solutions to the nation's multiethnic tensions. But, for reasons of its own, the West didn't take the risk, another fact that is on the list of things the men of Karlovac will never forget. "If 100,000 animals of some special breed were being slaughtered like this," one told me, "there would have been more of a reaction."

(JANUARY 25, 1993)

Dateline Bosnia: Beyond Pale

CHARLES LANE

On the day after the Bosnian Serb parliament voted to reject the Vance-Owen peace plan, I found myself sitting down to a St. George's Day feast at the Serb home of Slavisa Guja, 29, and his extended family in Pale, a ski resort just a dozen miles east of Sarajevo. The table was laden with home-made bread, Russian salad, smoked meat, chicken, steak, bread, pastries, and jugs of *slivovitz*. Slavisa turned on the TV and popped a tape of his own band's music videos called "Fatherland" into the VCR. Mournful tunes and Slavisa's wailing voice mingled with images of blood and war: Slavisa's special forces unit training on horseback in the snow; Serb refugees fleeing the suburbs of Sarajevo; Christ on the cross.

A shot of the Statue of Liberty rolled by, accompanied by a warning: "America, this is where our destiny is. This is the fatherland of a Serb." The scene from New York harbor dissolved into footage of Hitler's troops, as Slavisa sang: "Angry Germans, you have shed enough blood. We haven't forgiven this yet." Finally, Slavisa addressed his Serb brethren across the Drina: "White eagles soar, leading the people to freedom. Serbia, mother, do you hear? This is where you are being defended as well. This is where your destiny lies, too." Over and over, Slavisa's voice chorused: "The Drina is running with blood; the Drina is running with blood." He pointed to the automatic gun hanging from a peg on the wall. "That is my future," he said with what I thought was exaggerated solemnity. "I have traded my guitar for this." But couldn't more war have been avoided if the Bosnian Serb assembly had accepted Vance-Owen? "No," he said, resuming his tone of injured gravity, "no matter how we voted, what the world powers decide will be done."

The fatalism, nationalistic rapture and feelings of victimization of people like Slavisa cast a long shadow over the already dubious referendum in which the Bosnian Serbs will vote on whether to accept the Vance-Owen plan to end the war in Bosnia. The more territory the Serbs cleanse in Bosnia, the more they protest their own vulnerability to genocide. On the way from Pale to Belgrade, I drove the two-lane mountain highway from Vlasenica in Eastern Bosnia to Zvornik on the Drina. It is a road through ruin. Muslim village after Muslim village stands burned and abandoned, red-tiled ghost towns tucked into the green hills. The remains of a mosque lay in a neat pile, the crushed minaret still discernible amid the white rubble. Circular holes, made by tanks and grenade launchers fired from short range, gape in the sides of houses. Jagged black smoke smudges ring smashed-out windows. Graffiti scream "Fuck you" in Cyrillic Serbian characters. A few items of property, left behind by looters, sit on the sidewalks: a table and chairs, a washing machine, bits of clothing. The Serbs' campaign in this area ended more than a month ago. But even now, a couple houses are still burning.

A
t a checkpoint in the charred and looted center of Nova Kasaba, an old Muslim town, Serb militiamen stood guard amid the destruction and told me of the suffering inflicted on their people by the Muslims. (There were atrocities by Muslims during an ill-fated winter counteroffensive in the area.) But down the road, in Milici, a Serb village, children could be seen walking home from school and skipping rocks in a river, as if the war were a million miles away. The men insisted that what I saw around me was a last-ditch defense against Muslim fundamentalism. The area was designated for Muslim control under the Vance-Owen plan, but they said they would rather die than live together again with their former neighbors. "The American media lie," said Ljubo, 28. "No one asks Serb mothers who lost so many children. What about the Serb women in Sarajevo being kept in brothels?" Ljubo's partner, who wouldn't give his name, chimed in, "Would you want to convert to Islam? Would you want your wife to wear a veil?"

Serbian President Slobodan Milosevic is for Vance-Owen not because he fears for the "destiny" of the Bosnian Serbs, but because he fears that international sanctions and the threat of Western air strikes have turned the Bosnian war from a boon to his rule into a threat. Angry and humiliated by his erstwhile Bosnian clients' repudiation of his advice at Pale, Milosevic has cut off the Bosnian Serbs' supplies and angrily summoned their leaders to Belgrade.

T
his fit of pique has done little except to draw attention to Milosevic's loss of control over Serbia's Bosnian brothers. General Ratko Mladic, the square-jawed commander of the Bosnian Serb army, is the new Bosnian Serb strongman. He seized that role from Milosevic at three o'clock in the morning on the conference's second day. That was when he mounted the podium to deliver his own military-style briefing on the plan. Delegates watched trans-

fixed as he superimposed a transparent map of the Vance-Owen plan on a map of the Serb's current holdings, showing how much strategic territory the Serbs would give up. Serbs would be confined to islands of territory with only untrustworthy United Nations troops to protect their lines of communication, he said. Then Mladic unveiled his clinching argument: the Vance-Owen map bears a striking resemblance to one that appears on page 32 of a book written in 1970 by a historian from the mixed Bosnian Muslim-Croat town of Vitez, he said—proof that the whole thing is yet another genocidal plot devised by the Serbs' historic local enemies. Unlike Milosevic, Mladic speaks in words the local Serbs can relate to. "We can't forget about the graves of those who were lost in war," he told the Belgrade daily *Novosti*. "No matter how the world and our neighbors view this, we have to respect our victims. In this crucial moment, we are threatened by the total extermination of the Serb people."

It's anyone's guess whether Mladic really believes his own rhetoric. But already he's pursuing his own alternative to Milosevic's strategy. By negotiating a cease-fire with Sarajevo's forces last week, he seems grudgingly to be willing to tolerate demilitarized safe areas in Muslim enclaves like Srebrenica and Zepa that have already been starved and shelled into submission. Why should Serbs live in U.N. police enclaves, he seems to be saying, when they still have the muscle to make the Muslims do so instead? Such a plan assumes twin risks: the severing of supplies by Serbia proper, and the risk of eventual international military intervention. But the dithering of the international community has given Mladic little reason to fear foreign bombing will actually materialize. And in any case, Bosnian Serbs have gone too far to turn back now. For the general himself, the alternative to war could be a war crimes tribunal. For Serbs in areas that Vance-Owen would return to the Muslims, like those at the checkpoint in Nova Kasaba, it is the return of the very neighbors whom they have just shed so much blood to expel. For both, confrontation, whether with their brothers across the Drina or with Western forces, is preferable.

Of course, not every one in Mladic's dominion is enthusiastic about the road he would have them take. In quiet moments among family and friends, ordinary Serbs in Bosnia will sigh and concede to you that they think the thirteen-month-old war has gone on long enough, at a high enough cost in lives—Serb and Muslim alike. They know that casualties on the Serb side have risen steadily, as the Muslims have recovered from the initial Serb onslaught, captured or bought weapons, and learned to fight. Some even speak wistfully about the days in which Bosnia's nationalities lived together. Why not accept Vance-Owen, if it will bring an end to this nightmare? they say. Funerals, especially, draw doves. In Pale, Nada Pandurovic and her soldier son, wearing a uniform and carrying a gun, were hitchhiking home from the last rites of her friend Milos Kusic, 48, killed fighting on the front lines in Sarajevo. "What would you do with a Serb republic when you don't have any youth in it any longer?" Nada wondered aloud. But under their current leaders, there's little chance that the Bosnian Serbs will find their way to a sensible answer. Destiny beckons, and white eagles are soaring overhead.

(MAY 31, 1993)

Dateline Sarajevo: Boom Town

ANNA HUSARSKA

There are ample reasons for grief over here—blood-covered sidewalks, bombed-out hospitals, overcrowded cemeteries—yet the only time my eyes got misty was when I met Sadik Besirevic, the general director of Bosnia and Herzegovina Railways. Besirevic received me on a Sunday morning in his spacious office. He went out of his way to make a positive impression: he wore his Sunday best (a sharkskin suit, purple shirt, and a red paisley tie), offered coffee and vodka, and gave very detailed answers to my questions.

It was painful to hear Besirevic list all the losses that his company has suffered: 200 out of 500 passenger cars destroyed, thirty-five of 200 locomotives wrecked, 800 freight cars missing, twelve railway bridges destroyed. He estimated the total damage at $500 million. He told me about his family, which had been decimated in this war: his two brothers (Muslims) were killed by Serb nationalists—one left a Croat widow, another a Serb widow. His four nephews and brother-in-law also died in the fighting.

But the tale became unbearably pathetic when Besirevic started talking about his plans for Bosnia and Herzegovina Railways: "The new tickets will be ready soon," he boasted. But they will be tickets to pretty much nowhere; of the pre-war 660 miles of track, only six miles are currently in use. "The new uniforms for the rail personnel are being designed, so as to conform with our new image," he enthused. Never mind that there is no fabric to sew *any* kind of clothing in Sarajevo. Besirevic wants the new Bosnian trains to be "as elegant as the Austrian ones, which is necessary since we will be rejoining Europe."

He was particularly proud of the company's redesigned logo and letterhead. "With these we're showing a more European image. We think it's good for the company," he bragged as he unrolled a poster bearing the elegant new image: two interlocked blue and green arrows. On the bottom of the poster were photos of the destroyed railway station in Sarajevo. In the center the message read, "The future is in front of us," and just below it, in smaller letters, a simple appeal: "Support Us!"

"Very international, no?" he said, fishing for a compliment. I nodded energetically and blamed my tears on the cigarette smoke. Expressing any doubt that there is a future in the railway is like telling a child that there is no point in writing to Santa Claus. The truth is, in Sarajevo, whose 380,000 inhabitants are barely surviving, even Besirevic's job is not the most surreal. Think of postmen with no letters to deliver, drivers with no trams to drive, guides with no tourists to lead, librarians whose collections of books have been burned or stored away. Paradoxical as it may sound, the one area of activity that has best preserved a semblance of normality in spite of the war, and against all odds, is culture and the arts.

At studio Trio Dizajn, Dada Durakovic (a Muslim) and her husband, Bojan Hadzihalilovic (a Serbo-Jew), who designed the logo and the poster for Besirevic (in exchange for Meals-Ready-to-Eat), have their work interrupted all the time by blackouts: a candle can replace a bulb, but the computer and laser printer need electricity. When the war started they moved the studio from the front room of their apartment—too exposed to snipers—to the kitchen. They cook in the bathroom.

Like Besirevic, Dada and Bojan work to forget about the war. Of course, the goodies they receive in exchange come in handy, especially since they share their apartment with half a dozen friends and relatives whose houses have been destroyed. When Dada and Bojan designed new ID cards for the Bosnian army and the police, they were presented with oil, sugar, feta cheese, and peas. As payment for drawing the covers of the weekly *Dani* (Days), the publishers bring them booze. They received reams of paper for producing a fancy invitation for a book party. (The book: *Mom, I Don't Want to Go to the Basement,* a collection of children's drawings and writings about the war.)

When they designed the package for a new brand of cigarettes, the company offered them 30,000 ciggies. The design is very handsome—a Bosnian coat of arms from 1340 that Dada found in a historical book about Yugoslavia. On the back of the pack is printed a short text. Not about the danger of smoking, but about democracy: a quote from the 1910 Bosnian constitution saying,

"All citizens are equal before the law." When I mentioned the "surgeon general's warning," Bojan joked that in Sarajevo it would be more fitting to print a different warning: *Pazi Snajper*—Beware of Snipers. "The new brand of cigarettes will be called 'Bosnae,'" Dada said, but the others in the room corrected her: "*Would* be called." And they laughed, because all know that in a few months the tobacco company will run out of tobacco.

Dada gave her cigarette logo to Cika Fahro, the most famous jeweler in Sarajevo, who produced beautiful cigarette cases for the planned new brand. Cika (who is a Muslim) and his wife, Teta Radmila (a Serbo-Croat), have no children of their own, but five young people have lived with them since the beginning of the war and five others come to work in the attic of their house in the Old Town, depending on the intensity of the shelling. Four are Muslims, three are Serbs, two are Croats ,and one is a Serbo-Croat, though it's a hassle to get them to tell me their ethnic origin because they all identify themselves as "Bosnian." So much for the impossibility of the three ethnic groups living together.

"In this household we lost 252 pounds all in all," explains Cika when I remark that they've all become slim since I saw them last year. "Bogi lost the most, eighty pounds," says Mladen, the Serb. "I did not lose it," objects Bogi, "they stole it from me. Just imagine, I would be a rich man if I could peddle all this meat at twenty-five deutsche marks a pound," the current price here. They don't buy meat nowadays; it is too expensive. "We eat it in playback; one speaks about it, the others eat bread or rice," jokes Mladen. To enrich their diet they grow salad greens and onions on the balcony in plastic boxes and empty food cans. (Cika is in charge of that.) Bogi, who lives in another part of town, picks *zara,* a weed rich in iron, that they add to the salad. One of Cika's nephews buys the bread, and Bruno (the Croat) brings to the household the food he gets as humanitarian aid. "Sarajevo should be renamed 'Lotograd'— because survival and food distribution are both a lottery," he says.

Survival is certainly a time-consuming occupation, but at least there is plenty of work for jewelers in this war. They produce pendants, earrings, and pins with the fleur-de-lis insignia (the symbol of Bosnia) for women, and decorations for the police and the army.

The jewelers and the graphic designers are not exceptions. Most of the cultural community of Sarajevo is very active: there is an army orchestra (it plays Glenn Miller tunes and military marches from memory—all of their sheet music was lost during the war); the Kamerni Theater, which has six plays in its repertoire; fashion shows, rock concerts, disco nights, chess tournaments, photo exhibitions, a Miss Sarajevo contest. The Obala Theater had an exhibition of visual art, and when Miro Purivatra, the manager, finds fuel for the generator, the Obala even shows movies (*Thelma and Louise* was a recent hit). Every evening the local television station has an excellent cultural broadcast called "RAT ART" (*rat* means "war").

Just staying alive in Sarajevo is difficult, but the city's artists push the challenge even further by trying to keep the cultural life alive. They are neither ignorant nor naive: they know that their country is slowly being destroyed as the outside world stares on, passively. But Sarajevo's artists treat their creative work as a way of beating the enemy: they are a dramatic and very literal embodiment of what André Malraux meant when he wrote: *l'art est un anti-destin*—"art is a revolt against destiny."

(AUGUST 16, 1993)

Dateline Pristina: The Next Bosnia

ANNA HUSARSKA

Waiting at the bus terminal in Skopje, Macedonia, I took out my digital wristwatch, which holds telephone numbers, and entered the names of my contacts in Pristina, the capital of the southern Serb province of Kosovo. I must have looked slightly ridiculous, because Marco, an Italian photographer accompanying me to Pristina, stared at me, bemused. So as not to seem paranoid, I handed him a stack of reports and press clippings on human rights abuses in Kosovo. Several cited cases of journalists having their notebooks confiscated.

No sooner had we crossed the border from Macedonia into Kosovo than the bus—filled entirely with Albanians—was stopped at a checkpoint. Serbian policemen came on board and, at random, dragged off two men and searched them thoroughly. Then the policemen ripped up the address books that the

Albanians had in their wallets. The two men returned to the bus and sat without a word. When I asked them what happened, they shrugged. It obviously was not the first or the last time such a thing had happened to them; they, too, said they had made copies of their addresses.

My interest in their fate won Marco and me some sympathy among the passengers. When we arrived in Pristina, a couple of them offered to show us the way to the municipal bus stop. But when we started the usual chit-chat, they kindly asked us not to speak to them in public, and to walk at some distance. Befriending foreigners can bring them trouble. (I had read about that in my stack of reports, too.)

We waited a good half-hour for the bus: the embargo imposed on the whole of Serbia has hit Kosovo as well, stymieing municipal transportation, electricity, and most other utilities and public services. During those thirty minutes, two convoys of cars decorated with "Just Married" streamers passed by honking. Both were adorned with flags bearing a double-headed black eagle on a red background. This is the Albanian flag, and—as the people at the bus stop explained to us—except for weddings, Albanians in Kosovo cannot display it.

One does not have to be an habitué of repressive regimes to feel the tension here. The Serbian militia is everywhere. (Our contacts in Pristina instructed us to meet them on a back street close to the Grand Hotel, but not in front of it. The hotel, they explained, is the hangout of the Serb army and secret police forces.) While the Serbs continue their war in Bosnia, here in tiny Kosovo (population 2 million) they apply a subtler combination of oppression and repression. The oppression is patterned after apartheid: a minority denying all rights to a majority (in Kosovo, Albanians outnumber the Serbs nine to one, but the Serbs outgun the Albanians ten to zero). The repression is reminiscent of Polish martial law: Serb forces (black and blue camouflage, bulletproof vests, walkie-talkies) patrol the towns and villages, arresting and beating Albanians with little regard to the law. The Albanians' response is a nonviolent resistance à la Solidarity.

When we finally hooked up with our contacts, they led us to a small wooden hut that stood in a muddy wasteland next to the central police station. A few expensive Japanese cars were parked outside. Plaques on either side of the door read: "Albanian PEN Center" and "Kosovo Writers Association." It did not look like a base of the Albanian resistance (especially given its proximity to the police), but it is one. Although there is no plaque announcing it, this is the headquarters of the Democratic League of Kosovo (LDK), the leading party of the republic. Inside, amid humming faxes and photocopying machines, a staff of well-dressed young men who look like they're fresh from Wall Street prepares statements, translates bulletins, and informs the world about the persecution all around them.

• • •

The normality is deceptive. The Serbs avoid hurting Albanian leaders because it would get them bad publicity; but they do not shy away from beating and arresting civilians, raiding houses and stealing jewelry, foreign cash, and cameras from ordinary people. Adem Demaci, president of Kosovo's Council on Human Rights, says that in the town of Glogovac (population 6,000), 171 houses were raided, 403 people were beaten and 156 arrested in reprisal for the deaths of two Serb policemen.

This sort of thing has been going on for nearly four years, as Kosovo's status as a de facto autonomous republic within the Yugoslav federation, granted by Josip Broz Tito in 1974, was gradually taken away. Ever since he came to power, Serbia's President Slobodan Milosevic saw the Kosovo issue as a way to increase his own power by inflaming Serb nationalism. He dissolved the local parliament in July 1990, and Belgrade embarked on a wave of mass purges of "disloyal" Albanians. According to Muhamet Hamiti of the Kosovo Information Center, more than 130,000 ethnic Albanians, or Kosovars, have been dismissed from jobs in government, the police, media, schools, and hospitals since 1989. Hamiti, formerly a professor of English literature at the University of Pristina, was thrown out from his job and replaced by a Serb.

The Albanians' response to the Serbs' seizure and monopolization of Kosovo's public institutions was to boycott them and create their own. The parliament went underground (it now operates from Stuttgart); in October 1991 it declared the region's independence. In May 1992 secret parliamentary and presidential elections were held in Kosovo: LDK won 76 percent of the vote, and Dr. Ibrahim Rugova, a poet and literary critic, was elected president of the republic.

Under the independent government, Kosovars set up their own schools with Albanian curriculums and their own clinics and hospitals where Albanians (denied health care in Serb-run hospitals) are attended by Albanian doctors, most of whom were fired from their previous posts. These institutions, plus the welfare system for those who lost their jobs, are financed by the Kosovo Central Fund, whose money comes from Kosovar émigrés. (Last year, it received more than $1 million in donations.)

President Rugova is 48 years old; his hair, balding on top, is long and disheveled on the sides. When he received us in his office in the LDK hut, he was uncharacteristically without the trademark kerchief that he wears around his neck. Rugova says he is very proud of Kosovars—"we succeeded in leading a nonviolent fight and in surviving"—but is rather pessimistic about the future of the region. "The bloodbath would be worse here than in Bosnia, because of the higher population density. And besides, we have nowhere to go. The border with Albania is all mountains."

Rugova says he is counting on international support to avoid being swallowed by the Serbs. "We want preventive measures. We have asked for the establishment of an international trusteeship or a protectorate." His demands sounded faintly unrealistic, coming just a week after the Serbs expelled from Kosovo a group of observers from the Conference on Security and Cooperation in Europe. "The Serbs now want all of our territory," he says matter-of-factly. "In Bosnia, they grabbed the land because of ethnic rights; here in Kosovo they claim historical rights."

Indeed, for the Serbs the region is the cradle of their civilization. In 1389, under czar Lazar, the Serbs battled the Ottoman forces. They lost, and the defeat ended the medieval Serb Empire. Six hundred years later, Milosevic pledged to more than 1 million Serbs gathered for the anniversary of the battle that never again would anyone beat the Serbs. Until now, he has been proved right. The Serbs are getting away with creating a Greater Serbia. With the war in Bosnia almost over, they may look for other outlets for their aggression. Kosovo is in their sights.

(NOVEMBER 15, 1993)

Falling Down

SLAVENKA DRAKULIĆ

I have three photos of Mostar in front of me. One is a postcard, a sepia-colored photo printed on poor, cardboardlike paper. It is dated September 1953, when my father sent it to us on his first visit to Bosnia-Herzegovina. In the center of the photo is the Old Bridge—all postcards of Mostar have that bridge on them, of course—and a part of the old city. "I think of you as I walk over this beautiful bridge," he wrote to my mother and me in Rijeka, Croatia. I can imagine him walking there on a warm autumn day. Coming to the middle, to the place where young boys used to jump into the river to prove their courage, he must have leaned over the stone railing and looked into the Neretva below, quick and silent as a snake. He must have stopped there, overwhelmed by the elegance of the stone construction. When his hands touched the bridge, he must have felt its smoothness and warmth, as if he had touched skin instead of stone. It was as if the bridge had a life of its own, a soul given to it by the people who had crossed it in its almost 400 years of existence. It was erected in 1566 during the Turkish Empire and, the story goes, the stones were stuck together with mortar that had been mixed with the whites of eggs. Serbs and Turks, Croats and Jews, Greeks and Albanians, Austrians and Hungarians, Catholics, Orthodox, Bogumils, and Muslims—all had stopped at the same spot, rested on the same stone. I was 4 when he wrote that postcard, and I know that he was certain that one day I would see and touch the Mostar bridge, too.

My father was wrong. I did not make it. I foolishly thought the bridge would be there forever. So, I never went to Mostar, never walked from one bank of the river to the other. The bridge that saw so many wars, survived so many years, no longer exists. It collapsed in a second on November 9. All I have to remember it by are these three photos: before, during, and after. And I wonder what my father, dead for years now, would have said if he had seen this other photo, the last before the bridge was destroyed. Would he recognize it, ragged and pitiful as an old beggar, with a makeshift wooden roof, black automobile tires and sandbags piled in a futile effort to protect it from the occasional shelling that had started with the war?

When the bridge collapsed, it was Tuesday morning. A pleasant, sunny day, much like the one when my father visited Mostar. The town is only about seventy miles from the Adriatic sea, so winter comes rather late. The bridge had been shelled since Monday afternoon. People who saw it say its collapse did not last long: at 10:30 A.M. the bridge just fell. As I look at the second picture, I try to imagine the sound of the Old Bridge falling down. A bridge like that doesn't just disappear; its collapse must have sounded like a swift, powerful earthquake, the kind that people in Mostar have never heard before. Or maybe it sounded like an old tree splitting in two—a hollow crack followed by a long silence. Whatever the sound, the river swallowed it in a single morsel. A while later, it was as if the bridge had never existed.

The third photo of Mostar is one I cut out of a newspaper and carry around with me. It is in color and, paradoxically, the most beautiful of the three that I have. The sun shines over the rooftops of the old city, painting the stone houses white. The slightly swollen river, a rich, deep green, rubs along its banks like a lazy, satiated animal. Absent from this beauty, however, is the bridge. There's the beginning of its long stone arch, but if that portion were only ten feet shorter, there would be no trace of the structure at all. Only the sheer logic of the place, a feeling that a bridge belongs there, over the river, between two halves of a medieval town, tells us that something is missing. It's been a little more than two weeks, and I'm still surprised when I look at the photo. When I remember what is no longer there, I feel a spasm in my stomach, a knot in my throat. I feel death lurking in its absence.

I've heard that people in Mostar, even adults, cried when they saw that the bridge had fallen. I believe the reports, for I have seen people who are not from Mostar cry as well. An elderly journalist. A lawyer. A singer, who wept for the first time since the war started. Not so long ago the newspapers published photos of a massacre in the Bosnian Muslim village of Stupni Dol. One picture showed a middle-aged woman with a long, dark knife-cut along her throat. I don't remember anyone crying over that photo or others like it. And I ask myself: Why do I feel more pain looking at the image of the destroyed bridge than the image of the woman? Perhaps it is because I see my own mortality in the collapse of the bridge, not in the death of the woman. We expect people to die. We count on our own lives to end. The destruction of a monument to civilization is something else. The bridge, in all its beauty and grace, was built to outlive us; it was an attempt to grasp eternity. Because it was the product of both individual creativity and collective experience, it transcended our individual destiny. A dead woman is one of us—but the bridge is all of us, forever.

The war in Bosnia-Herzegovina is well into its second year now. You would think that nothing new could happen, that, after the concentration camps and the mass rapes, the ethnic cleansing and the slow, cold death of Sarajevo, there would be no room left for imagination. But this war seems to have neither rules nor limits. Just when you think nothing could possibly surprise, something happens—even more violent, more painful, more surprising than before.

Finally—who did it? The Muslims are accusing the Croats, the Croats are accusing the Muslims. But does it even matter? For four centuries people needed that bridge and admired its beauty. The question is not who shelled and demolished it. The question is not even why someone did it—destruction is part of human nature. The question is: What kind of people do not need that bridge? The only answer I can come up with is this: people who do not believe in the future—theirs or their children's—do not need such a bridge. For me, this is the chilling measure of the photo of Mostar without its Old Bridge. This is why I would say that those people—whoever they might be— do not belong to this civilization, civilization built on the idea of time, civilization built on the idea of a future. Even if they rebuild the Mostar bridge and reconstruct it meticulously, they are barbarians.

Holding the old postcard in my hand, I regret that I have not been there. My father is dead. The sepia color is washed out; the existing postcards of

Mostar with the Old Bridge in the middle will probably disappear, too. My daughter will only remember a story about a beautiful stone bridge that, once upon a time, existed in a far away country shattered by a long, long war. And I myself have no memory of my own of the bridge now, when I need it the most.

(DECEMBER 13, 1993)

———————— ❖❖ ————————

Dateline Sarajevo:
Back on Track

ZLATKO DIZDAREVIC

Sometime last summer, when we still used to try to imagine the day when everything would finally stop and we could head south, toward the sea, one of my friends said: "As far as I'm concerned, I'll know the war is over when the trolleys start running again and, like in the old days, I can get on the No. 2 and take it to the end of the line, right to Villa Cengic. And we can pass all the way across 'Sniper's Avenue,' but no one will be shooting at us."

We laughed then, looking over the twisted tracks, the fallen power lines, the wrecked and burned-out trolleys. The trolleys remained exactly where grenade and mortar shells had stopped them dead in their tracks in May of 1992. It seemed like everything else—the end of the war, a return to normal life—would come before the trolleys started running again. We figured that we'd get to the sea by car, or maybe even somewhere farther by plane, before we'd be able to make it to Villa Cengic on the No. 2 red line.

Things turned out differently. The conflict made fools of us again. When it comes to forecasting war and peace, politics and life, we have to admit, once more, that we're complete amateurs. The trolley is running. The tracks have been straightened out. The power lines have been put up and a few red cars, in mint condition, have been hauled out from God knows where. But none of this has anything to do with the end of the war we had imagined. And it has nothing to do with what our trip on the No. 2 would have meant. There is still no peace waiting for us at Villa Cengic.

What stands out most about the No. 2, as it makes its way through dead neighborhoods, is the route's senselessness. The trip is nothing more than movement from one place to another within the same concentration camp, the same prison. Once upon a time we used to sit in the No. 2 and head down to Bascarsija, the heart of the Old City of Sarajevo. Today the area is just a gaping hole, empty and calm. We used to get on the No. 1 and head for the railroad station and then go on from there, by train, to other places. Like people. Now there are no trains; there isn't even a railroad station. If they start the No. 1 again, what good will it be if it only serves the same bogus purpose as the No. 2? There were times when we used to pile into the No. 3 and somehow make it to Ilidza. And from there we could go wherever our hearts desired: down the old tree-lined avenue to the source of the Bosnia River, up to Mt. Igman or even to nowhere in particular. Thanks to the world's kindness and affection, Ilidza now belongs to "them"; it is at the other end of the world, somewhere on another planet. You can't get there, as everyone well knows, by trolley. A revived No. 3 won't be able to do us much good either.

The No. 2 is off and running, and everything else stays still, with very little hope that anything is about to change. What a blunder it was to think that, one day, a trolley would take us to freedom. For the rest of the world—especially for the politicians and diplomats who try to get us to accept their lies, who try to get us to tell the world how happy we are—the resurrected trolley is a triumph. But what is it to us? How can we even begin to explain that we've always liked going to Ilidza, the railroad station, Mostar, the sea? And that we'd much rather go to these places on foot than have the ability to "freely" roll to nowhere on a trolley. As the No. 2 stops at every station on its aborted route across nothing, it creates an illusion that is equally senseless, revolting, and desperate.

Of course, it isn't easy trying to explain this to people who think that the only aim in life is to fill your stomach and your pockets, and that you can be as happy as a cow in five square meters of living space as long as you have your mercy provisions—the gift of a "landlord" or humanitarian organization. It's also tough to put a damper on the warm feelings of all those who helped get "Operation Trolley" underway by sending money, technicians, and even cameramen, just to make sure it was recorded for posterity. The "international community" also kept its honor intact and showed its strength, so its leaders have good reason for a victorious toast over a glass of whiskey. A great night-

---

This essay was translated by Ammiel Alcalay.

mare no longer bears down on them in quite the same way or in quite the same place. That nightmare hopped onto the red line, Sarajevo's No. 2, and it's making the rounds now, to the general contentment of some of the exhausted and depleted citizens of Sarajevo.

But it's slightly more difficult to sell this story to those in Sarajevo who are still using their own heads to think with, something that, apparently, may constitute this disobedient city's gravest sin. A few days ago Afan Ramic, an artist, was talking with some people from Japan who had come to visit his studio, which is in an abandoned building that used to be a printing plant. They were a fine bunch, very serious, dignified, and sincere. They listened carefully, spoke carefully, and made offers even more carefully. For hours they studied the canvases, took pictures of the works. Then, with great tact and meticulously chosen words, they conveyed a message to the painter: their TV station, as well as their government, would be honored if he, the Sarajevan artist Afan Ramic, would come to Japan with his paintings. There would be exhibitions, and all expenses would be paid. In short, they saw no problems except, of course, whether this "extremely interesting" painter would be willing to accept their invitation. Would this trip upset any other plans he might have made? Did he find the concept to his liking? Were there any special conditions that needed to be met?

"I looked at them for a while without really knowing what to say. I wasn't really sure, to tell you the truth, whether or not they were pulling my leg or whether they were serious," Afan said later. "I always admired the Japanese for their seriousness. Could it be that after 700 days of imprisonment, hunger, personal tragedy, and every other kind of misery imaginable, they were really asking me whether or not I wanted to go to Japan and have a show? And what's more, did they have any idea what they were saying when they claimed that everything would be OK as far as traveling was concerned? Then I decided to ask them what, around here, always ends up being the most important question: 'That's all well and good as far as Tokyo and Osaka go; I have no doubt that it's also nice in Nagoya and Yokohama, but how am I going to get past the Serb barricades on Ilidza?' I got the feeling that they felt confused and didn't quite grasp what I was asking them. I actually began feeling sorry for them. Then I said, more to myself: 'Forget about it, don't worry, I'll get to Ilidza by trolley.'"

The Japanese went off happy that they had gotten Afan to come to their country. The painter was left to wait for the trolley to Ilidza, or some other mode of transportation the international community could arrange. After all, when you get past Ilidza and that last barricade, everything is a lot easier. From there to Japan isn't far at all.

(APRIL 4, 1994)

Dateline Macedonia: Fear

MISHA GLENNY

A confused bunch of people stare as police and firefighters sift through what is left at the scene of the crime. The minaret still stands like a small rocket pointing to the sky, but the rest of the building has been burned beyond recognition. The gutted mosque has become a common, almost mundane sight in Bosnia. But this is Veles, a dusty, unpleasant industrial town in the center of the former Yugoslav republic of Macedonia.

The mosque was the only one in Veles. It served Albanians, Bosnian Muslims, and the local Islamic Roma community. It went up in flames on March 11. Two days later the government learned that the cause was arson. For four agonizing days government ministers debated whether or not to release their findings. On March 18 they made the information public. "The police don't know who did it," explains Guner Ismael, the minister of culture. "It could have been any number of groups, Christian or Muslim. It is the sort of incident we have to be very careful about."

As an unhappy peace edges slowly toward Bosnia, Macedonia is creeping inexorably toward an internal collapse similar to that which preceded other wars in the former Yugoslavia. "The dominant political party in Macedonia is the Party of Fear," maintains Kole Casule, one of the country's most famous writers and a leader of the 1941 Macedonian uprising against Bulgarian and Nazi occupiers. "There is fear in Parliament, and you can feel the fear on the streets." And with good reason. Macedonia's neighbors—Albania, Serbia, Bulgaria, and Greece—regard it with varying degrees of contempt. Worse, the country's domestic fabric is being severely strained by the deteriorating relations between its Slav majority and its huge Albanian minority (between 20 percent and 40 percent of the population, depending on whom you believe).

Macedonia's problems took a turn for the worse on February 15, when Greece imposed a commercial blockade on the country, cutting off its main oil supply line. Western diplomats considered this a reaction to the American decision to recognize Macedonia. Greece, by contrast, asserted that the former Yugoslav republic's use of the word "Macedonia" implies territorial claims on Greece's northern province of the same name. Athens also wants Macedonia to remove the sixteen-point Sun of Vergina from its flag, maintaining that the symbol is Hellenic cultural property.

The results of the blockade are most visible in the south. At Gevgeljia, a border crossing between Greece and Macedonia, ten lanes of passport and immigration control lie idle. The enormous complex, built to handle thousands of vehicles a day, now sees only a trickle of diplomats and private visitors. Until three years ago, it was among the busiest crossings in Europe, with Turkish *gastarbeiter* and German, French, Dutch, and Scandinavian tourists. In one of the duty-free shops on the Macedonian side, the catatonic staff lolls about, surrounded by thousands of unsold bottles of liquor, cartons of cigarettes, and giant chocolate bars. "On a very good day, we'll get maybe fifty customers," says a cashier, barely reacting to questions. "But since the blockade, trade has more or less collapsed completely."

On one level, Greece's fear of Macedonia is understandable. Like all modern Balkan countries, Greece has been tossed about on the sea of nineteenth- and twentieth-century history, its borders chopped and changed on the tempestuous voyage. The last time this happened was during the Greek civil war, which followed the Second World War—Communist guerrillas, with the support of Slav Macedonians and Serbia, fought to incorporate the Greek part of Macedonia into a Balkan federation. In the latest round of Balkan diplomacy, however, Greece's efforts have succeeded only in making it seem like a bully: a member of NATO with a huge standing army picking on a tiny, landlocked country with four tanks.

According to a Western diplomat in Athens, "The Greeks imagined that it would be a matter of days before the blockade would begin to bite and gas lines to form. It would then be a matter of months, they believed, before the country was brought to its knees." To judge from the streets of Skopje, Macedonia's capital, you would not know it. There are no gas lines (Macedonia is buying oil from Bulgaria and Albania), and the city retains its status as ex-Yugoslavia's curious economic miracle—the shops are full and the dinar, the local currency, is steadily rising against the dollar and the German mark. "Over the period of a year, the blockade will have an impact," says Macedonian President Kiro Gligorov, "but not immediately."

Far more worrisome than the blockade are the tensions between Slavs and Albanians. Tetovo, the center of Macedonia's Albanian community, lies twenty-five miles to the west of Skopje. The drive there cuts through some of the less imposing peaks of the Balkans before revealing the majesty of the Sar mountains. Directly behind them lies Albania; across them to the north is the southern Serbian province of Kosovo, populated largely by Albanians. An erstwhile Ottoman settlement with tiny shops selling the region's culinary goodies—*burek, cevapcici,* and baklava—Tetovo is also home to a new radical movement that dominates the main Albanian political organization in Macedonia, the Party for Democratic Prosperity.

The focus of the movement is 29-year-old Menduh Thaqi. Thaqi has caught the imagination of the western Macedonian Albanians. When he speaks, other Albanians in the room exude a silent respect: "If we do not receive full constitutional parity after the elections," he warns, "then we will begin a campaign of civil disobedience. We will also establish our own political structures, including an Albanian assembly."

It is this threat that worries the authorities in Skopje. After all, the creation of alternative political structures by one national community in Croatia and Bosnia started a war. "Macedonia has succeeded in keeping the peace for two years," says Robert Norman, chief of the U.S. Liaison Office in Skopje. "It faces serious problems, both economic and ethnic. Failure to address either could lead to [what] we have witnessed elsewhere in the former Yugoslavia." The country's future should be clearer after the elections in November. Still, Norman adds, "There is no guarantee that the situation will remain stable that long."

Since Macedonia declared its independence in 1991, the Slav-dominated government has worked harder than any other in the former Yugoslavia to accommodate minority rights. Nevertheless, progress has been slow. Although there are five Albanian ministers in Macedonia's coalition government, Albanians still account for only 3 percent of government employees. In addition, teaching in Albanian remains dreadfully inadequate. In the Tetovo region, only forty-two secondary school classes are conducted in Albanian, although Albanians make up 70 percent of the province's 135,000 inhabitants.

Macedonia's prime minister, Branko Crvenkovski, is one of a number of exceptionally capable young politicians in the government. He has no illusions about the delicacy of the situation. "There is no doubt that if a conflict breaks out here in Macedonia, a Balkan war, involving Albania, Serbia, Bulgaria, Turkey, and Greece, is unavoidable," he says.

According to a Macedonian military adviser, "The third Balkan war in Macedonia would see a three-way carve-up between the Albanians in the west, the Serbs in the north, and the Bulgarians in the east." This is why Greece's decision to impose the blockade has come in for so much flak from the European Union. "The blockade accelerates the possibility of an internal collapse," says another Western diplomat in Athens. "The resulting war would almost certainly end in an expanded Albanian state, an expanded Bulgarian state, and an increased Turkish influence—the blockade runs directly counter to Greece's long-term interests."

If war comes to Macedonia, and it is not unlikely, southeastern Europe will again lurch toward a bloody mire. And like the overwhelming majority in Bosnia, the innocents in Macedonia, who want nothing but peace, will doubtless shoulder the brunt of the conflict's inevitable misery.

(APRIL 25, 1994)

Dateline Sarajevo:
War and Peace

DAVID RIEFF

To anyone who spent much time in Sarajevo before the cease-fire, returning to the city comes as something of a shock. For openers, one can walk around. Since the Serb siege began in April 1992 this is an activity that Sarajevans have undertaken only out of necessity—most often to get food and water—and it has cost many of them their lives. Almost as startling is the fact that a city that was once more expensive than Tokyo is now relatively cheap. When I left Sarajevo at the end of January, a kilogram of coffee cost eighty deutsche marks (DM), a pack of local cigarettes went for six marks, and an egg cost five marks. Now coffee sells for around fifteen DM, cigarettes are a mark and a half and a dozen eggs cost seven DM. And, for the moment at least, prices are still falling. You see bananas in the marketplace and potatoes and half-eaten ends of bread in the garbage.

Although the recently reopened road connecting the Bosnian capital with Bosnian-controlled territory on the other side of the Sarajevo airport is little more than what in the United States would be called a farm route, at present it is jammed with private commercial traffic. It is generally agreed that some 800 private convoys have made the journey from the Dalmatian coast to Sarajevo since the February cease-fire. In part, this is because of a miscalculation by Sarajevo's black marketeers, who apparently reckoned that since every commodity had cost so much during the siege, prices would somehow remain just as high once they could bring in more. Instead, an oversupply was created, and prices fell.

The result is that on the streets of the city, one sees all sorts of foodstuffs (and clothes and consumer goods) at prices that are often cheaper than those in Zagreb, let alone in Serbia. Some, like the shiny new cars that have begun to reappear on Sarajevo's streets, almost certainly were in storage throughout the siege. With every week, at least a semblance of normalcy is being restored to Sarajevo. Once, it was an oddity for there to be silence for more than a short time; now, a burst of automatic weapons fire—for so long the unremarkable background noise of life in the city—is exceptional.

Many people, myself included, have been appalled and disgusted by the policy of the United Nations in Bosnia, believing that the presence of both the Blue Helmets and the humanitarian relief workers has served as a fig leaf for the refusal of the great powers to do anything to prevent the genocide of the Bosnian Muslims and the destruction of the Bosnian state. Yet even we have to admit that U.N. Protection Forces (UNPROFOR) troops have finally begun to improve the lives of Sarajevans. UNPROFOR soldiers are collecting the garbage and repairing the city's tramlines and electric grid. (Most Sarajevans now have some electricity, whereas during the first two years of the fighting most did not.) More important, the soldiers stand guard at key points in the city that used to be free-fire zones for Serb snipers.

Not that the fighting has stopped. Peace is a relative term in Sarajevo. In the four months of the cease-fire, according to doctors at the city's Kosevo Hospital, at least forty people have been killed by Serb snipers and more than 100 have been wounded. But compared to the more than 10,000 who died in the first two years of the siege, the toll of late has been low. Indeed, some Bosnian government officials fear that ordinary Sarajevans have come to take the absence of war so much for granted that if the shelling were to resume again, even for a day, hundreds of pedestrians newly crowding the streets would be killed or injured in the first salvos.

Sarajevans are adapting to the peace as quickly and as resolutely as they did to the shelling and the sniping. Only this time they are applying their ingenuity to the restoration of a civilian environment, albeit a peculiar one. Not a day seems to go by without a new café opening up. In Bascarcija, the old Ottoman center of the city, the owners of the stores that once catered to tourists have unshuttered their shop windows and sit in the summer sun as if expecting business to begin again. Young lovers cuddle together in the parks, and when one sees children running it is after an errant soccer ball—not, as before, in an effort to escape an exploding mortar bomb. Sarajevo is still in ruins, of course, but the people strolling the streets behave almost as if they were in Saint Tropez or Piraeus rather than in a destroyed city that is still under siege.

Indeed, the more one insists on thinking in the present rather than the future tense, as so many ordinary Sarajevans have come to do, the more what is happening in the city seems like an unqualified improvement. As far as the future is concerned, however, there is plenty to be apprehensive about. The United Nations High Commission for Refugees (UNHCR) has reduced its relief effort in the city. John Fawcett, a Canadian relief expert who has been in Sarajevo on and off for almost two years, says there has been no serious attempt to stockpile the kind of fuel people will need next winter. And the Serbs could cut Sarajevo's tenuous lifeline at any moment, at which point the city would again be all but entirely dependent on aid from the UNHCR. In any case, when winter comes the road will become impassable a good part of the time, even if the Serbs hold their fire.

A nd this they are unlikely to do, Bosnians and foreign aid workers alike seem to agree, since by fall the war is almost certain to have begun again in earnest. Whatever hope for a final settlement is held out by officials from UNPROFOR or the so-called contact group of Britain, France, Russia, and the United States, most Bosnians believe that the cease-fire is only a prelude to more fighting. Already in Central Bosnia, Bosnian government troops under the command of Gen. Mechmet Aligic, a former tank officer in the Jugoslav National Army, are nibbling away at Serb positions around Mount Blasic. Aligic has what must be called a pragmatic view of cease-fires: for him, they mean open roads through which trucks laden with weapons can travel freely.

Commanders such as Aligic are often cited by U.N. officials as being the main obstacles to peace. UNPROFOR commander Lt. Gen. Michael Rose, in particular, is said to be outraged by Aligic's intransigence, but as has been the case so often, the U.N. is indulging once more in its favorite sport: blaming the victims. They are right, of course, to insist that if only the Bosnians would accept the partition plan the contact group is now offering, the fighting would stop and the kinds of humanitarian gains that are evident in Sarajevo could be extended to much of the rest of Bosnia. And, from a strictly humanitarian point of view, the Bosnian government's refusal to accept maps based on ethnic cleansing, and its continuing resistance, was always the problem. Many

U.N. officials do not understand why the Bosnians don't surrender and make life easy for themselves, just as a British officer like Rose does not understand why a fighter like Aligic not only goes on resisting but goes on the offensive when the odds are so clearly against him.

The answer is to be found in northern Bosnia, in the area along the Croatian border known as the Bosanska Krajina, one of the first taken by the Bosnian Serbs. It was there, near the cities of Banja Luka and Priejdor, that the secret Serb concentration camps of Manaca, Omarska, and Trnopolje were located. And it was in this region—once home to almost 600,000 Bosnian Muslims—where some of the worst ethnic cleansing took place. By the start of 1994 only a little more than 50,000 non-Serbs remained. In the past few months these people have been forced out at a rate, according to the UNHCR, of almost 500 people per week. In other words, whatever the negotiators and the U.N. officials may wish to believe, or wish the world to believe, the genocide of the Bosnian Muslims has not abated. To the contrary, in Serb-controlled areas it is being stepped up.

If anything, Sarajevo has become a Bosnian Potemkin village writ large and underwritten by the U.N. for its own purposes. There were always two "free" Bosnias—Sarajevo and the rest of the country—but, if anything, improvement in conditions in the capital has only made the divide deeper and more apparent. It is safe to predict that the longer things in Sarajevo continue to improve, the more its citizens are likely to support an end to the war at almost any price. But in Central Bosnia, which is once again deluged by legions of destitute Muslim refugees bearing their tales of evil and atrocity, the only peace most people want is the vengeful kind that comes with victory. And they are beginning to believe it is within their grasp, whatever their fellow citizens in Sarajevo are feeling, and no matter how often UNPROFOR officers tell them the Bosnian cause is lost.

(JULY 18 & 25, 1994)

Dateline Bihac: Picked Pocket

CHARLES LANE

On front lines a few miles west of Bihac, a young soldier named Osme recently explained why he joined Serb forces from next-door Croatia in their assault on the United Nations safe area. Driven from his home three months ago by the Bosnian Army's V Corps, Osme believes the Bihac pocket will never have peace until "war mongers" loyal to the Sarajevo government have been driven out. "The V Corps must be defeated," he told the Associated Press, parroting Bosnian Serb leader Radovan Karadzic. The odd thing is that Osme, like hundreds of other soldiers now moving on Bihac, is a Muslim himself. He is loyal to Fikret Abdić, the renegade Muslim tycoon-cum-warlord who broke with Sarajevo over his decision to make a separate peace with the Serbs, and who has been waging a Serb-backed campaign to wrest the pocket from V Corps ever since.

The world's outrage over Bihac reflects the widely held, and broadly accurate, view of the Bosnia war as a case of Serbian aggression against largely defenseless, mostly Muslim, civilians. The prime culprits in the pending demise of the safe area are the Serbs and a Western alliance that, buckling to Serb threats, has failed to defend the U.N. safe area or even enforce a cease-fire in Croatia that was supposed to disarm Serbs there. But as Osme's story shows, there is more to the Bihac tragedy than the failure of outsiders. It is neither a simple tale of unprovoked aggression nor a case of ancient and unfathomable ethnic hatreds. And when the history of Bihac's fall is finally written, a chapter must be reserved for the blundering of Bosnia's squabbling Muslim leaders themselves.

Bihac is bordered on the north and west by the Krajina, a historically Serb-majority and currently Serb-held area of Croatia; it is hemmed in to the east and south by largely Muslim Bosnian lands that have been ethnically cleansed and occupied by Bosnian Serb forces. Bihac also contains the last link in a rail line that would connect Belgrade with the Krajina capital of Knin. Still, the Serbs have no historical or ethnic claim on the pocket; thanks to the ebb and flow of the Ottoman Empire, the area's population is overwhelmingly Muslim, and has been for as long as anyone can remember. In every peace plan so far the Serbs have acquiesced in awarding "Turkish Croatia," as the area was once known, to the Muslims.

The Bihac pocket has a more Islamic atmosphere than the rest of Bosnia. It's the first place I saw green and white crescent-and-star flags flapping from minarets, and even a few young men wearing fezes to a religious festival. Still, Bihac's Muslims have long had a pragmatic, almost accommodationist, outlook befitting their unique geopolitical situation. Serbian-Muslim cooperation in World War II helped make Bihac a stronghold of the Partisans. In 1954 Serbs, Muslims, and Croats teamed up to join in an ill-fated peasant revolt against Tito.

No man embodies these Bihacian traits better than Fikret Abdic. The former Yugoslav Communist government jailed him in 1987 for allegedly issuing phony bonds in the name of Agrokomerc, a food processing company that he built into an economic powerhouse during his twenty years as director. But to thousands in the Bihac pocket, where Agrokomerc was based, "Babo" (Daddy) Abdic was a font of jobs and money, and a hero. Acquitted and released in 1989, he was elected to represent Bihac on Bosnia's ten-member collective presidency. When Serb-Muslim tensions flared in the spring of 1992, Abdic mediated between nationalist Bihac Muslims and mainly Serbian Yugoslav National Army officers dug in at the city's strategic military airport. Abdic won the Serbs safe passage out of town—though they detonated explosives at the airport before leaving.

After the war in Bosnia began in 1992, Bosnian Serbs dug in on the Grabez Plateau to the east and shelled Bihac for a couple of months—killing hundreds and stopping the V Corps from acting against the genocidal campaign going on behind Serb lines in northern Bosnia. But the Serbs never seriously tried to take the town. And from the fall of 1992 on, Bihac remained peaceful, even prosperous. From his castle near Velika Kladusa, at the north end of the pocket, Abdic built a vast smuggling operation that brought meat, fuel, and a host of other supplies from Croatia's Adriatic ports, through the Krajina, to Bihac. Abdic's old Serb and Croat connections, nurtured in his Agrokomerc days and now freshened by payoffs, made it possible. The U.N. got into the act: French peacekeepers guarded Abdic's convoys from Zagreb in exchange for the use of Agrokomerc real estate as a camp.

Abdic's racket thrived because it was expedient for all concerned. Serbs and Croats got money to buy arms to use on each other (or on Muslims elsewhere in Bosnia). The U.N. got a safe area success story. The government of Bosnia in Sarajevo, busy with other matters and unable to maintain contact with distant Bihac, tolerated Abdic's scam as a means to stabilize one of the few large areas under its nominal control. But Abdic grew increasingly contemptuous of what he saw as Bosnian President Alija Izetbegovic's futile effort to build an Islamic state. He even began advertising his operation as a model of how Yugoslavia might rebuild interethnic cooperation through trade. "We see ourselves as the Cayman Islands of the Balkans," one of his lieutenants later told *The New York Times.*

The end began in June 1993, when Abdic's willingness to cooperate with the Serbs caught the attention of David Owen, the European Union's peace mediator for Bosnia. At the time, Owen was pushing Izetbegovic to agree to the latest of his plans to chop up Bosnia along ethnic lines. To put pressure on Izetbegovic, Owen began promoting Abdic as a leader of "dissidents" on the Bosnian presidency who were willing to settle the conflict. This was tantamount to an Owen-orchestrated coup, and Abdic, well aware of this fact, cheerfully played along.

Izetbegovic, fearing that other regional Muslim leaders might follow Abdic's example, engineered the Bosnian parliament's rejection of Owen's plan and moved to isolate Abdic politically. Abdic countered by declaring himself president of "autonomous" Bihac and signed peace treaties with Radovan Karadzic of the Bosnian Serbs and with the Croats. With the help of the surrounding Serbs, he began arming a militia (including deserters from the V Corps) in Velika Kladusa. Sarajevo ordered the V Corps to crush Abdic.

The former Yugoslav National Army officer who commanded the 15,000-man V Corps, Captain Ramiz Drekovic, was only too happy to oblige. He had never even pretended to be defending the ideal of a multiethnic state. The one time I met him, in May 1993, I realized that not all Serbian propaganda about Muslim extremism was unfounded. In an office bedecked with Islamic paraphernalia and Arabic-language diplomas, Drekovic threatened terrorist attacks in Europe as retaliation for the genocide against his people. Drekovic wasn't even from Bihac, but from the Sanjak, a Muslim-majority area of Serbia known as a hotbed of Muslim nationalism. Drekovic ran a tight ship: his spirited units were the first Bosnian forces I saw who saluted their officers.

From September 1993 on, Bihac was the scene of a bloody fratricidal sideshow to the Serb-Muslim war in the rest of Bosnia. Both sides committed terrible abuses. Abdic, acting less and less like a sugar daddy and more and more like a dictator, opened a prison camp in which hundreds of Muslims suspected of opposing his rule were brutalized. The V Corps, for its part, harassed and mistreated the 1,000 remaining Serbs in Bihac until they begged the U.N. to get them out. Three months ago, the V Corps, now commanded by Gen. Atif Dudakovic, finally took Velika Kladusa, driving 17,000 of Abdic's followers into Serbian Krajina.

The V Corps might have stopped and consolidated its control over the pocket. But both Dudaković and Sarajevo were feeling their oats. The Serbs in Krajina and Bosnia were still struggling to cope with the cutoff of aid from the Milosevic regime in Belgrade. Thanks to the support of the United States, Bosnia and Croatia were once again allies, ending the Bosnian army's crippling struggle with the Croats and opening the way for new arms shipments through Croatia from Iran and elsewhere. U.S. support for lifting the arms embargo against Bosnia gave the Bosnians an incentive to demonstrate their improving prowess on the battlefield.

In October the V Corps staged a dramatic breakout from Bihac, driving the Bosnian Serbs from 100 square miles of adjacent territory—and, it should be noted, that would have belonged to them under most international peace plans. About 10,000 Serb civilians fled, telling foreign journalists of looting and other abuses by the Muslim troops. Bosnian Prime Minister Haris Silajdzic (who recently has demanded NATO air strikes against the Serbs and blamed the U.N. for a pending massacre in Bihac), crowed that V Corps victories meant that the military momentum had shifted to the Muslims, and that now the Serbs would have to bargain seriously.

But the Serbs did not oblige. Running low on fuel, and sensing that the U.S. decision to stop enforcing the arms embargo presaged greater American steps to help their enemies, they chose to strike back while they still could. Gen. Ratko Mladic made two audacious decisions. To make up for lost artillery positions on the Grabez Plateau, he attacked Bihac from the air, in open defiance of the U.N.'s NATO-enforced no-fly zone. And he broke the U.N. rule against staging actions from Serb-held areas of Croatia, attacking Velika Kladusa with the help of Abdic's rebel Muslim army. Having somehow failed to anticipate that U.N. flaccidity would enable Mladic to make such a pincers move, the V Corps lost the ground it had just won and is now waging a last-ditch defense of its own headquarters.

Once again, Mladic and the Serbs have won by calling the international community's bluff. This, along with Owen's ill-conceived Abdic gambit, constitutes the heart of the outside world's culpability in the destruction of Bihac. Yet international actors, the U.S. especially, also bear another kind of responsibility. By appearing willing to do more for the Muslim-led Bosnian government than it actually was, the American government encouraged Sarajevo to launch an ill-considered and ultimately disastrous military campaign that has cost it not only territory, but also moral standing. Yet after so many past promises of outside help had proved false, how could Bosnian leaders have gambled so much so recklessly on them this time?

The Serbs' objective now is the unconditional surrender of the V Corps. Since no outside power seems willing to stop them, they will probably fight on until they get their way. The ethnic cleansing of the Bihac pocket's 180,000 Muslim residents and Croatian intervention to stop it could follow—though Mladic may eventually find it more expedient to control Bihac and its Muslims through a reinstated Abdic. At the war's outset, people in Bihac joked that the fighting would lead to the creation of three new countries: Velika Srpska (Great Serbia), Velika Hrvatska (Great Croatia), and Velika Kladusa. Thirty-one months and an ocean of blood later, that witticism has become prophecy.

(DECEMBER 19, 1994)

------------------------------------ ✦✦ ------------------------------------

Dateline Sarajevo:
Greater Serbs

SAMANTHA POWER

Nesho Malic is a Serb. He is also a nerd. At 18, he speaks better English than I do, better French, perhaps, than the U.N. sector Sarajevo commander from Nantes. When he translates, he annoys me by claiming goat herders on "Snipers' Alley" have used words like "perspicacious" and "forlorn." His earnest brown eyes flash from behind thick lenses. "Well, geez, you asked me to be precise," he says, "Now I'll have to reassess my approach." Nesho, a young man who worships multiethnic Bosnia even more than books, who has chosen, like 30,000 other Serbs, to stay behind in besieged Sarajevo, is one of 4 million reasons Serb brutality in Srebrenica matters.

He got his brains from his mother. An M.D. and Ph.D., she finished at the top of her class and rocketed to the top of the Yugoslav medical establishment. She is now unemployed, and her position at the faculty stands vacant. Nesho, who is nearsighted in one eye and farsighted in the other, just completed high school ("naturally at the top of my class," he says) and received a draft notice for the improved-but-hardly-inviting Bosnian army. Without his glasses he would mistake a Serb T–55 tank for a stalled Sarajevan tram, so he was initially told he could put his languages or his knowledge of physics to use in army intelligence or communications. But, because of his name, he believes, he was assigned to infantry duty and must report for front-line service next month.

Nesho was desperate to volunteer for the multiethnic army when his nominal brethren began shelling his family and his town in April 1992. Too young to enlist, however, he decided to stay in Sarajevo and bide his time writing novels and military assessments by candlelight. "I had fifty chances to leave, but I used to believe in this place," he sighs. His mother's slight hand trembles as she pours Turkish coffee in their downtown flat. "Why should my son fight for a country in which we have no rights?" she asks. But she knows the answer. Because, bad as it might seem on this side of the confrontation line, it is as good as it gets. Their nationality may not be explicitly mentioned in the Bosnian federation's new constitution, and they may not feel embraced by neighborhoods they now must scour for a familiar face, but the Serbs remaining here have at least earned the distinction of being the best-treated minority in the former Yugoslavia.

Nesho says, "I am so tired of being told I should be grateful I'm not a Muslim in Banja Luka. That's like telling blacks who are prejudiced against in America, 'Yeah, but you should be grateful you aren't living under apartheid in South Africa.' I'm selfish. I have to think about my life." Yet he wouldn't dream of defecting to join the Serbs who are destroying his Bosnia.

Not that they would need his help. Before Srebrenica fell, one senior Bosnian official bragged of army gains in the Serb-held suburb of Grbavica. When asked what had been captured, however, he answered shyly, "Uh . . . two houses." This is the pace of Bosnian successes, and Sarajevo is dying in the meantime. The streets are empty, not because of the government ban on outside gatherings or the hourly air-raid sirens, but because of a thirty-nine-month soul-sapping exodus. "The only people who live here now are the poor, the refugees, and the intellectuals with ideals," says Nesho's mother. Well over half the city's population comes from outside, mostly from the countryside, and that has changed the cosmopolitan character of Sarajevo in large and small ways. Unthinkable in urbane Sarajevo before the war, hefty, baggy-trousered farm-women are now ubiquitous, hanging laundry outside their windows or yelling across the street to friends. To the few *gradjani* (citizens) who have stayed, the newcomers are known as *seljaci* (peasants). It is the rural *seljaci,* not the cosmopolitan *gradjani,* who tend to mistrust people like Nesho and his family.

Bosnia's other major towns have also had to absorb refugees by the tens of thousands. After the biggest, most efficient and, by all accounts, most vicious Serb ethnic cleansing operation in more than two years (and that is saying something), some 25,000 more Muslim refugees have arrived in Tuzla, which shelters 200,000 displaced already and is now the country's most populous town.

They are not first-time refugees. In April 1993, Serb "irregular" Tigers and White Eagles—whom even their pathologically perfidious sponsor in Belgrade faults for war crimes—mowed through predominantly Muslim eastern Bosnia, slaughtering non-Serbs in their path and forcing tens of thousands of terrorized Muslims into Srebrenica, a quaint river-side town that boasted three mosques, two Orthodox churches, and one Catholic church. Renowned for its silver mines and its plum trees, Srebrenica suddenly became notorious as a "nightmarish, ethnic ghetto." When U.N. cattle trucks attempted to relieve the pressure on the town by relocating some of those sleeping in fields, thirteen civilians were crushed in a stampede to earn a place, Serb women stoned the refugees, and the evacuation was abruptly halted. The U.N. commander general at the time, Philippe Morillon, devised a stop-gap demilitarization accord that required the enclave's Muslim defenders to hand their weapons and fates over to the world. In 1993, when he installed blue helmets in the first ever Bosnian "safe area," Morillon proclaimed that "an attack on Srebenica now would be an attack on the whole world."

But, two years later, the world watched and some 400 Dutch peacekeepers scurried for cover as Bosnian Serb Commander Ratko Mladic personally oversaw Srebrenica's "sanitization" on July 11. As many as 10,000 fighting-age men, as well as dozens of young girls, vanished. Of those Bosnian fighters who had attempted to break free, Bosnian Serb radio said "most were liquidated" and the rest captured. The women, children, and elderly eastern Bosnians left behind are now on the run for the second or third time. They wanted to be left alone but they are being taught how to hate. They hate the West. They hate the Serbs. It is hard now to blame them.

Western policy may become a three-pronged self-fulfilling prophecy. The U.S. and Europe said they didn't want the war to spill over; but Croatia sees the world's half-hearted commitment to borders and has massed its troops to pounce. The U.S. and Europe said they didn't want to lift the arms embargo because it would force the U.N. Protection Force (UNPROFOR) to withdraw and would spawn a "humanitarian catastrophe"; but, after watching as Srebrenica's scant defenses faltered, UNPROFOR's days are numbered and the humanitarian catastrophe is here. And the U.S. and Europe said they didn't want a Muslim state in the heart of Europe; but if the money and guns come from Allah, the advice can't be far behind.

Haris Silajdzic has a waking obsession. Tucked in a drawer in his office at the windowless presidency is a manila folder marked "Embargo." The folder is bulging with notes from White House meetings and Xeroxed copies of old congressional resolutions that say "nonbinding" in small letters. His crusade hasn't achieved much. But, while diplomats roll their eyes and say the dapper prime minister must stop "droning on" about Serb fascism and the Bosnian right to self-defense, Silajdzic is indefatigable. "I know I talk about these things ad nauseam," he admits, visibly exhausted, "but I have to believe that someday, somewhere I might be heard."

At midnight on the Tuesday Srebrenica fell, Silajdzic eagerly recounted the details of a phone conversation he'd just had with Bob Dole and Joseph Lieberman in which the senators assured him they had enough votes "from both sides of the aisle" to rid him of his obsession. Silajdzic is too smart not to know that he, and Bosnia, will again be disappointed, but he has few friends left and, to quote the U.S. president, few good options.

UNPROFOR would hardly seem to be one of them. Mission Impossible has melted into Mission Invisible, prepared to defend only its inability to defend the five remaining "safe areas." "We were never put there to protect the safe areas; we were put there to 'deter attacks' against them," officers say, always adding, "Don't blame us. We requested 36,000 troops to enforce the 'safe areas' and we only received 7,000."

The soldiers are humiliated, and their commander, General Rupert Smith, who was prepared to escalate against the Serbs, has been rebuffed. Together, as they await some shred of guidance from the capitals beyond standing orders "not to destabilize," they are living off rations: spam for breakfast, lunch, and dinner. Their headquarters is shelled so regularly now that, when the Grand Prix was broadcast on television recently, most of the peacekeepers in the TV room dove for cover, mistaking the scream of race cars rounding their first bend for the whistle of incoming homemade rockets. The seventh veil that shrouded the mission has been lifted and, with the "safe area" of Zepa on the verge of falling, peacekeepers do not pretend. "We can only watch and see how the battle develops," says U.N. spokesman Lieutenant Colonel Gary Coward.

Anticipating a Serb attack and the usual dose of U.N. protection, Bosnian soldiers raided Ukrainian compounds in Zepa and Gorazde, where they stole everything from armored personnel carriers and flak jackets to medical kits. Officials at headquarters were not even notified for two days. "The reason we didn't know about it earlier is the Bosnian army also stole the Ukrainians' radios," shrugged one official. With no leverage on the Serbs, U.N. spokesmen condemned the Bosnians. "The Bosnian government is stooping to the same level as the Bosnian Serbs," one official said. "They are going to lose the world's sympathy if they keep this up."

Clumsy Nesho Malic will don a Bosnian uniform next month, but he will not stop dreaming about the Bosnia that the Serbs ("I'm a Serb with a lower-case 's,'" he explains. "The guys in the hills are Serbs with a capital 's.'") and the West destroyed.

He consoles himself with the saying, "Oh Lord, give us the serenity to accept what cannot be changed, the courage to change what should be changed, and the wisdom to understand the difference." He will never quite resign himself to the reality: that his former heroes in the government have accepted that Bosnia's complexion has changed, that Western leaders have no courage to change what should be changed, and that only he, a pen-toting teenager, has the wisdom to understand the difference.

(AUGUST 7, 1995)

Dateline Zagreb:
The Fall of Srebrenica

CHARLES LANE

The barking of dogs filled the air around Srebrenica on the night of Tuesday, July 11, just hours after the United Nations–declared safe area fell to the Bosnian Serbs. To Warrant Officer Be Oosterveen of the Dutch unit assigned to protect the enclave, it was clear what the sound meant: Serb soldiers were using dogs to hunt down Muslim men who had fled to the surrounding hills. After daylight, he heard the sound of shooting coming from those same hills. "It was not fighting," he recalls. "It was shot by shot. There's a difference between fighting and executing. You can hear that." Soon, there was proof. A frightened refugee boy approached Oosterveen, gesturing toward the hills and drawing a line across his throat. The boy led Oosterveen and a fellow soldier to a group of nine men, Muslim civilians, face down in a row at the edge of a stream. Oosterveen's colleague snapped a couple of quick pictures of the bodies. Then the two soldiers, weaponless because Serb troops had disarmed them, hastened back to camp. "The Serbs were close," Oosterveen says. "It was dangerous."

So thorough was the Western humiliation in Srebrenica that a thirty-year veteran of a NATO army found himself reduced to furtively documenting war crimes that had occurred on the perimeter of his own base, crimes that he had been powerless to prevent. But the story is even worse: a review of the events leading to the fall of the enclave shows that it need not have fallen so easily, meaning that at least some of the horrors perpetrated against its former inhabitants were quite possibly preventable. There are many to blame, including Srebrenica's Bosnian army defenders, who failed to put up a serious fight. But most of the fault lies with the rubber-willed politicians of the West and the U.N.–dominated system they devised for purportedly protecting the safe area. That hybrid of peacekeeping and warfighting made it impossible for the Dutch to use all their military assets, including NATO air power, to full advantage against the Serbs. The result was that authorized representatives of the international community stood by as certainly dozens and probably hundreds of civilians were either murdered—some by Serb forces wearing stolen U.N. garb and driving stolen U.N. vehicles—or led away to face death in Serb custody. Srebrenica is a case study in how Western dithering at the highest levels translated into humiliation and murder on the ground.

The full story of this scandal begins in Spring 1992, when Serbian paramilitaries began the ethnic cleansing of the Drina valley. The area, directly abutting Serbia, was strategically vital to Greater Serbia; yet most of its population, inconveniently, was Muslim. The majority-Muslim town of Bratunac, on the Drina just nine miles north of Srebrenica, was occupied by the Serbs on May 10. According to eyewitness testimony reported by Misha Glenny in *The Fall of Yugoslavia,* several hundred of the town's Muslim men were murdered in two days; some 6,000 or 7,000 more Muslim civilians were crowded into the town's sports stadium and then expelled. Many of them wound up down the road in Srebrenica.

On a visit to Bratunac on May 11, 1993, one year after this pogrom, I found an eerie, half-empty town whose remaining population appeared to be entirely Serb. Most of the shops in the former Muslim quarter had been looted and their windows smashed. The mosque had been razed; goats grazed in the weed-choked Muslim cemetery. Locals told me that the mosque had been hit by a Muslim bomb.

The sacking of Bratunac set the stage for a fierce Muslim counterattack and the most serious documented atrocities committed by Muslim forces in Bosnia. Muslim guerrillas, including survivors of the Serb rampage of the spring, operated throughout the winter of 1992–93 from Srebrenica and its surroundings, using an abandoned mine as a fortress. They burned several Serb villages and killed hundreds of Serbs; most were soldiers, but many were civilians. In February 1994 Nasir Oric, the commander of the Bosnian army in Srebrenica, showed John Pomfret of *The Washington Post* a videotape that, Oric proudly explained, depicted a burned Serb village and a pile of headless Serb corpses slaughtered by Oric's men.

During this period, Serb forces refused to permit humanitarian relief convoys into refugee-swollen Srebrenica. They attempted to seize the town outright in April 1993. That offensive, including a Serb shelling attack which left thirty-six people dead in a Srebrenica school yard, eventually prompted the U.N. to declare Srebrenica a "safe area." The Serbs accepted, on the condition that the Muslim soldiers in the town relinquish their weapons to a company of Canadian U.N. troops; most of the Muslims did. For the next two years, Srebrenica's population, stretched to about 42,000 by the continuing influx of "ethnically cleansed" Muslims from elsewhere in the Drina valley, lived in ghetto-like misery but relative quiet. Supplies came first via NATO air drops, then from U.N. convoys and the black market.

Oric, who in his prewar incarnation as a Yugoslav police officer briefly served as one of Serbian President Slobodan Milosevic's bodyguards, established himself in the enclave as yet another of Bosnia's Robin Hood–style warlords. Zipping around the minuscule territory in a shiny black Volkswagen, he organized a thriving trade in fuel and goods smuggled across Serbian territory with the help of Ukrainian U.N. peacekeepers in nearby Zepa. Oric also presided over the reinfiltration of Muslim guerrillas into the enclave—as well as their partial rearmament. This was, as the Serbs say, a violation of the safe area demilitarization agreement, though it must be added that the agreement itself had been negotiated at the point of a Serbian gun. General Ratko Mladic of the Bosnian Serb army seems to have finally gotten fed up with Oric and decided early this spring to get rid of the Srebrenica enclave once and for all.

But Mladic had to contend with the 400-odd soldiers of the Netherlands 13th Air Mobile Infantry Battalion, under the command of Lieutenant Colonel Ton Karremans. The Dutch had replaced the Canadians in January 1994; before the assault, though, they still only had about 60 percent of their full strength, because the Serbs had refused to allow the entire battalion to enter the enclave as previously agreed. The Serbs also exploited U.N. peacekeeping rules to cripple the Dutch military capability. According to a senior Western officer, the Dutch unit was equipped with TOW missiles capable of destroying Serb tanks. But, by the time the Serbs attacked the town, the TOWs were inoperable. Serb officers had confiscated vital TOW spare parts as the Dutch were bringing them into the enclave; U.N. procedures permitted the Serbs to do so. Nevertheless, the Dutch, with light weapons and armored personnel carriers, had succeeded in establishing observation posts around the enclave and did their best to monitor the cease-fire, to look after Srebrenica's civilians, and to deter a Serb attack.

The Dutch were the on-the-scene embodiment of the will of the international community, and Mladic, contemptuous though he is of the West's threats, was careful not to succumb to overconfidence. His troops began to gather around the enclave in April. Colonel Karremans reported suspicious troop movements to U.N. headquarters in Zagreb, but no special steps were taken to counter them. On June 3, the Serbs launched a brief attack on a Dutch observation post, but this, too, was dealt with passively.

On July 6, according to Karremans's account, Mladic's troops began seizing the Dutch observation posts one by one—using carefully directed tank fire that landed just close enough to threaten the Dutch but not close enough to kill them. "That was done in a very neat way by the Serbs," Karremans recalled. "Like Pac-Man." As the Dutch abandoned their posts (following U.N. rules of engagement that permitted them to fight back only if their lives were directly threatened), the Serbs took some of them hostage. They stole the peacekeepers' weapons, body armor, and vehicles and, in some instances, their fatigues, blue helmets, and berets.

The U.N. Security Council resolution establishing the safe areas permitted the U.N. to use all means, including NATO air power, to protect the enclaves and the U.N. troops in them. That included both wide-ranging punitive air strikes and close air support, defined as a carefully targeted attack on a particular weapons system threatening U.N. troops. Close air support must be requested by a commander on the ground, approved by Bosnian theater commander Lieutenant General Rupert Smith of Britain in Sarajevo and then agreed to by U.N. special representative Yasushi Akashi and his top military man, Lieutenant General Bernard Janvier of France, in Zagreb. Then the request is communicated to NATO Admiral Leighton Smith of the United States, who is based in Italy, to be carried out.

If a large-scale air attack had come, it might have been enough to shore up the Dutch and the enclave itself and to rebuff the Bosnian Serb attack. But air power did not come in an effective and timely fashion. Karremans formally asked for close air support on the afternoon of Saturday, July 8. By this time, his observation posts were collapsing and about thirty Dutch soldiers had been taken hostage. But the request, according to a senior Western military source in Zagreb, was turned down by Smith and his staff in Sarajevo. "They felt the U.N. in Zagreb would see it as too early and not worth the risks," specifically the risk of further hostage-taking by the Serbs, the source says. This was a reasonable fear, given that the Serbs had responded to an air strike on their capital, Pale, in May by seizing 320 peacekeepers. Janvier, who had been delegated full authority over air power by Akashi (who was out of town), spent hours in elaborate consultations with his staff in Zagreb, General Smith in Sarajevo and Admiral Smith in Italy.

By Sunday evening, the bulk of Janvier's staff was recommending that the Dutch troops be given close air support. But he balked: European Union mediator Karl Bildt was in Belgrade trying to negotiate with Milosevic for the recognition of Bosnia, and Janvier feared that an air raid on Bosnian Serb troops would upset those talks. He argued, as one source present at the meeting puts it: "If Karremans can hold out without close air, let's try it." Instead of launching close air support, Janvier ordered Karremans to set up a blocking position just south of Srebrenica town. Karremans dispatched fifty soldiers armed with light anti-tank weapons—but not the more effective TOWs. He relayed Janvier's threat to Mladic: any attack on the blocking position will result in the use of NATO air power.

Sure enough, on Monday, July 10, Mladic's soldiers attacked—and the Dutch drove them back. This was perhaps the crucial moment in the entire test of wills. Suddenly Mladic was knocked back on his heels. Some of Janvier's staff advised him to seize the moment and make good on his threat of air attacks. We will never know if the one-two punch of Dutch ground resistance and NATO air power would have bought more time for Srebrenica and its civilians. Janvier, still eager to avoid upsetting the political balance, opted not to use the planes. He justified his decision, in part, the source told me, by pointing out that the Dutch unit had already driven back the Serbs.

To be fair, Janvier's decision was made on the basis of incomplete intelligence. U.N. peacekeeping rules require U.N. forces to operate in a neutral, "transparent" manner and, thus, forbid them from running clandestine intelligence networks. As far as Janvier knew, the Serb forces consisted solely of what Dutch troops had personally seen up to that point: a tank and about a company's worth of infantry. In fact, as the Dutch learned Tuesday morning, when Mladic poured reserves into the fight, the Serb force consisted of 1,500 men backed by tanks—a four-to-one numerical advantage over the Dutch defenders.

Mladic attacked remaining Dutch observation posts from all points around the enclave. One post retreated, another stopped the Serbs. Unaware of the machinations in Zagreb, bewildered Dutch soldiers looked to the sky and wondered what was keeping the NATO airplanes. Finally, at noon, Janvier decided he had no choice but to order close air support. At about two o'clock, a first sortie took out a pair of Serb tanks as they were menacing a Dutch unit.

But at that point, Mladic took to the radio and gave Karremans an ultimatum of his own: any more air strikes and his artillery would flatten both the Dutch compound and the civilian population of Srebrenica. He would also execute all Dutch hostages. Monitoring the situation in Holland, Dutch

Defense Minister Joris Voorhoeve immediately called Akashi and demanded that the air strikes be called off. Akashi, back in Zagreb, complied—and the battle to save Srebrenica was effectively ended before it had truly been joined.

In the aftermath, Defense Minister Voorhoeve insisted that Mladic's threat to the Dutch hostages and to civilians had been paramount in his decision to, in effect, let the Serbs have the safe haven without further opposition. But he and other Dutch military officials also emphasized a second reason: the fact that the Bosnian army itself was mounting so little resistance. "At the moment fighting started, they all fled," said Dutch Lieutenant General Hans Couzy.

Where, indeed, were the 6,000 or so armed men of Srebrenica, who, together with a battle-ready Dutch group and NATO aircraft, could presumably have at least blunted a Serb force of 1,500 even if they were out-gunned in artillery? Throughout the war, the Serbs have been notorious for their reluctance to risk casualties to their own personnel by seizing positions with infantry; their specialty is shelling civilians into submission. Besides, Nasir Oric had sworn "Srebrenica will never be Serb as long as I'm here."

But on the day Srebrenica fell, Oric was not in town. He was, it seems, fifty miles northwest in Tuzla, on unspecified business. Indeed, his whereabouts in the months leading up to the Serb attack are a bit of a mystery. The Dutch forces had noticed a sharp deterioration in Bosnian morale and discipline throughout the spring—a deterioration of which Mladic, whose own spying capability is unconstrained, surely was aware.

In any case, military cooperation between the Bosnian and Dutch defenders was effectively precluded by the absurd contradiction inherent in U.N. policy toward the safe area. On the one hand, U.N. member states had refused to supply sufficient ground troops to actually defend against a Serb attack and had agreed to rules that let the Serbs weaken the capability of those troops that were introduced. On the other hand, they were supposed to enforce the U.N. arms embargo and its formal, if ineffectual, commitment to maintaining the Srebrenica safe area's demilitarization. The implicit message to the Bosnians was: we *cannot* defend the safe area, but you *may* not defend it. According to Oosterveen, Dutch troops refused several requests from the Bosnians to fight on their behalf. Not surprisingly, this led to increased tensions between Dutch and Bosnian forces. In one incident, Couzy said, Bosnian soldiers threatened to kill Dutch troops if they ever abandoned their posts—a threat carried out on July 8, when the Bosnians killed one Dutch soldier as his unit retreated from an observation post it had just surrendered to the Serbs.

The Bosnian men were divided between a minority for whom Srebrenica was home and a vast majority for whom defending Srebrenica would mean fighting for an unwanted refugee camp. Weak and hungry after months of

Serbian siege, poorly armed, pressured by the final Serb push, and without Oric around to whip them into shape, the Bosnians fell to fighting among themselves. Dutch troops witnessed two firefights between factions of the army that wanted to stay and protect the town and factions that wanted to flee. The Bosnians succeeded in mounting only a single major firefight against the Serbs before thousands of them began fleeing with their weapons and ammunition along the dangerous route through Serb-controlled territory to government lines near Tuzla.

What, then, has become of the roughly 42,000 people who once lived in the now-liquidated Srebrenica safe area? About 75 percent of them have made it to safety in Tuzla, according to the United Nations High Commission on Refugees (UNHCR). The other 25 percent appear to fall into two categories. The first consists of 5,200 men (this number comes from the Bosnian Serbs' own Pale Radio) who were either captured as they escaped from Srebrenica with the remnants of the Bosnian Army or, in a minority of cases, remained behind in Srebrenica and were then separated from their families by the Serbs. These people have been confined by Serb forces in Bratunac. The second group consists of the remaining 5,000 or so, a figure that may include some stragglers who will turn up in Tuzla over the next few days and even a handful who may have escaped to Zepa or Gorazde. But the few reliable accounts from outside observers that have emerged so far suggest that many, many of these people are dead.

Once their brief struggle with the Serb army was over, the Dutch troops and about 15,000 refugees fell back to the Dutch compound at Potocari at the north end of the enclave. When the Serbs brought in vehicles to take people to Tuzla, the Dutch tried to negotiate for at least one Dutch soldier to ride on every truck or bus, but the request was refused. When they attempted to escort the refugee buses, the Serbs stole fourteen of their jeeps and several armored personnel carriers. As a result, the Dutch could only mount four or five stationary observation posts along the entire fifty-kilometer route the refugees were traveling.

Even with their monitoring capability systematically curtailed by the Serbs, the Dutch alone *saw* about twenty people murdered by Mladic's men. In addition to Oosterveen's account, two other soldiers report witnessing atrocities while confined by the Serbs to the Dutch compound. In one case, a Muslim man was taken away to a house, put up against a wall, and shot by Serb troops. In another, a Dutch officer, having earlier seen men taken away from the compound for interrogation, saw the bodies of nine dead Muslims lying in a row, shot in the back.

The UNHCR, after interviewing refugees in Tuzla, has also documented that Muslims, both soldiers and civilians, were ambushed and shelled by the Serbs as they fled Srebrenica, leading to unconfirmed reports of hundreds of bodies lying scattered along the road to Tuzla. The UNHCR has confirmed cases in which a total of ninety-nine people were murdered outright, including twenty to thirty women and children killed by Serb soldiers who, wearing the blue helmets and driving the white jeeps they stole from surrendering Dutch troops, lured the refugees out of hiding to their deaths. Raymond Bonner and Stephen Kinzer of *The New York Times* spoke with more than 100 refugees in Tuzla and have documented cases in which a total of sixty Muslims were murdered. Kinzer's informants recounted how, before dawn on Wednesday, Serbs dressed as U.N. soldiers took people away from the Potocari compound, and the next day the bodies of nine dead boys were found—seven with their throats cut and two hanging from a tree. Robert Block of *The Independent* has seen videotape taken in Srebrenica on July 13 by the Belgrade independent station Studio B; the tape shows the bodies of about twenty-five young Muslim men who have been lined up against a wall and executed.

And what about the 5,200 Muslim men from Srebrenica confined in Bratunac? There, the sports stadium is once again being pressed into service as a detention center for the ethnically cleansed. The Serbs have systematically refused access to Bratunac, despite appeals from UNHCR, the International Committee of the Red Cross, and the chief of staff of UNPROFOR. In every case, the Serbs have promised access and then withdrawn the offer. No journalists have been allowed into the town.

Yet the reports that have so far trickled out of Bratunac, if they can be confirmed, suggest that most of these men have met an awful fate. Through Western diplomatic sources, I learned that UNHCR in Tuzla has received the first account from a Muslim man who escaped from Bratunac. The 35-year-old man told the relief agency that he had fled Srebrenica with a group of 100 or so fellow Muslims before the town was occupied by the Serbs. But their group was captured and herded into several tiny abandoned houses outside the enclave. During the night Serbs removed men in groups of four and executed them; the man saw the bodies.

The survivors were then taken to the stadium in Bratunac, where they were held with their hands bound behind their backs and forced to look only at the ground. Mladic himself appeared and harangued the group, telling them that this is what they got for putting their faith in President Alija Izetbegovic of Bosnia and trying to break away from Yugoslavia. He promised them they would be reunited with their families if they cooperated. Upon Mladic's departure, trucks arrived and took the men to a field, where they were made to lie down. Serb soldiers opened fire on the men with machine guns. The witness, however, was only wounded and managed to escape with another Muslim by hiding in a ditch. They watched as Serbs used earth movers to cover the dead bodies.

Though it cannot be independently confirmed, both the UNHCR aide who recorded it and the U.S. Embassy in Zagreb regard this story as credible. Rope burns around the man's wrists and a minor head wound seem to support his account. So does additional information gathered by Block of *The Independent,* one of the few Western reporters covering the crisis from Belgrade. He has seen additional video footage, taken by independent Serbian TV, which shows hundreds of Muslim men standing on a football field in Bratunac with their hands tied behind their backs. He has interviewed *Serb* witnesses, recently returned from Bratunac, who say that these men were on their way to the slaughter. The witnesses told Block of as many as 4,000 captured Muslim men murdered by Serb troops. One woman told Block that her brother-in-law, a soldier, counted 1,600 killed on Monday, July 17, alone. Other Serbs told Block that the Serbs were using trucks to transport corpses and an earth mover to bury them in mass graves.

It is vital that the truth behind these frightening reports be established. So far, however, there has been no demand from the United Nations Security Council that the Serbs grant outside relief agencies access to Bratunac. Meanwhile, the assessment of U.N. officials and Western governments is that Srebrenica was militarily indefensible—that there was no way to prevent the enclave, hemmed in by Serb-held high ground, from falling. This is about half true. Srebrenica was militarily indefensible—but only because the U.N. military deterrent operated under ambiguous and unwieldy rules designed less to protect Bosnians than to avoid Western casualties and obscure the accountability of Western governments. It would be more accurate to say that Srebrenica fell not because it was militarily indefensible but because it was politically indefensible. Which is also a pretty fair description of the West's policy toward Bosnia.

(AUGUST 14, 1995)

PART III

—❧❧—

Indecision and Impotence

Europa Nervosa

NIALL FERGUSON

Anyone who's been following the wretched Balkan saga already knows the official reasons for European queasiness. But what the Europeans are not saying is just as important as what they are saying. The subtext of their nervousness is historical, not logical; and the arguments of the European powers, from Britain to Russia, are extensions of a historical experience, different from that of Americans, which alone explains the Atlantic rift. The United States has yet to grasp this. Even *The New York Times* threw up its editorial hands, writing, "Why European governments remain so complacent about all this remains a mystery." Some history might help.

Current events are merely the latest episode in the oldest and most difficult story in European diplomacy: the Eastern Question. In essence the question was based on the fact that the Ottoman (i.e., Turkish) Empire, which in 1815 stretched from Morocco to Armenia and included most of the Balkans, was crumbling. First the Greeks and then the Serbs successfully challenged Ottoman rule, followed closely by Egypt in the 1830s. To which of the other empires—British, French, Habsburg, or Russian—should go the spoils? Or should the subject peoples be encouraged to seek independence?—though this really meant dependence on one of the Great Powers and was therefore the same question. The present positions of the European states are the most recent answers to this Eastern Question; and each reflects its answers of the past.

Britain's first bad Balkan experience began in 1853 with the Crimean War. Although there had been British support for Greek independence, by the 1840s the official line was that the Ottoman Empire had to be preserved. The reason for this was a fear that Russian expansion in the eastern Mediterranean might threaten lines of communication to Britain's Indian colony. Thus the British decided to intervene (in alliance with France) when the Russians occupied Moldavia and Wallachia and declared war on Turkey, ostensibly because of ill treatment by the Turks of Christians in Jerusalem. The war was popular: the poet Tennyson exulted that "The Peace that I deem'd no peace, is over and done. . . . It is better to fight for the good than to rail at the ill"; the government called it a "battle of civilization against barbarism."

But the invasion of the Crimea in 1854 was a bloody mess, exposed in the media by the London *Times*'s William Russell. Having lost 22,500 men (including most of the Light Brigade) and one prime minister (Lord Aberdeen, who resigned in 1855), the British were content to be able to negotiate peace at Paris in March 1856.

Twenty years later (by which time most of the terms of the Paris Peace had been forgotten), the Balkans returned to British politics after a revolt by Bosnian Serbs against Ottoman taxes. The Bulgarians in Eastern Rumelia joined in, only to be massacred by Muslim irregulars (the *bashi-bazouks*), who killed thousands of civilians. The British government of Benjamin Disraeli, rather like George Bush's, attempted to sit it out. One diplomat sneered, Kissinger-like, at "shallow politicians . . . who have allowed their feelings of revolted humanity to make them forget the capital interest involved"—interests that were "not affected by the question whether it was 10,000 or 20,000 persons who perished." However, this misread the public outrage sparked by lurid media stories in the *Daily News* and *Northern Echo,* which united such diverse figures as Queen Victoria and Thomas Carlyle. Realizing that "the game was afoot . . . the iron was hot and the time to strike had arrived," the retired Liberal leader William Gladstone (in an eerie premonition of the retired Conservative leader Margaret Thatcher) dashed off a pamphlet titled *Bulgarian Horrors and the Question of the East.* It sold 200,000 copies within a month. It did not, however, impress Disraeli, who quipped that the pamphlet was, "of all the Bulgarian atrocities, perhaps the greatest."

When the Russians intervened on behalf of the Bulgarians and defeated the Turks, Disraeli countered by threatening war, a policy so domestically popular that it coined the phrase "jingoism": "We don't want to fight, but by jingo if we do, We've got the men; we've got the ships; and We've got the money, too." In fact, the British didn't need to fight: the Russians were duly brought to heel by the Treaty of Berlin, and Disraeli returned with Cyprus—and "peace with honor."

British involvement in the Balkans between 1900 and 1945 reflected fear of German rather than Russian influence, but this in no way simplified the Eastern Question. Ultimately, the British were drawn into the Great War of 1914 on the side of Russia, to head off German domination of Western Europe. British troops also became involved in the fighting in the eastern Mediterranean—with disastrous results at Gallipoli. In the Second World War, they found themselves in Serbia itself, as they backed resistance to the Axis occupation of Yugoslavia. Once again, it was a mess, as the British had to choose between two Serb groups: Tito's Communist Partisans and the royalist Chetniks under Draza Mihajivoc. If one adds to this the expensive bog into which the British got themselves in Cyprus, it becomes easier to understand the reluctance of the Major government to get embroiled in the current trouble.

The Germans, in their own way, have equally troubling Balkan antecedents. In 1876 Chancellor Otto von Bismarck declared that the Balkans were not "worth the healthy bones of a single Pomeranian musketeer." "The Eastern Question," he maintained, "is an area in which we can help our friends and harm our enemies without being inhibited to any great extent by direct interests of our own," a pretty good summary of the policy of the current German chancellor, Helmut Kohl.

Between 1876 and 1887 Bismarck sought to act as the "honest broker" between the other powers. It was he who brought them together in Berlin in 1878 to avoid war between Britain and Russia, negotiating the deal that reduced the independent Bulgaria in extent (returning Eastern Rumelia to Turkey) and gave Cyprus to Britain to put Bosnia-Herzegovina under Austrian protection. It was he who opposed German intervention in Bulgaria in 1885, when its German-born king, Alexander von Battenberg, appealed for help in his war with the Serbs. And it was he who, in 1887, secretly promised to respect Russia's "historically acquired rights" in the Balkans.

But after Bismarck's fall in 1890, there was a gradual shift in German policy. First, the Germans themselves began to cultivate the Turks as allies, proposing to link Berlin and Baghdad by rail and sending military advisers like Liman von Sanders to Constantinople. Second, the Germans encouraged their Austrian allies to take a hard line against Serb ambitions to create a united South Slav state, which clearly threatened Austria's hold over Slovenia, Croatia, and southern Hungary. In 1908, 1912, and 1913, the Germans supported Austrian threats of war against Serbia, a tactic that finally plunged Europe into war when it was repeated after the assassination of the Archduke Franz Ferdinand in Sarajevo. (The assassins were Bosnian Serbs protesting against the annexation of Bosnia by Austria in 1908. They had been trained by the Serbian secret service.)

It might be said that, in one respect, the Germans stuck to Bismarck's Balkan policy. In both world wars, few of the millions who died in Yugoslavia were Germans, and not many Pomeranian musketeers left their bones there. Even in the Second World War, German military involvement in Yugoslavia was limited after the initial, crushing invasion of April 1941 (which itself cost the Germans just 151 casualties); of the twenty-six divisions stationed in

Yugoslavia, twenty were Italian. Much of the Nazi horror in the region was contracted out to the Croatian regime of Ante Pavelic. Nevertheless, Yugoslavia was a headache for Hitler. The need to overrun it probably delayed the launch of Operation Barbarossa by around six crucial weeks; and after the Italian collapse in 1943, Tito was a thorn in the German side. Fifteen thousand Germans died when Belgrade fell to the Communists.

The German position today is therefore easily understood. There is, as there was between 1900 and 1945, a geopolitical argument for exerting German influence in the Balkans. And indeed, the pressures within Germany for intervention are probably stronger than anywhere else in Europe. The government most likely to support Clinton's plans to lift the arms embargo is Germany's, just as it was Germany that was most eager to recognize the independence of Croatia in December 1991. But the memory of the bloody war-time occupation rules out the use of German troops, the sight of which do more than anything else to lend credence in Serbia to Milosevic's propaganda.

Of all the ex–Great Powers, France has been the most consistently disinterested in the Balkans. The French have long focused on ex-Ottoman regions elsewhere: Algeria, Tunisia, and Morocco in North Africa, and Syria in the Middle East. More by accident than design, Napoleon briefly acquired from Austria the "illyrian provinces" (the west coast of present-day Croatia) in 1809. But the region was peripheral to his grand design. In marked contrast to Britain, the Crimean War was deeply unpopular in France; and while Louis Napoleon tinkered with pet schemes to assist the war effort (e.g., to improve the design of tents for his cavalry), the pressure for peace was intense. Likewise, when Gladstone was whipping up British indignation over the Bulgarian horrors, the French—with the exception of Victor Hugo—responded with a Gallic shrug.

Where France did express an interest, the motive was mercenary. After 1870 French lending to the new Balkan states was substantial: the Serbs got around 600 million francs, the Greeks 630 million, and the Romanians 3.6 billion. This was largely a reaction to German investment in the region, which threatened to exclude France from the eastern Mediterranean. That old Prussophobe Raymond Poincaré summed up the French attitude in 1912, when he commented: "The time will come when the partition [of the Ottoman Empire] will take place . . . and we will have to organize ourselves in advance so as not to be absent." During the 1930s French policy was to counter the resurgent German threat by making alliances with the other beneficiaries of the 1919 peace treaties. This meant cultivating the king of Yugoslavia, Alexander, who in 1929 had abolished democracy and increased Serb dominance of his country (initially called "The Kingdom of Serbs,

Croats, and Slovenes" in 1918). In October 1934 he arrived in Marseilles to meet French Foreign Minister Louis Barthou. Both were shot dead as they traveled through the city in an open carriage by a Macedonian assassin hired by Croat separatists. The event has not been forgotten.

Throughout April of this year, it was argued that taking a tougher line with the Serbs over Bosnia would weaken Boris Yeltsin and strengthen his opponents. This argument rests on the idea that the Russians are the Serbs' "natural" allies. But history suggests a more complex relationship. It was Czar Nicholas I who coined the phrase that the Ottoman Empire was the "sick man" of Europe (though what he in fact said was "dying bear"); and it was Russia who long showed the greatest interest in Turkey's Balkan provinces. So frequent were clashes between Russia and Turkey that the war of 1853 was the seventh. But the price of this policy was considerable. The Crimean War cost Russia dearly and denied the czar the prize of Moldava and Wallachia; and supporting the Serbs in their fight with Austria-Hungary after 1908 led Russia into a war with Germany that killed czarism off for good. Stalin also found Yugoslavia an equally awkward ally after the Second World War. Having agreed, in a weak moment, to pull the Red Army out of the Balkans, leaving Tito in charge after the German surrender, Stalin was initially well disposed toward Belgrade. But when Tito began talking about a Balkan Federation with Bulgaria and Albania, Stalin changed his mind, expelling Yugoslavia from Cominform for "boundless ambition, arrogance, and conceit." But Tito remained a Soviet headache for decades to come.

In the light of this experience, it would be odd if Russia were to commit itself seriously to the Serb side now. Such expressions of pro-Serb sympathy as there have been are best seen as moves in the far more important game of blackmailing the West for aid, now the principal goal of Russian foreign policy. In truth, the most the Russians can do is to block resolutions on the U.N. Security Council, or neglect to enforce sanctions on their own exporters, threats the West can easily counter.

Compared with the above, direct American experience of the Balkans has been trifling. In 1941 Colonel William ("Wild Bill") Donovan was sent by Roosevelt to advise the Yugoslav government to resist the Germans—advice reminiscent of the old *Beyond the Fringe* line: "At this stage in the war, we need a futile gesture." Five years later, in 1946, a U.S. Air Force plane was shot down by Tito for violating Yugoslav airspace. And that's about it. Small wonder there's more enthusiasm for "doing something" about Bosnia in Washington than in Europe. The lesson the Europeans have drawn from history is that Bismarck was right: the Balkans are more trouble than they are worth.

Yet it may be that this is a case in which the historic parallels are misleading. In the past, intervention in the Balkans tended to go wrong because another great power would invariably intervene on the other side: Russia versus

Britain and France in the Crimea; Austria and Germany against Russia, Britain, and France in 1914; and so on. Discounting the exaggerated fears of a Russian backlash, that would not happen today if Britain and France took decisive action to impose peace with German financial backing. Of course, it would not be easy. And some American help would be essential. But it would certainly not be as big a mess as previous interventions in the region. And a century and a half after it was posed, it might even answer the Eastern Question.

(MAY 31, 1993)

See No Evil

PATRICK GLYNN

The behind-the-scenes story of the creation of American policy on Bosnia, which is only now emerging—thanks partly to the angry resignations of so many officials involved—calls into serious question the ability of the United States to cope with the complex problems of the post–cold war era. It also calls into question the morality of American foreign policy. At a time when a museum to Holocaust victims was opening in Washington to great fanfare, history will record that two administrations refrained, in the face of overwhelming evidence, from countering a blatant program of genocide in Bosnia whose scope and nature they fully understood.

Most Americans assume that the United States was surprised by the war in the Balkans. On the contrary, at every stage American officials understood what was taking place in the disintegrating Yugoslavia. In 1990 the Central Intelligence Agency correctly predicted the violent breakup of the country; at the beginning of 1992 it foresaw the spread of the war to Bosnia. The failures of U.S. policy in Yugoslavia lay not in a lack of intelligence or even in the absence of feasible options, but rather in a conscious decision by high officials to avoid involvement.

Indeed, interviews with current and former officials involved in the Bosnian situation, some of whom spoke on the record and others of whom insisted on anonymity, suggest that the Bush and Clinton administrations deliberately distorted the picture of events in order to defuse public pressure for American involvement. The pattern of behavior is oddly reminiscent of the policy surrounding the prosecution of the Vietnam war: in Vietnam, the government concealed bad news to blunt public outcry against the war; in Bosnia, the government manipulated information to stem popular support for intervention.

Government officials knew that the central problem in Yugoslavia was aggressive Serbian nationalism—despite frequent public statements suggesting that all sides were somehow equally to blame. In the fall of 1990, the CIA prepared a national intelligence estimate predicting the potentially violent breakup of the country as early as mid-1991. The estimate, whose basic contents were reported in *The New York Times,* laid the primary blame on Serbian president Slobodan Milosevic (an assessment with which then-Deputy Secretary of State Lawrence Eagleburger publicly agreed).

The United States was by no means oblivious to problems in Croatia, where Franjo Tudjman's nationalist ruling party had alienated and frightened the Serbian minority; the government was equally aware of the growing secessionist feeling in the republic of Slovenia. But State Department officials in 1991 regarded the Slovenian, Croatian, Macedonian, and Bosnian leaders as at least nascently democratic and pro-Western in orientation. It was, as American officials well understood, the still-Communist regime in Serbia that was repressive and prone to violence.

"It was no big secret in the State Department or the [Central Intelligence] Agency that the Serbs were responsible and were going where they were going," says George Kenney, who resigned in protest as acting head of the State Department's Yugoslavia section last year. "We knew perfectly well what was going on over there. CIA and INR [the State Department's intelligence bureau] knew exactly what was going on." Other officials involved in policymaking at the time confirm Kenney's view.

Ironically, numerous public statements by the Bush administration accurately reflected this understanding of the war. But such clear-headed official statements of Serbian responsibility were inevitably followed by conspicuous silences or off-the-cuff remarks designed to muddy the waters, spread the blame and reduce pressures for decisive U.S. action. For example, as early as September 25, 1991—three months after the outbreak of the Yugoslav war— Secretary of State James Baker scathingly criticized Serbia before the U.N. Security Council, stating that "the Serbian leadership" and "the Yugoslav military" were "working in tandem" to "create a 'small Yugoslavia' or 'greater Serbia.'" Baker went on to deplore such "repression" and "use of force." But afterward, according to one former official who spoke on the condition of anonymity, "Baker clammed up for three months." "There was a general understanding in the [State] Department that the secretary was uncomfortable with what he had said" and had gotten "way out ahead" on Yugoslavia policy, he says.

Repeatedly, according to officials who participated in the policy, the Bush administration found that an honest portrayal of events in warring Yugoslavia created political pressure for American action. As a result, in the words of the same former official, it inevitably sought to "tamp down" the impression it had created through such forthright statements. This explained what the former official calls the "toing and froing" of the Bush rhetoric on Yugoslavia, sometimes citing Serbian aggression, at other times depicting the struggle as the product of age-old ethnic tensions or "civil war."

No one was more effective in complicating the picture of the struggle than Deputy Secretary of State Eagleburger, a former U.S. ambassador to Belgrade, who played a central role as both policy-maker and public spokesman on the issue. Appearing on "The MacNeil/Lehrer NewsHour" in April 1992, as war was beginning in Bosnia, Eagleburger acknowledged that the Serbs were the "principal culprit," but argued that they were "not the only culprit by any means." He portrayed the war as one in which the sides were not yet "tired of killing one another," and reminded viewers of the "very close historical relationship" between America and Serbia, which dated from World War II, when the two countries were "allies."

According to several present and former officials, Eagleburger's assessment of blame was calculatedly ambiguous—and clearly at variance with what the State Department and intelligence agencies knew at the time. "It was cynical, disingenuous, whatever you want to call it," says Marshall Freeman Harris, who resigned in protest three months ago as the State Department's Bosnia desk officer. The purpose, he and others say, was to counter growing pressure, stemming from media reports of the war, for decisive U.S. action.

Yet nowhere was the pattern of distortion clearer than on the issue of the Serbian concentration camps. According to several former officials, State Department officers knew of the existence of Serbian detention centers for Bosnian Muslims as early as April and May of 1992; by the end of June, they knew of full-fledged concentration camps. Yet it was not until August 3, after *Newsday*'s Roy Gutman revealed the camps and their cruelties in stories written from Bosnia, that a State Department spokesman acknowledged their existence. And even then, Assistant Secretary of State Thomas Niles went to Capitol Hill the next day to testify that evidence concerning the camps was inconclusive. By the fall of 1992, according to several former officials, the State Department had enough evidence to produce a legal finding of "genocide" against Serbia—but such charges were blocked, for fear the United States would be required to intervene under the 1951 Genocide Convention.

All the while, a struggle persisted within the State Department: working-level officials tried to make public the appalling information on Serbian atrocities; mid-level officials thwarted their attempts in an effort to keep in place the Bush policy of nonintervention. The information flow was even blocked internally. Kenney says that a "Night Note" he composed on Serbian concentration camps for President Bush's reading was altered by Eagleburger's office to make it appear, incorrectly, that all three sides were *equally* engaged in operating camps. (Croat and Muslim fighters were known to have carried out atrocities, but on nowhere near the vast scale of the Serb forces.) Other former officials cite a similar pattern of evasion and distortion.

Also, throughout 1992, when Eagleburger was publicly encouraging hopes for American businessman-turned-Yugoslav–prime minister Milan Panic to end the war, intelligence agencies and State Department officials all but unanimously came to the conclusion that Panic would simply be used by Milosevic and would have no appreciable impact on Serbian policy. During the whole Panic episode—nearly six months—the chance for more decisive American action was put on hold.

The same conflict was replicated in the U.S. embassy in Belgrade, where Ambassador Warren Zimmerman, in accord with the dominant policy line, put the best face on Milosevic's susceptibility to mere diplomatic pressures even while analysts in his embassy consistently argued that the Serbian leader would only respond to force.

Amid the many shifts in public posture, the one constant in the Bush policy was the objective of avoiding involvement. This taboo on military action colored the whole intragovernmental process. Kenney and other former State Department officials tell of an utter absence of overall strategic discussion of the Balkans and a debilitating lack of communication between analysts familiar with the situation and top officials. For example, when recognition of Bosnia was under consideration in early 1992, the CIA predicted that such a move could trigger war—at least in the absence of some larger effort at containing or deterring the aggressive Serbs. Nonetheless, top policy-makers proceeded with recognition despite the CIA warnings.

Intelligence agencies, which provided excellent interpretation of political trends, offered characteristically cautious assessments of possible action. These appraisals—based on sparse information about the military situation, particularly the composition and morale of Serbian forces—were readily accepted by leaders eager to find reasons for inaction. For example, in the fall of 1992, when pressure was building to lift the arms embargo on Bosnian government forces, intelligence suggested that training lead-times (in many cases, of four to five weeks) would make arms supplies to the Bosnians ineffective—even though the war was to continue for nearly a year.

Clearly, decisive action involved political risks—especially for an unpopular president in an election year. But this was not the same as saying options were unavailable. It is worth remembering that, during the 1980s, the fateful decision to arm Afghan resistance fighters with Stinger missiles—ultimately leading to the USSR's defeat in Afghanistan—involved overcoming powerful bureaucratic resistance in both the Defense Department and the CIA. "A lot of things are doable when there's a commitment to it," says one unhappy former State Department official, reflecting on the pattern of inaction. "There was never anybody who sat down and said what would it take."

Notably, some high-level civilian officials in the Bush Pentagon, including Undersecretary of Defense Paul Wolfowitz and Assistant Undersecretary Zalmay Khalilzad, a participant in the successful Afghanistan policy under Reagan, repeatedly pushed in interagency meetings for lifting the arms embargo on Bosnian government forces during 1992. They pointed not only to the Afghan success but to the example of the war in Croatia, where gradual acquisition of illegal arms by the Croatian army had produced a military stalemate, and ultimately an enduring cease-fire, between Croat and Serb forces in December and January of 1991 and 1992. Top-level State and NSC officials opposed lifting the embargo on the simple grounds that more arms would prolong the war in Bosnia. The aversion to risk and the resistance to action were overwhelming, former officials say.

Interestingly, after the election, Bush himself experienced a change of heart and sent Eagleburger to Europe to argue for lifting the embargo. But Eagleburger, whose strong personal opposition to lifting the embargo was well known, gave a deliberately unenthusiastic rendition of the president's message, according to a former official familiar with the discussions. Faced with such mixed signals, European governments had little incentive to endorse a change in policy.

Despite heady campaign rhetoric on Bosnia, the Clinton administration has essentially repeated the Bush pattern of inaction and obfuscation—only in a more obvious, embarrassing, and potentially destructive fashion. The administration's overall review of options on Bosnia produced similarly cautious briefs from intelligence agencies, which argued that arming the Bosnians would make for a bloodier war and warned that air strikes might embolden Albanians to revolt in Kosovo. Officials say President Clinton early on was persuaded of the risks of action. Nonetheless, unwilling to admit that it was washing its hands of Bosnia, the administration has combined bold declarations about American "strategic interests" there with weak initiatives guaranteed to produce no results, while at the same time damaging U.S. prestige and credibility. In May 1993 Christopher traveled to Europe to offer a decidedly— some speculate deliberately—unenthusiastic case for Clinton's proposed "lift and strike" option (combining an end to the arms embargo against Bosnia with air strikes against Serb forces). Since then, the administration has taken to arguing that the president wished to act in Bosnia but was prevented by the allies.

Lately, the administration has begun to engage in its own all-too-transparent brand of revisionism. Lacking the subtlety shown by Eagleburger, Secretary of State Christopher's clumsy efforts to distribute blame for the war equally ("there are atrocities on all sides") provoked an angry memo from a State Department analyst, leaked to *The New York Times,* pointing out the blatant inaccuracy of the secretary's assessment. More recently, administration officials have taken to arguing disingenuously that we should "respect" the surrender that the Bosnians have "freely" accepted—despite the fact that the Owen-Stoltenberg partition plan is plainly being imposed on the Bosnian government, not least by behind-the-scenes pressure from Washington. Indeed, the decision of the Clinton administration to begin pressing the Bosnian government to accept surrender and partition precipitated the final spate of resignations by Harris and two other officials at State.

The Bush administration succeeded in distancing itself from the Bosnian debacle, at least for a time. Having condemned the Bush policy on moral grounds, the Clinton administration is now in the position of quietly sponsoring Bosnia's surrender to aggression. No wonder nobody wants to admit it.

(OCTOBER 25, 1993)

Curses

LEON WIESELTIER

Dodging has given way to shrugging, in Washington, about the crime of the Serbs; to shrugging, and to a particularly obscene kind of diplomatic pressure, in which the Americans who failed to save Bosnia are demanding that the Bosnians save America, by signing on the dotted, self-immolating line and taking the world's only superpower off the hook. Some of our suits are also beginning to get a little jittery about the historians who will follow them, and so the number of senior officials whose ardor for action against the Serbian aggression was impeded by other senior officials is growing daily. Even the president counts himself in the company of the blocked. (At the opening ceremonies of the Holocaust Memorial Museum in the spring, when Clinton tried to please the crowd of survivors by speaking grandiloquently about Bosnia and insisting that "never again" would the United States allow a genocide to happen in Europe, my mother turned to me and mordantly said: "He talks about Bosnia like he's somebody else.")

It appears to be the local view that the time for action is past, that realism is all that remains; but realism, in the case of American policy toward Bosnia, is just a fancy name for complicity with reality. It is too late, I am sure, for "lift and strike," for the arming of the Bosnians and the disarming (from the air, by Americans) of the Serbians. At the White House, and at the Pentagon, and at the Department of State, "lift and strike" long ago crashed and burned. But is it too late also for "sign and lift"? After all, a partition whose parties cannot defend themselves is not a peace, it is a pause in war. Surely the Bosnians must not be left, eternally and as an element of policy, defenseless. At this late date in the dying of Bosnia, indeed, the arming of the Bosnians is not a way of prolonging the war, it is a way of fixing the peace. It might even be a way of inducing the Bosnians to take the deal; and it poses no threat to Serbia. (Poor, threatened Serbia.) Of "sign and lift," however, I hear nothing.

The time for epic cursing is not past. Readers of the Bible will remember the epic curse (I take the term from the scholar David Quint) as an imprecation of special magnitude, a linguistic response to wickedness that seeks to match its scale, a prayer that the punishment share the finality of the crime. "Ye corridors of Foggy Bottom, let there be no dew, neither let there be rain, upon you. . . ": that sort of thing. Czeslaw Milosz's poem [see page *ix*] is a fine example of an epic curse. The Balkan disaster has provided rather a large number of objects for rage. Not least among them is, speaking coarsely, Europe. For this much, therefore, Slobodan Milosevic has my thanks: he has exposed Europe for what it really is, which is the part of the civilized world that is second to none in its horror of otherness.

Fifty years ago there was no room for Jews in Europe. Now there is no room for Muslims in Europe. Those who are shocked by the indolence of the Europeans in the Balkans are forgetting history, and I do not mean the history of the fifteenth or sixteenth or seventeenth century. I mean the history of the twentieth century. This was the century in which more innocent people were slaughtered by European armies in the name of European values than were ever slaughtered by any armies in the name of any values. And the morning after the slaughter, the cunning of history kicked in. The cold war appeared as a brilliant disguise for the killing field.

No sooner had Europe perpetrated the most spectacular genocide in history than its eastern half could pose as a group of tolerant nations suffering tyranny and its western half could pose as a group of tolerant nations opposing tyranny. Of course, the eastern half did suffer and the western half did oppose. But the tyranny turns out to have frustrated not only the hunger for freedom. It turns out to have frustrated also the hunger for sameness. Over here we thought that the Soviet empire was evil because it forbade the mind and shackled the spirit. Over there they thought that the Soviet empire was evil also because it forced people to live with people not like themselves. And these outbursts of collective subjectivity should not be dignified as "nationalism." They represent the hoariest, the shabbiest, tribalism.

How, then, expect the Europeans to confront Serbia? They would have first to confront themselves. I know that I am exaggerating. There is a difference between the torching of a few Muslim homes in Germany and the murder of hundreds of thousands of Muslims in the Balkans. Still, the difference is not so large as to make the similarity trivial. And so I propose that we learn a few ashen lessons from the destiny of Bosnia. First, that the condescension of "the West" toward the rest of the world must end. For many years, and especially during the Reagan and Thatcher years, it has been the custom to describe the states of the post-colonial world, with pity or with contempt, as essentially awash in blood, in ethnic and religious savagery. In the matter of ethnic and religious savagery, however, "the West" has no justification for its strut, no ground for its triumphalism. A contemporary citizen of Sarajevo and a contemporary citizen of Colombo would understand each other perfectly. Second, that the liberalism of "the West" is not a fact of nature, but a fact of culture; not a fate, but an accomplishment. "The West" was not always like this, and in many of its precincts it is not yet like this. When we admire European democracy, we are admiring the self-overcoming of Europe; Spinozas and Mills did not fall from its every tree. Third, that there is no such place as "the West." There is Europe and there is America, and they are distinct chapters in the history of decency. Consider the European tradition of nationalist thought. There is no vision of heterogeneity in that tradition, there is only the anxiety (an admirable one, too) about minorities; but the anxiety about minorities is just a scruple of homogeneity. Its premise is still that otherness is a problem. The distance between the ideal of minority rights and the ideal of a multiethnic society is vast; and it is the distance between the democratic dispensation of Europe and the democratic dispensation of America. If my god was Allah and my skin was brown, I would try the States.

These speculations are not all that attenuated. They go to the heart of one of the administration's alibis. It was because the divergence between Europe and the United States was not properly understood that there arose the mistaken notion that the United States could not act except together with Europe. There were many who believed that something should be done, but that the Europeans should do it; but they may as well have believed that nothing should be done. And so nothing was done. An American, I am not at all proud. A Jew, I am not at all surprised.

(OCTOBER 25, 1993)

Who Lost Bosnia?

ROBERT WRIGHT

"As Sarajevo came under some of the worst shelling by Bosnian Serb forces in more than a year, the United Nations said today that it had again overruled calls for a NATO air strike. It sent a letter of protest to the Serbian commander instead."

—The New York Times, *May 9*

Oh good. When it comes to stopping rampaging Bosnian Serbs, I've always found that nothing works quite like a letter of protest. And you can't beat the price.

If I sound bitter, it's because I periodically entertain the idea that someday the United Nations could play a central role in preserving world peace; and reality periodically reminds me that I'm hopelessly naïve. This year, as spring brings its annual renaissance of death in the Balkans, I refuse to get my hopes up. Instead, I'll sublimate my idealism in a merciless apportionment of blame for the world's failure in Bosnia. Bring on the suspects.

Robert McNamara. One of the great barriers to action in Bosnia has been the misapplication of "lessons" from Vietnam. As if bringing us Vietnam itself weren't bad enough, McNamara has now resurfaced to endorse the misapplications. Counseling against intervention in Bosnia, he lectures: "You cannot confront the powers of nationalism with external military force after the state has begun to dissolve." Granted, it's hard for an outside power to beat indigenous nationalism, especially amid chaos. But in Bosnia, unlike Vietnam, nationalism works for us as well as against us. Our ally isn't some puppet government with a dubious claim to popular allegiance; it is an ethnically and religiously distinct group whose security and identity are deeply at stake. Motivation is not a problem.

A related bit of confusion is the insistence that "air power alone" doesn't win wars. To repeat: we aren't alone in Bosnia—and we'd be even less alone if the Bosnian Muslims were better armed. Combined with NATO air support, an armed indigenous force could have repelled Serbian aggression long ago. Casualties to NATO fliers would have been appreciable, but not so high as to make an air war politically unsustainable. (In these pages I've touted this as a general formula for bolstering peace in the post–cold-war world: the rich, high-tech, but risk-averse West provides air support and arms to victims of aggression, but refrains from sending ground troops because high Western casualties would render the operation politically undoable. Hopes of making my mark in the annals of punditry by dubbing this the "Clinton doctrine" have been complicated by the Clinton administration's lack of interest. See below.)

Boutros Boutros-Ghali. From the beginning, Boutros-Ghali saw conflict in Bosnia as a civil war—and thus saw the U.N. as an impartial "peacekeeper." Certainly Yugoslavia's meltdown was in some ways a civil war. But once the world had recognized Bosnia as a sovereign nation, the Serbia-sponsored assault on its government was also an act of transborder aggression. And the U.N. doctrine of collective security is clear on what this means. The victim is the good guy, the aggressor is the bad guy, and the world community joins the fray (even if only by bombing and providing arms). Collective security, by the way, isn't just part of the U.N. Charter; it was the basic impetus for creating the U.N. after World War II. Is it too much to ask that the secretary general have an affinity for the animating spirit of the United Nations?

One reason some people are reluctant to take sides in the Balkans is that which side is in the right depends on when you started watching the movie. Atrocity is a tradition there, and all groups have shared in it. One virtue of the doctrine of collective security is that it legalistically sidesteps the issue of historical grievance, and all the fruitless debates about who slaughtered whom first. Whatever history's various outrages, borders are borders. Violate them and you're the world's enemy. There are many problems collective security can't address—including most civil wars—but Bosnia wasn't one of them.

George Bush. First, the good news: with the Persian Gulf war, the Bush administration revived the doctrine of collective security. After decades of cold war irrelevance, the Security Council sanctioned transnational reprisal against an aggressor. The bad news is that this magic moment seems to have been a Mr. Magoo–type accident. To be sure, Bush seemed at first to see the significance; he started using the phrase "new world order." But when people asked what it meant, he fell silent. And when war broke out in the Balkans, the reason for his reticence became clear: he had no fondness for collective security when U.S. interests didn't seem directly at stake—which is to say, he had no fondness for collective security.

Early on, with Bush in full post-Gulf glory and Russian nationalism fairly quiescent, Security Council backing for swift and strong NATO air strikes was probably obtainable. And, anyway, Bush could have prodded NATO to action without the U.N. Collective security needn't be the exclusive province of any one acronym. His failure to act was an unconscionable squandering of the precedent set in Iraq. Such precedents are vital to collective security: at great human cost, you convince would-be aggressors that the world won't tolerate aggression, and thereafter deterrence is much cheaper—a few devastating air strikes, say. But Bush never grasped the meaning of the Persian Gulf war, so he couldn't build on it.

General Michael Rose. Rose, former head of U.N. forces in Bosnia, can't be blamed for inheriting a hopeless mission—playing impartial peacekeeper in wartime. But he can be blamed for being an "impartial" with pro-Serbian sentiments. A recent ABC News special on the U.N.'s failure in Bosnia featured videotape of an unguarded conversation with a subordinate in which Rose basically calls the Muslims lazy bums who want the United Nations to do their fighting for them. Good luck.

President Clinton. Clinton is only marginally culpable. By the time he showed up, things were a mess. In particular, "peacekeepers" (read: hostages) had poured into Bosnia, paralyzing both NATO and the United Nations. Besides, to his credit, Clinton has called for air strikes and for multilaterally lifting the arms embargo. Still, he hasn't done so in a full-throated way. And though he mentioned "collective security" in his presidential campaign, he has shown few signs of devotion to it, or of vision generally. Indeed, the move to expand NATO eastward is a rightish cold-war reflex that may seriously dilute the alliance's character and reflects a poverty of imagination. A more progressive idea is one that nobody at the White House seems to take seriously: transforming NATO from a mere mutual defense league into an instrument of collective security beyond its borders. Policeman is a role that, I'm beginning to suspect, we can't always count on the United Nations to play.

(MAY 29, 1995)

Call to Arms

CHARLES LANE

Should the arms embargo against Bosnia be lifted? For the first four months of his administration, President Clinton built his Balkan strategy around a "yes" answer. The idea was, roughly, to fortify the military capability of the Muslim-led Bosnian government and, hence, raise the odds of a relatively fair settlement between the government and the Bosnian Serbs. Clinton's plan was "lift and strike"—to end the embargo and support the Bosnians with air strikes while they re-armed. But the administration abandoned it after the British and French rejected Secretary of State Warren Christopher's muted pleas in May 1993.

Instead, for the last two years, the administration has been following Europe's lead. The European policy keeps the embargo and limits Western involvement to the use of neutral U.N. peacekeeping troops and humanitarian relief. Though rarely stated so baldly, the policy assumes that the West's interest lies not in punishing aggression, or in securing the integrity of Bosnia, but in muting intra-NATO squabbles and stabilizing the chaotic Balkans on just about any terms. (Just below the surface lies British and French fear of Muslim influence on the continent.) Since the Serbs are the strongest party, the best hope is to give them what they want. The Muslims' role is to accept their fate. The embargo pressures them to do just that.

It's clear now that this strategy has failed. The Serbs simply would not be appeased. They rejected both the 1993 Vance-Owen plan and the 1994 Contact Group plan, though both were accepted by Sarajevo and both ratified Serb ethnic cleansing. After the humiliating Serb hostage-taking in response to pinprick air strikes, the United Nations Protection Force (UNPROFOR) has lost what remained of its humanitarian credibility: it bargained away the air strike option and assured Serbian commander General Ratko Mladic that its new "rapid reaction" force will leave him alone. The heavy weapons exclusion zone around Sarajevo has collapsed.

Basically, the Serbs rejected the peace plans because they felt strong enough to get away with it. "As long as the planet Earth has been in existence," Mladic has said, "borders between states and peoples have been determined by the shedding of blood and the cutting off of heads." Mladic's dealings with UNPROFOR only reinforce his view that no force on Earth can cut off more heads than his. Yet the British and French cling to their old strategy. And so does Clinton. Resisting Republican calls for a unilateral lifting of the embargo, he wants to help pay for the rapid reaction force, insisting the U.N. troops are still doing more good than harm. Vice President Al Gore claims, based on invisible evidence, that the five-nation Contact Group is "still making some progress toward a negotiated settlement."

Yet, while "unilateral lift" is certainly a morally defensible policy (Clinton himself labeled the embargo an "injustice" last year), it's not exactly the free lunch many Republicans seem to think. For one thing, it would exact a high price in diplomatic disruption. On the other hand, a modified version of "lift and strike," launched in concert with European allies, might still work. For a president who said April 11 that he'd favor a "multilateral lift" if "other measures fail to bring about a political settlement" this would require only some consistency—and a modicum of risk-tolerant cleverness.

One reason such a strategy might work is that, contrary to European expectations, the Bosnian Muslims have turned out not to be so weak. Their army survived both the initial Serbian onslaught and the bloody 1993–1994 Croat-Muslim war. Even the arms embargo has eroded over the last two years. When a U.S.–brokered agreement ended the Croat-Muslim struggle in February 1994, the Bosnian Army could once again import black-market weapons from Iran and elsewhere, via Croatia.

The Serb Army is on the strategic defensive. Spread across 70 percent of Bosnia, plagued by desertions and on uncertain terms with their suppliers in Belgrade, the Serbs can neither easily defend their turf, nor mount a tactical retreat without undermining morale. Since late 1994, when Muslim forces attempted to break out of the enclave at Bihac, the Bosnians have initiated most fighting. Around Sarajevo now, for example, a more aggressive Bosnian Army appears to be advancing. Croat gains against the Serbs in Croatia add to the momentum.

The Serbs retain one decisive advantage, however: heavy artillery and tanks. Until this advantage is neutralized, the balance of forces—a resurgent Bosnian-Croat alliance against a weary but still potent Serb Army—will remain a formula for bloody stalemate. The solution is to persuade the Europeans to amend, lift, or sidestep the embargo and get heavy weapons to the Bosnians. It doesn't require a formal declaration by the U.N. Nor does it demand a massive U.S. airlift like the intentionally self-discrediting $5 billion "plan" that the pro-embargo Pentagon leaked last fall. If the British and French want to preserve plausible deniability, the transfers can be done semi-covertly—disguised as shipments to the Croats, perhaps. The Saudis have offered to buy East-bloc weapons for the Bosnian army. Such gear is compatible with what Bosnia has now; to use it wouldn't require much, if any, American training.

There are risks. "There would be an interval before the heavy weapons were delivered to the Bosnian government and before they were trained in their use," Gore said recently, "during which the Serb forces would attempt to surge and overrun Sarajevo and the eastern enclaves of Gorazde, Srebrenica, Zepa, and the carnage could potentially be just horrific." Such a development could require retaining the threat of NATO air strikes—already allowed under U.N. resolutions—but not necessarily a massive campaign as envisioned in the original "lift and strike" proposal. Anyway, Gore's scenario "is a bit of a myth," according to a U.S. official who monitors the Bosnian forces. If the Serbs massed to take Srebrenica, they'd have to divert forces from elsewhere, exposing themselves to a counterstrike from Bosnian and Croatian troops. This is what happened last December, when the Serbs lost the town of Kupres to the Croats while they pushed back the Bosnians at Bihac.

More significant would be the impact on the U.N. peacekeepers. This has been the Europeans' trump card against lifting the embargo: their men are at risk, Americans aren't. But this threat, too, may be overblown. Many of the peacekeepers are deployed in Muslim-Croat areas, less exposed to Serb reprisals. The danger to the others could be reduced by intelligent redeployment: recalling U.N. military observers from scattered positions; declining to replace British and Dutch units in Srebrenica and Gorazde when their rotations expire this fall; and withdrawing the underequipped Bangladeshi battalion from Bihac. U.S. ground troops should assist in these relatively discrete tasks. It is the threat of air strikes, more than the presence of foreign troops, that has provided the "safe areas" what little security they now enjoy, as Professor Norman Cigar of the Marine Corps School of Advanced Warfighting points out in a recent paper, for a modified "lift and strike."

Belgrade might intervene. But Serbian President Slobodan Milosevic and his Yugoslav National Army are much weaker now than they were two years ago. Though Milosevic has continued to help the Bosnian Serbs, the power struggle between him and the Bosnian Serb leaders is real. Crippled by sanctions and enmeshed in a wrangle over borders with Croatia, the last thing Milosevic needs is full-scale war in Bosnia. He recently let the Croatians rout Croatian Serb forces from Western Slavonia. Having spent two years trying to get his Bosnian cousins to cut a deal, Milosevic might even secretly welcome new military pressure on them.

It's time for another high-level trip to Europe. Unlike Christopher's, the purpose would be to explain that the United States gave Europe's approach a shot and is now ready to chart a different course. It is prepared to use air cover and even a modest number of ground troops to protect European forces from threats that may arise when weapons begin to flow. The American objective would be pragmatic: to force the Serbs to negotiate, not to roll back all Serb conquests. Bill Clinton, understandably, is reluctant to open his re-election campaign with a new Bosnia policy. The payoff, however, could be a second term whose first 100 days are not consumed by yet another agonizing debate over how to stop the war in Bosnia.

(JULY 17 & 24, 1995)

Nationalism and Before

MARTIN PERETZ

In the summer before my freshman year in college, I was assigned, as preparation for the coming heavy-think, E. H. Carr's *Nationalism and After*. The emphasis was on the "after" since Carr was one of those subtle "historical necessity" apologists for Stalin who thought that the nation-state expressed nothing authentic and that it would soon pass into oblivion. That's what most intellectuals believed then, at least as regards Europe. But, in the decolonizing countries, instead of the displacement of nations by ever larger units, the heady trend was the process of what was called "nation-building." Graduate students wrote dissertations about this irresistible phenomenon. Foundations summoned the wise to give counsel. Nehru, Nkrumah, Seku Toure, these were the historic nation-builders. You have only to utter the word "Nigeria" or "India"—let alone "Somalia"—to grasp immediately what a failure that enterprise has been, almost everywhere.

I wrote once in these pages that "the great revenge of imperialism was nationalism." It was the modern stage on which antique hatreds were played out, clothed in contemporary costume. But in the industrialized world, where nationalism was long ago supposed to have been supplanted by socialism or some such universalism, it is very much alive, in many places altogether decently, and in others murderously. This is befuddling to the post-national theorists and policymakers. They have seen their most ingeniously crafted designs for betterment and uplift—the European Union, say—frustrated continually by national sentiment.

But, if the nation is a difficult concept for these rationalists to appreciate, the resilience of religion is, quite simply, incomprehensible. But it is religious passion that still exerts the most volatile authority over the minds of men and women. If you cannot understand that, you cannot understand the grim news from Bosnia.

The Serbian war against the Bosnians is a religious war not only because most Bosnians are Muslims but because the Serbs are Orthodox Christians. The best scholarship I have been able to find about Serbian Orthodoxy and Serbian nationalism is the writing of Sabrina Petra Ramet. (A professor of politics at the University of Washington, she is the author of *Balkan Babel: Politics, Culture and Religion in Yugoslavia, Cross and Commissar*, and an essay on Yugoslavia in a book edited by Pedro Ramet, *Religion and Nationalism in Soviet and Eastern European Politics*.) Ramet discloses some small but telling details. For example, the mug of ex-Communist Slobodan Milosevic, who seized power in Serbia eight years ago and turned himself into a nationalist, is carried aloft in Orthodox services as a religious icon, along with the saints.

The post-Communist states are particularly prone to religious revanchism, because it was there that God and His servants were most persecuted. It is true that in many countries, Yugoslavia included, certain "patriotic clergy" were indulged by the regime in return for service. But the church was still the most stable refuge for ideological resistance and memory. Serbian nationalism is rich in symbols of the past, humiliating symbols like battles, in Kosovo and Constantinople, lost centuries ago. These were battles lost to infidels as those fought today, however brutally, are victories of the faithful avenging the past.

The Russians have supported Serb aggression and want Bosnia diminished because they, too, are Orthodox Christians, which is also the fuel that fires

Moscow's war against the Chechens and others. It is true, of course, that Stalin, who was not motivated by religion at all, inflicted the most excruciating suffering on the Chechens. But in so far as Yeltsin's war against them is a gesture to his ultra-nationalist right, it is also a gesture to the church for which Russification has always meant Christianization. The harmony of church and state was the very definition of pre-Communist rule, and Yeltsin has tried to evoke that harmony. And it should not be overlooked that the nostalgists share not only memory but fears. These fears rivet on the Muslim outlands of Russia, geographically close to the Turks and the Persians, old enemies of the czars and their dreams.

The other Slavic churches (and the states they sway) are, to a greater or lesser extent, all now allied in the Orthodox revanche. The border with Bulgaria, one of these states, is the porous frontier through which international sanctions against Serbia are violated. Even the Greeks are involved, cheering on fellow faithful of the Eastern rite against "the Turks," a phrase applied indiscriminately to virtually all neighboring Muslims.

Balkan cartography is patchwork. But one clear psychological line running through it is the line between the Orthodox churches and Islam, that is to say, the line between their believers. It is now a line drenched in Muslim blood. There is, of course, another dividing line in this region, and it is the one that runs between Orthodoxy and Rome. This line runs deep, and not only in the former Yugoslavia. A Serbian victory in Bosnia does not leave the Catholics of Croatia safe. The shadow of clerical fascism in Nazi-era Croatia is now stalked by the reality of clerical fascism in present-day Serbia.

So what about the Muslims? Once upon a time the Libyan tyrant Muammar Qaddafi helped pay for a mosque-building program in Yugoslavia. But that was a long time ago. The oil-Arabs are, of course, poorer now. The Islamic states have been eerily quiescent about the agony of Bosnia's Muslims. To be sure, Saudi Arabia has sent some money and maybe, just maybe, some arms. Saudi men of the particularly pious persuasion have also gone as volunteers. The Organization of Islamic Conference, composed of fifty-two Muslim member states, has campaigned against the arms embargo but has not attempted to break it. That's it: Bosnia, after all, is not Kuwait, either to Riyadh or, for that matter, to Washington.

Turkey, because of ethnic affinities, history, and the presence of a small Bosnian lobby, is the one Muslim country that has been significantly touched by sympathy for the Bosnian Muslims. When it tried to move against the genocide, its initiative was squashed by the NATO alliance. Still, it has a much better record than other Muslim countries. Take Iran: it sent mullahs to the Bosnians, but it was caught red-handed selling oil to the Serbs. The Muslims of Bosnia are, in fact, very Europeanized. They drink beer and even abide women in the clergy. They are tolerant, so tolerant that Muslims elsewhere think them heretics. But this has not kept the Serbs from waging a holy war against them. They are the ultimate victims of a jihad: too complicated to be defended, too alien to be tolerated.

(AUGUST 7, 1995)

Beyond Words

FOUAD AJAMI

"It's beyond words," a man of Tuzla said of the refugees who have been herded out of Srebrenica. "These people have lived through an unbelievable terror. Something completely evil happened in Srebrenica." That is where we are, beyond words, where every good and urgent thing has been said and has scattered into the wind and been trampled by the killers and knights of Greater Serbia. There, amid those columns of misery on the road out of Srebrenica, lies the promise of American primacy and benevolent power, which in Bill Clinton's hands had turned into a tarnished and uncertain inheritance.

We shall, of course, never know for certain whether the callousness toward the people of Bosnia would have been the same had these men and women and children taking to the road not been people of the Muslim faith. In the vast expanses of Islam, the inescapable conclusion has been drawn: the Bosnians have been marked for destruction because of their adherence to Islam. For those who love their civilizational and racial lines straight and unambiguous, the people of Bosnia must be a bit odd. There is a jarring quality to those columns of misery: the head-scarves of the women speak of Islam, the pigmentation and the features are those of Europe. The rituals of grief and bereavement have an Islamic echo to them in a crowd neither decidedly "Eastern" nor wholly European. Ours must be reckoned a terrible time for miscegenation.

We can exonerate the Clinton administration and its Bosnia policy of any civilizational bias or prejudice or religious favor. Ideology of any kind, a moral passion, is alien to this crowd. They are equal opportunity shirkers. Judging by their entire attitude toward America's role in the world, the Clintonites would let down people of any color and creed and faith and national origin. They are a decidedly ecumenical lot.

Though we think of the president and his closest advisers as forever seared and defined by Vietnam, it is another, a far more proximate intervention, that has shaped much of what they have done in Bosnia: the expedition to Somalia. It is the lessons of Mogadishu that the Clinton White House have projected onto the Balkans. Somalia was the poisoned chalice handed the Clintonites by their predecessors, the Bush people, and by Boutros Boutros-Ghali, who was keen to use the cant of multilateralism to hunt down Mohammed Farah Aidid and settle an old account with the Somali warlord from his time in the Egyptian bureaucracy. The trauma of Somalia happened on Clinton's watch. We had rushed unaware into a place we did not fully understand, into a war of clans and bandits. With the gear we carried on that expedition we carried fantasies about reconstituting a place that had broken beyond repair. When we were rebuffed and exited with nothing to show for the effort, the expedition became a warrant for abdication elsewhere. It would be easy, henceforth, to project Somalia onto other foreign commitments. (Haiti was the exception. But that was a police operation forced on Clinton by a tide of refugees.)

For thirty long, cruel months, the thrust of the Clinton Bosnia policy would be reduced to what truly mattered: damage control. The one thing we would never grant the Bosnians was our candor. The one thing the Clinton people would not do was stand up in broad daylight and assert that, for them, Bosnia was a place of no consequence to America's vital interests. The cavalry was always on the way. We would always promise to be there, with our guns and our war tribunals, after the next massacre. We would lift the arms embargo on the Bosnians if only we could, if only the Europeans and Boutros Boutros-Ghali would permit it. We would unleash the terrifying air power that broke the will of the Iraqis in the Gulf, if only we would be asked to do it. We would roll back the Serbian gains if only that division of authority (the "dual key," in officialspeak) between NATO and the United Nations were to be resolved. Genocide is always handled by the next desk.

Power—great political, military, and moral power—had passed to these men, but they don't wish to use it. It is odd, this ambition and yearning for power and the reluctance to deploy it. Something Clinton himself said in accepting the Democratic nomination in the summer of 1992 is a fitting description of his own administration. In staking the claim of his generation to power, he ridiculed George Bush's lethargic presidency by quoting Abraham Lincoln's admonition to General George B. McClellan, the commander of the Army of the Potomac, who was forever refusing to engage the Confederacy: "If you're not going to use your army, may I borrow it?" That is where the Clinton presidency now finds itself. Its Bosnia policy is but an embodiment on cruel display of its general abdication of America's leadership in the world. In Lincoln's words, the bottom is out of this tub.

It is easy to see the method in the mix of abdication and spin that constitutes Clinton's policy toward Bosnia. The words would tire, the Clinton advisers reasoned, the outrage of the critics would be spent, the safe-havens would fall, and Bosnia would be consigned to memory, a victim felled by those famed Balkan ghosts that are said to haunt that peninsula: the curse of the place having its way. Now all would be well if the conquest of Bosnia were to be completed before the 1996 campaign kicked in.

There have been endless pretexts and warrants for the American abdication. Most shamefully, we passed off our acquiescence to the Serbian project of conquest as something we owed Russia, an act of deference to the pan-Slavic spirit that was said to be blowing through that land. We fell for this great legend because it suited our needs. There is a Russianist, and a Russophile at that, in the inner circle, Deputy Secretary of State Strobe Talbott. But no Russianist was needed to see through that shameless pretense. Pan-Slavism has never run deep in that presumably mystical Russian soul. It was the calling of a few romantics and priests and literati; the Russian state looked at the pan-Slavic sentiment with cold-blooded disdain and caution. A cursory reading of the Congress of Berlin's diplomacy, which settled the first great Balkan Crisis in 1878, ought to put an end to the legend of Russia's commitment to the Serbs. Alexander II hated Balkan revolutionaries and their ruinous radicalism; St. Petersburg played the game of the Great Powers when the scramble for the Ottoman Empire's European domains had begun. Serbia got very little of its grandiose ambitions fulfilled; the Serbs had no sponsor among the powers. They had wanted Bosnia; it was ceded to the Habsburgs. They had wanted Novi Pazar, a territory separating Serbia from Montenegro; it, too, was denied them.

We gave currency to the pan-Slavic idea, summoned it from the world of the dead, when it should have been blatantly clear that the Russians were in this enterprise as a way of simple financial blackmail, of squeezing the best for themselves out of the industrial democracies. There was never an explanation why a ruined society on the ropes like Russia, riddled with all kinds of troubles, struggling to keep a political center alive amid plunder and chaos, was owed favors in the Balkans. That our concern for Russia had to be demonstrated by sanctioning genocide in Bosnia carried "Russia-firstism" beyond the call of duty. Were we serious about helping Russia get beyond autocracy and failure and chaos on that road toward political democracy and market reform that we say we want for her, the last thing we would do for Russia would be to indulge the darker, more atavistic part of her temperament. We ought to have given the Russians a choice: the company of outlaws and pariahs or the decent company of nations at peace.

A policy of spin and appeasement with thirty months on its hands gets to be good at playing the game of exculpation. It finds the pretexts and squeezes them as they come. Nor is this policy above seeing hidden victories and accomplishments in the ruins. The Clinton advisers have taken to claiming for the Bosnia policy an amazing defense: whatever its faults and cruel harvest in Bosnia, their policy, they say, has prevented the spread of a wider war in the Balkans. The killing rages in the northern Balkans, but peace (of sorts) reigns in the southern end of the peninsula. Greece, Turkey, and Albania, we are told by the Clintonites on the Sunday talk shows, have stayed out of the fight, and all is quiet in Kosovo and in Macedonia between the Slavs and the Albanians. But the troubles in the southern Balkans haven't happened simply because they haven't happened, not because the southern Balkans have been incorporated into our zone of peace or been awed by the display of our might. The Serbs have no interest in a wider war. They have secured the submission of Kosovo and disinherited its Albanian population. Why risk a wider war when you can get what you want with a smaller, less costly enterprise? The warlords of Belgrade and Pale may be cruel, but they will take victories on the cheap when they come their way.

Future chroniclers of this Balkan crisis will puzzle over the disparity of (real) power between Pax Americana at the zenith of its influence in the aftermath of its twin victories in the cold war and in the Persian Gulf and the Serbian revanchists who stepped forth to challenge it and got away with their brazen defiance. They will be at a loss, the historians: they will have to write the history of this Bosnia calamity either as an epic of Serbian bravery or as one long chronicle of a generation's failure to see that there were things that truly mattered in these sad hills and towns of Bosnia.

In one of the best scholarly accounts and histories of the former Yugoslavia, *Bosnia and Hercegovina: A Tradition Betrayed,* historians Robert Donia and John Fine tell us that America's performance in the Gulf war made a deep impression on the Serbs. An analysis and a strategic review by the general staff of the Serb-dominated Yugoslav People's Army, the two historians observe, concluded that Desert Storm was a "true paradigm" for interventions after the cold war but still held out the possibility that the Serbs could pursue their project of conquest without triggering the kind of response that thwarted the Iraqi bid. Grant the warlords of Greater Serbia their due: they read the world as it was. Luck came their way in the Western leaders they drew. Pity the man in his bunker in Baghdad: he must envy the Serbs' exquisite sense of timing. Hitherto there had been a strong element of martyrology and self-pity at the core of Serbian history, their narrative of their history one long tale of sorrow and denial, material for the folk poets and the singers with their *guslas* (the one-string musical instruments). In their annals, they must make room now for the great change in their fortunes, for that one long season when they rode out and left a trail of misery and high crimes behind them and were never made to pay a price.

(AUGUST 7, 1995)

After Srebrenica

ZBIGNIEW BRZEZINSKI

The following is the speech that might have been delivered immediately upon the fall of Srebrenica if the post of Leader of the Free World were not currently vacant.

My fellow Americans, my fellow citizens of the democratic world: I address you tonight about the crisis in Bosnia, because both our sense of moral outrage and the long-term interests of the democratic world call for immediate and decisive American action.

The fall of Srebrenica is a defining moment. The prolonged and brazen defiance of the international community by an armed mob of Bosnian Serbs can no longer be tolerated. The suffering of hundreds of thousands of innocent civilians, and the murder of tens of thousands of them, can no longer be passively observed by the civilized and democratic world. You have seen the pictures of the atrocities in Bosnia. If our shared commitment to human rights means anything to us, as Americans and as decent men and women, the United States has to react.

There is no other choice. Over the last three years the United Nations has been unable to protect the victims or to deter the aggressors. Repeated violations of U.N. resolutions have gone unpunished. The United Nations Protection Force, or UNPROFOR, originally deployed to protect the helpless, the unarmed, and the vulnerable, has itself been subjected to humiliation, intimidation, and fatalities.

When the conflict in the former Yugoslavia first broke out, our European allies insisted that it was Europe's responsibility to resolve it. Acting under a United Nations mandate, the UNPROFOR was deployed in order to provide humanitarian assistance and to make secure the several U.N.–designated safe-havens. A U.N. negotiator and a negotiator appointed by the European Community sought to find a peaceful solution. They actively discouraged any military pressure on the Serbs, particularly by the United States, on the grounds that it would be counterproductive.

The result has been a moral and a political calamity of historic proportions. For some three years now, ethnic cleansing, massive brutality, and persistent contempt for the international community have characterized the conduct of the Bosnian Serbs.

We can no longer maintain the pretense that the conflict in Bosnia is merely an extension of ancient ethnic feuds, justifying the world's moral indifference and political passivity. The historic facts are to the contrary. Over several centuries, ethnic and religious coexistence, not ethnic and religious conflict, has been the predominant reality in Bosnia and Herzegovina. Even the current violence did not begin with the support of the majority of Bosnians, whether of Muslim, Croat, or Serb origin. It is the product of an organized, brutal, and fanatical minority.

The international community has the obligation to distinguish between victims and aggressors. Not to do so is to reduce the U.N. Charter to a farce. But the issue is not only a matter of morality, or of principle, or of simple justice. The character of the international order is also at stake. A world unable to make the distinction between victims and aggressors, and especially a world unwilling to act on that distinction, is a world in which the United Nations becomes the object of derision—on the part not only of the aggressors but of all free peoples. World peace will be the ultimate casualty in Bosnia.

After some three years of sustained brutality, no one can deny that the U.N. has proven incapable of coping decisively with the forces of aggression in Bosnia. Even worse, the impotence of the U.N. has so constrained any attempt at an effective response by NATO that both the unity and the credibility of our alliance are now at stake. On a number of occasions, retaliatory NATO air strikes at Bosnian Serb targets, requested by the UNPROFOR commanders, were emasculated by U.N. officials to the point that they became mere pinpricks of no deterrent value. They emboldened, rather than constrained, the aggressors.

NATO's inability to act assertively is now generating increasing tensions within the alliance itself. The alliance triumphed in the course of the cold war. Yet indecision and disunity in regard to Bosnia are undermining the most successful coalition in history. It would be ironic if Europe's longer-range security and stability were to join the growing list of victims of the unchallenged aggression in Bosnia.

The United States, therefore, must act—and act now. The failures of the U.N. and NATO reward aggression and encourage its repetition. Continued inaction by the United States would gravely jeopardize America's global credibility. It would be tantamount to a piecemeal abdication of America's world role. We have no choice but to step into the breach.

Accordingly, I am today announcing the following three major policy decisions:

(1) The United States is notifying the U.N. Secretary as well as our allies and other states participating in the UNPROFOR that it favors the UNPROFOR's immediate withdrawal.

Unable to protect safe-havens, the U.N. force is becoming a shield for the Bosnian Serbs, inhibiting more decisive responses. This is all the more tragic because many UNPROFOR soldiers have already perished at the hands of the Bosnian Serbs in the fulfillment of their thankless task. We pay tribute to their heroism, but the reality must also be faced that UNPROFOR's vulnerability is being exploited by the aggressors.

The United States is prepared to deploy its ground forces immediately to render secure the UNPROFOR's withdrawal. In doing so, the United States reserves for itself the right to protect the process of extraction also with its air power, with American air strikes conducted on a scale and directed at targets determined exclusively at American operational discretion.

Let me warn the belligerents that any hostile interference with U.S. military forces engaged in this effort will precipitate immediate and significant retaliation.

(2) I am asking the Congress of the United States to pass a resolution, which I will immediately sign into law, endorsing the lifting of the embargo on the delivery of arms to Bosnia.

Bosnia, as a member of the United Nations, is entitled to the right of self-defense. The arms embargo against Bosnia deprives the victim of the necessary means for self-defense. It benefits the aggressor, who enjoys access to the large stocks of heavy weaponry of the former Yugoslav army.

• • •

I am asking for bipartisan congressional support, since the lifting of the embargo will have major international consequences. Both the U.N. and our principal allies participating in the UNPROFOR have stated that the lifting of the embargo would precipitate the UNPROFOR's withdrawal. It is essential, therefore, that this critical step be taken with the fullest congressional support. The world must know, our friends must know, and the aggressors must know that we Americans are united in taking this critical step.

There is every reason to believe that the lifting of the embargo will significantly help the Bosnians in their effort to defend themselves. Their army, which is eager and willing to fight, is larger than the army of the Bosnian Serbs. With the arrival of more modern and plentiful arms, the Serbian advantage on the battlefield will be erased. A number of states have indicated their willingness to finance and to deliver to the Bosnians the needed arms. The arming of the Bosnians need not be a unilateral American undertaking.

(3) I am asking the Congress to endorse, on a bipartisan basis, my decision to warn the Bosnian Serbs that U.S. air power will be used in a sustained, strategic fashion to retaliate against any Serbian offensive designed to take advantage of the UNPROFOR's withdrawal to assault the safe-havens and to preempt the delivery of arms to the Bosnians. Congressional support on this critical issue will signal to the world America's determination not to tolerate aggression, not to look away from ethnic cleansings.

Let me make it absolutely clear that the goal of American air power is not to win the war for the Bosnians. Nor is the use of American air power the first step toward an American engagement in the ground war. That war must be fought, and will be fought, by the Bosnians. They have proven their determination. The commitment to employ American air power is necessary at this stage of the conflict in order to prevent large-scale massacres and a Serbian effort to achieve promptly an outright victory. We will deter the Serbs from exploiting their current superiority in heavy artillery and tanks, or we will deprive them of that superiority.

There will be no more pinprick attacks. If need be, U.S. air power will strike, effectively and repeatedly, against Bosnian Serb concentrations of heavy weaponry, command and control centers, and hostile radar systems, wherever they are located, and also against Serb logistics, ground transportation and access to Serbia proper. American air strikes against the Serb machinery of war will inflict—again, let there be no doubt—massive costs and much pain. It will not spare the war criminals in Pale. It will be punitive, it will be retaliatory, it will be sustained, and it will help to equalize the balance on the battlefield.

As a result of these actions, the Bosnian Serbs may realize that compromise is preferable to continued carnage. They are more likely to reach that conclusion when it becomes evident that they cannot subdue the Bosnians and that continued warfare against the Bosnians, as well as the Croats perhaps, could even become suicidal.

I wish to address a few words directly to the people of Serbia: Americans admire the courage that the Serbian people displayed in World War II. We have no interest in waging war on Serbia. We know that many people in Serbia view the leadership in Pale and its supporters as adventurers and criminals. We urge you not to let yourselves be hijacked by them. They are not only discrediting Serbia in the eyes of the world, they are also threatening your own future. A wider war in Bosnia can bring to Serbia only more misery and suffering. We urge you to press your government to opt for peace so that Serbia, too, can become a partner in building a larger and more cooperative Europe.

And I also want to say a few words to the people of Bosnia: Americans are not indifferent to your suffering. We understand that you are the victims of an ugly war that is repugnant to us all. And we honor you for the spirit that you have shown in your dire circumstances. Please do not give up hope. We will not stand by idly and watch Bosnia, and decency, destroyed.

My fellow Americans, the steps I am announcing tonight are a token of our seriousness of purpose. I am conscious of their risk, but I am even more aware of the moral and political consequences of continued indecision and passivity. And I know that I speak for all of you in this great and free country when I say that the United States will not be passive in the face of genocide. Fifty years after America took a stand against evil in Europe, the words "never again" must not be allowed to become a mockery. That is why America will now do what it must.

(AUGUST 7, 1995)

PART IV

❖

The Abdication of the West

Rescue Bosnia

THE EDITORS

At least Bill Clinton has a plan for a U.S.–led military effort to punish the Serbian aggressors in Bosnia and Herzegovina: through the U.N. Security Council, the international community would charge Serbian leaders with crimes against humanity such as genocidal "ethnic cleansing"; the U.S. Navy would tighten the U.N. embargo against Serbia and its ally Montenegro by stopping and inspecting ships on the Adriatic; and the United States would participate in air strikes "against those attacking the [U.N.] relief effort" in Sarajevo.

Finally someone in this campaign has spoken seriously about a serious foreign policy question. What does George Bush think of the Clinton idea? "Reckless," harrumphed his spokesman, Marlin Fitzwater. It was a curious display of contempt from the very White House that Democrats had branded as reckless for taking on Iraq, and that, with Clinton's support, continues to threaten Saddam with military action for his shell game with U.N. nuclear inspectors. But apparently campaign point-scoring is a higher Bush priority than a small, besieged nation that looks to Washington for help. Yes, George Bush is still president and leader of the free world, which means he has greater responsibilities than candidate Clinton. But that only heightens our dismay over the attack on Clinton: it will have real effects in the real world, the most important of which will be to reinforce the pusillanimity of the European powers to which Bush has handed off the Balkan crisis—and to embolden the very Serbians who are attempting to bleed, pound, and starve the people of Bosnia into submission.

The Bush-Clinton tiff over Bosnia exemplifies the post–cold war paradigm shifts taking place in the foreign policies of the two parties. As Francis Fukuyama writes . . . the American foreign policy debate in the new world order seems likely to be in part a debate between Democratic interventionism in the name of high ideals and Republican world-weariness about potential quagmires called Bosnia. We agree with Fukuyama that U.S. foreign policymaking in the future will consist largely of selecting the best course between these two poles, on case-by-case basis.

Bosnia presents a particularly hard case. "It's clear [Clinton] is unaware of the political complications in Yugoslavia," sniffs Fitzwater. Fair enough: for centuries, the Balkans have confounded those who arrived to set the place right by Christmas. Our leaders have a duty to avoid commitments that would entail more risk to American life than the public is willing to tolerate—or than American interests merit. Clinton's proposal did not call for using U.S. (or European) ground forces in the Bosnian fray. But Clinton also doesn't explain how his program would remain limited to air strikes, which are never as surgical in practice as they are on the planning boards. What happens if, say, the Serb forces try to up the ante by shooting down our planes and helicopters, or by launching a massive attack on the U.N. troops in Sarajevo? Do we go in on the ground then?

Clinton's plan is also oddly silent on the question of helping the Bosnians help themselves militarily. Up to now, Bosnia has been subject to the same U.N. arms embargo as Serbia, in spite of the fact that the republic is clearly fighting a defensive war, one that its people seem willing to wage themselves. The government of President Aljia Izetbegovic has begged for the embargo to be lifted, meanwhile entering into a devil's bargain with the forces of Croatia for limited help. Allowing weapons transfers to Bosnia—and supplying U.S. weapons to balance the military forces in the war—offers a way to check the Serbs without unduly placing U.S. forces at risk.

The Balkan war is not so "politically complicated" that no judgment about its morality can be made. It is not merely an "ethnic conflict." It is a campaign in which a discrete faction of Serbian nationalists has manipulated ethnic sentiment in order to seize power and territory. It is an act of international aggression, an assault on a member of the United Nations. Despite the U.N.'s condemnation, there have been too many platitudes about the responsibility of "all factions" for the war. This lazy language is an escape hatch through which outside powers flee their responsibilities. Perhaps Europeans are just embarrassed by the spectacle of primordial violence on the edge of their own proudly postmodern continent.

The United States ought firmly to explain to its allies that we and they have a vital interest in the sanctity of internationally recognized borders. Instead, Washington continues to dither as the government of Bosnia loses more ground. It now controls little more than the area around the presidential building in Sarajevo and a few other towns. Serbs control most of the rest of the country, and are "ethnically cleansing" it on a monstrous scale. If the United States doesn't take the lead soon, Bosnia may find itself cleansed into extinction.

(AUGUST 17 & 24, 1992)

Clinton and Milosevic

THE EDITORS

Among the ironies of the Bush legacy is that, in retrospect, his record on the economy turns out to be somewhat better than on foreign policy. As we enter our third straight year of low inflationary growth, the results of the president's dithering in Russia, Iraq, and the Balkans are becoming damningly clearer. Iraq presents the most immediate challenge to the new administration, as the latest U.S. bombing illustrates. President Bush, seemingly still more outraged by an incursion into Kuwait than by the continuing plight of the Kurds and Shiites, has bequeathed Bill Clinton the fruits of his own indecision. Saddam is alive and sick and eager to test the young American president as soon as possible. Clinton should ready himself for an early, decisive use of force; and remember that Bush's mistake was not in using force, as Warren Christopher might counsel, but in not using enough of it and ridding us of Saddam for good.

It is in the Balkans, however, that the consequences of Bush's foreign policy are truly disastrous. The Vance-Owen peace plan is essentially a device to reward Serbian aggression and stall, rather than prevent, the destruction of an entire country, a destruction encouraged by the Bush-Baker-Eagleburger passivity. As we write, the Bosnian Serbs, pressed by Belgrade, have agreed in principle to the outlines of the Geneva plan, which allows for the withdrawal of heavy artillery from Bosnia, a restoration of the Bosnian economic infrastructure and the insertion of large numbers of United Nations Protection Forces to ensure a continuation of the cease-fire. Bosnia will be partitioned into ten separate provinces, with a deliberately weak central government and constitutional provisions designed to prevent Serb-majority provinces from simply seceding to Greater Serbia; there will be a constitutional court composed of a majority of non-Bosnians to settle intraprovince disputes. Given the alternative—the likely evisceration of the Bosnian state and the deaths of tens of thousands more Bosnian civilians—the settlement is a humanitarian achievement of sorts. We understand why the Bosnian Croats and Muslims have acceded to its logic.

But its logic is that territorial aggression and mass terror pay handsomely for the perpetrators. The deal rewards Serbia's murderous, barbaric assault on Bosnia; by deliberately weakening Bosnia's central government, it allows for the de facto, if not de jure, secession of the Serb-majority Bosnian provinces to the neighboring giant of Greater Serbia; it does nothing to reverse the horrifying ethnic cleansing that was the precursor to this agreement; and, after evidence of concentration camps, mass rapes, and other atrocities, the agreement absolves the villains from effective war crime prosecution. It does nothing about the central problem of the region: the aggressive regime of Slobodan Milosevic. It indeed gives him breathing space to consolidate power before moving on to cleanse Kosovo.

Why did the Serbs agree at this point? It was not, we believe, out of some change of heart. Serbia needs some respite from its onslaught and has in any case acquired three-quarters of what it wanted. More pertinently, the prospect of the Clinton administration rattled Milosevic. A member of the Yugoslav delegation to the "peace talks" in Geneva told *The New York Times* that Milosevic and Dobrica Cosic, president of the rump Yugoslavia, had informed the leader of the Bosnian Serbs that "if the war continued, it would no longer be a classic war, but a war in which the West would intervene, using weapons you can't even see." It was ultimately the threat of an Operation Balkan Storm that forced Milosevic to scale back his immediate plans of conquest.

We do not think he has scaled them back permanently. Geneva is a mini-Munich, granting the dictator most of what he wants, allowing him more time to gather his forces and giving the imprimatur of the international community to his war crimes. It is a classic product of Cyrus Vance and David Owen, men who have distinguished themselves by a mutual history of misjudgment and failure in foreign affairs, from Owen's failed negotiations over Zimbabwe to Vance's pitiful record with the Iranians.

If the agreement holds, President Clinton should ensure several things: that, in the continuing negotiations toward a final constitutional settlement, the Serbs do not squeeze out further concessions; that a decent number of American troops are included in the U.N. protection forces to give them credibility with Belgrade; and that the threat of U.S.–led military action remains foremost in the mind of Milosevic. So far, Clinton has shown an admirable ability to keep Belgrade nervous about U.S. intentions. If anything is to be rescued from Bush's Balkan morass, Clinton will have to make Milosevic more nervous still.

(FEBRUARY 1, 1993)

Stop Serbia Now

THE EDITORS

At the beginning, there was confusion. A state that was not a state was cut loose from an empire and convulsed itself in ancient hatreds. A civil war or an ethnic implosion? A religious feud or an imbalance of power? The status of Bosnia was, after all, historically problematic. It was not a "nation" as such; and the Europeans, with a long history of caution in such matters, advised caution. Besides, were not all the parties—Croats, Muslims, Serbs— morally tainted?

So the United States, exhilarated by the end of the cold war and consumed with an election campaign in which the arguments of retrenchment outweighed the passion for entanglement, let it be. The Europeans revealed themselves to be Europeans, incapable of united action, guided by separate historic and cultural temperaments, fearful of the larger truths that the Serbian war revealed about Europe's intolerance of tolerance, and addicted to the process of peace, which soon became the management of war. The United Nations, through its humanitarian efforts, indirectly facilitated the incursions of the Serbs, and by placing Western troops on the ground, provided a perfect excuse for the British and French to oppose military escalation. The U.N. thus assumed the role of the expediter of invasion, escorting the evacuees, shepherding the wounded, ushering in the victors. They do not wish to resist the Serbian conquest, they wish only to take the pain out of it. They are the cleansers of the cleansing, struggling to believe in decency in the face of unvarnished evil.

There may have been a point when the United States, confronted by what seemed to be an intractable internecine war, was right to pretend to stay aloof. We say pretend, because the United States has long been indirectly involved in the war. By upholding the arms embargo against Bosnia, we engineered a one-sided massacre; by halfheartedly supporting the Vance-Owen plan, we allowed the Serbs diplomatic space in which to pursue their military aims; by the policy of food air drops to those about to be slaughtered, we gave notice that we would do nothing to end the slaughter itself. Slobodan Milosevic, who follows the logic of force, rightly calculated that all the cards were his.

What we face now, however, is a new drama: the possibility not merely of new Serbian progress into Bosnian Muslim territory (and Macedonia and Kosovo), but the horrific possibility of genocide in those areas that the Serbs already control. The threat is thus both moral and strategic. Those who argue that this region is of no strategic importance are simply wrong. The entanglement of Russia and Greece, the mobilization of Islamic states in defense of the Muslims, the destabilization of Turkey, the possibility of mass migration on the edge of Europe, all are threats to European stability as a whole. But the moral signal that is now being sent by the American government (which, in the other side of its brain, is busy congratulating itself for its ethical activism in Somalia) is even more worrying: that international borders are movable by force of arms; that racial and religious terror will go unchecked.

As so often before, the fixation on multilateralism is restraining credible action. The U.N. has shown itself to be toothless; the British and French are as pusillanimous now as they were in a far greater but similar crisis in the 1930s. Russia's Serbian sympathies preclude helping Bosnia. (There is something really unpleasant about this sudden renewal of the great Russian people's tenderness toward the great Serbian people. Is this what the end of the cold war was supposed to accomplish?) If the United States can only act in concert with other powers, it simply will not act at all.

So we must act alone; but we must act. President Clinton should deliver an ultimatum to Milosevic and his strutting surrogates: that, by a certain date, all incursions are to cease; that genocidal actions must immediately cease (including what might be called "strategic rape"); that negotiations should begin on constructing a defensible and credible Bosnian state out of the ruins of Bosnia-Herzegovina; and that, if these actions are not taken, the arms embargo on the Bosnians will be unilaterally lifted and unspecified military action against Serbian military targets from the air and sea will begin. This declaration should be made after the April 25 referendum in Russia and should be a unilateral declaration that can give Yeltsin complete deniability. (We owe Yeltsin that much in this matter, but not more.) If the Western allies and the U.N. can agree to this, so be it. But if they cannot, Clinton should summon the will to go ahead without them. There are times when America, alone of nations, has an obligation to take a stand, and act where the self-styled angels fear to tread.

(MAY 10, 1993)

The Abdication

THE EDITORS

When blood is spilled, it is the responsibility of those who spill it, and the responsibility of those who could have stopped its spilling. For this reason, the carnage in the market of Sarajevo shamed also the White House, which should have been shamed long ago. Bill Clinton's dilatory, casuistic response to the great crime in the Balkans was not only shameful, it also marked a moment in the history of American foreign policy. This administration is transforming the only superpower in the world into the only abdicating superpower in the world. Poor Bosnia, it should have found itself in a trade war. Trade wars we fight. Wars of genocide we watch.

But it is not even clear to the American government that a war of genocide is what it is watching. In Houston a few days after the Saturday slaughter, Clinton smugly and fatalistically observed that "until those folks get tired of killing each other over there, bad things will continue to happen." It is true that Bosnian forces have recently retaken, and ethnically cleansed, some territory that Croatian forces had taken from them; but these ugly and foolish actions notwithstanding, it is not true that "those folks" are "killing each other." The Serbian (and Croatian) folks are attempting to exterminate the Bosnian folks. The war in the Balkans is not a civil war. It is a war of aggression, and its objective is genocide. So far 200,000 people have been killed in this war of genocide, and 2 million people have been made refugees.

It is important to understand that genocide is not quantitatively measured. The analogy between the European excruciations of the 1940s and the European excruciations of the 1990s, an analogy that was useful to Clinton on the campaign trail, is an apposite one. The standard is not 6 million. Before millions of Jews, gypsies, homosexuals, and dissidents were murdered, thousands of them were murdered; and before thousands of them were murdered, hundreds of them were murdered; and before hundreds of them were murdered, tens of them were murdered; and it was, the whole time, with every bullet fired and every switch thrown, genocide. Indeed, it is possible to kill a single man or a single woman and still be guilty of genocide, if you kill him or her as the beginning, or the middle, or the end of the extinction of the group to which he or she belongs; if killing is also cleansing. Historically speaking, there is nothing dirtier than cleansing.

But Clinton does not speak about the Balkan war historically. He is, you might say, failing the 1940s test, stumbling his way into history as the president who didn't get it. Consider his terse statement on the day of the slaughter in Sarajevo. Suddenly our prolix president was unable to put our struggle into words. "I am outraged by this deliberate attack on the people of Sarajevo." But this deliberate attack was no different from all the other deliberate attacks, except that the sadists got lucky. "There can be no possible military justification for an attack against a marketplace where women, men, and children of the city were pursuing their everyday lives." But there can be no possible military justification for any of the other attacks on the great and wretched city, which occur daily and so far have left 10,000 people dead. Indeed, there can be no possible military justification for the siege of Sarajevo, or the conquest of Bosnia. The president does not seem to grasp that the Saturday slaughter in Sarajevo was, for Sarajevo, a really quotidian catastrophe. It differed in degree, not in kind.

And then there was this grotesque sentence in the president's statement: "The United Nations should urgently investigate this incident and clearly identify those who are guilty." Identify those who are guilty! Maybe Representative Cooper did it. And again, the next day: "I have asked Ambassador Albright to urge the United Nations to accelerate the efforts to try to confirm responsibility for the strike in the market yesterday." Radovan Karadzic, the disloyal son of Sarajevo who is the leader of the Bosnian Serbs, is giggling. It was Karadzic who immediately announced that the Serbs were innocent, and that the Bosnians (or the Muslims, as he likes to call them, erasing Bosnia in language more thoroughly than in land) were killing and maiming themselves. It worked like a charm. In no time at all the air was filled with "crater analysis," which is the method by which the origins of distantly fired shells are identified. Since the mortar shell that turned the market into a charnel house struck the roof of a stall, which interfered with its hellish trajectory, it is impossible, according to the "crater analysts" of the United Nations, to confirm the location of the mortar that fired it. The little bomb fell, in the words of a British soldier, "in a range bracket that straddles both sides." The sadists, lucky again.

"When they kill me," the president of Bosnia said the day after the massacre, "they will probably say I committed suicide." With the authority, no doubt, of "bullet-hole analysis." This whole controversy is a Goebbels-like fake. Never mind that not a single "crater analysis" in the history of the siege of Sarajevo has established the guilt of anybody except the Serbians. . . . It plays right into the hands of The Big Lie (which, in the age of CNN, is The Extremely Big Lie) to regard the question of the responsibility for this massacre as a "debate" between the "view" that the Serbians did it and the "view" that the Bosnians did it. But this is how the president of the United States is regarding it, in his spirit of inclusion.

A t this writing, the response of the American government to the Saturday slaughter is approximately this: we are threatening an end to threats. This will stand as one of the representative formulations of Clintonism, and this will not ruin any Serbian gunner's day. The signals from the White House are confusing, and they are the measure of a confusion that is deeper than diplomatic. Some "senior officials" tell *The New York Times* that NATO will "give the Bosnian Serbs a week to lift the siege of Sarajevo or face air strikes by allied planes on their artillery positions in the mountains," even as other senior officials warn other reporters not to play the possibility of retaliation too big. The threat of strikes—this time we really mean it!—might temporarily restrain the Serbian onslaught, and it appears already to have resulted in a cease-fire— this time they really mean it!—and a withdrawal of the "siege guns" around Sarajevo; but even air strikes, if limited to the area around Sarajevo and understood as a single response to a single massacre, will not affect the balance of power almost at all; and nothing has been vouchsafed about the prompt lifting of the arms embargo against Bosnia. We admire the people of Sarajevo, of course, for their stoicism.

"The ultimate answer to all this killing," the president said, "is for the three parties to reach an agreement that they can live with and honor." This marks a shift in our dodge. In the weeks before the massacre, the administration was, to put it truthfully, in favor of war. The American government was opposed to a peace agreement, and it was angry at the French government for demanding one. A peace agreement, the Americans said, will make the Bosnians themselves complicitous in the conquest of Bosnia. But the administration was itself complicitous in that conquest; and so its skepticism about a settlement was just another bout of bad faith. (In the matter of Bosnia, in the course of two administrations, Washington has been bad faith city.) For a peace settlement will require an international force to police it; and an international force will require the participation of American troops; and the participation of American troops will require a political risk on the part of the president; and there the attraction of peace ended, until last week.

For Bosnia, peace means partition. And partition, too, has its requirements. The president seems willing to meet the requirements of peace, but not the requirements of partition. Unless all the parties to the partition have the power to defend themselves, for example, the partition will not be a peace, it will be a pause in a war. You cannot be for peace and against the arming of Bosnia. It is a measure of the moral seriousness of the Bosnians that they have asked only to fight their own battle. They do not want foreign troops with guns, they want foreign guns without troops. There are reports that the Bosnians are receiving weapons from the Saudis and the Iranians (and from profiteering Serbians, too; an archipelago of honor, is the former Yugoslavia), and this offends the sensibilities of some Westerners. The Bosnians are to be forgiven, however, if their survival is more vivid to them than our sensibilities. In any case, the United States can provide for their survival and our sensibilities by lifting the arms embargo against Bosnia. "Lift" used to be considered a step toward war. The time has come to consider "lift" more properly as a step toward peace.

And partition has another requirement, which is a demonstration of the West's deadly earnestness about it. By deadly, we mean deadly. There is no reason to believe that Slobodan Milosevic, the tacky, tribe-intoxicated thug who rules Serbia, will be dissuaded from his grisly advance by anything other than an experience of force. Air strikes, and only air strikes, will make the point. Unless the Serbian positions around Sarajevo are struck, and the United States makes it clear to the butcher in Belgrade that he must lift the siege of Sarajevo or have a taste of Sarajevo himself, we may expect the "strangulation" of Sarajevo to continue, and the metaphysical speculation in Western capitals about the meaning of "strangulation" to continue, until Sarajevo falls.

There have been a number of objections to air strikes, and to military action more generally. First, there is the objection that it is a difficult business. We do not doubt it; but we note that this administration is picky about difficulty. We do not see the president daunted by the complexity of deficit reduction or regional health alliances. Indeed, he basks in the complexity. And we understand why: complexity has a way of being diluted by urgency. Second, there is the objection that military action is, as Billie Holiday used to warn, all or nothing at all. Air strikes, it is said, will inexorably lead to the introduction of ground troops. This is silly. The projection of military power, unless it is hobbled in its conception by the utopia of Desert Storm or the dystopia of Vietnam, should be guided by the principle of calibration. Where there is intelligence, there are no slippery slopes. We have at our disposal a variety of instruments of force that may be matched to a variety of objectives of strategy. It is demagoguery to assert that we cannot make the cost of the siege of Sarajevo unacceptable to Serbia except at a cost unacceptable to us.

Third, there is the objection that it may not work. It may not. But the skeptics will have to do better than isolationism or Murphy's Law. After all, there is empirical evidence to the contrary. A little pin-striped noise was all it took to push Serbian guns out of their diabolical "range bracket." We know that Milosevic is not a brave man. He has already caviled at the prospect of American resistance, until the president dispelled the prospect. And Belgrade is not Baghdad; there is an opposition to its jingoist ruler, and a desire not to become the pariah of the post-Communist West. And the Serbian military is only the Serbian military. And the Serbians have something to lose, which is their foully gotten gain in Bosnia. There is something comic about all the talking heads on television who sagely advise that the instability in the Balkans is the shape of things to come and then demand guarantees. There are no guarantees; but from this rudimentary fact about human affairs, evil should not be allowed to draw encouragement.

This is not all. The United States will not act against the genocide in Bosnia unless it acts autonomously. It is one of Clinton's contributions to American foreign policy, however, to have stripped it of its autonomy. The difference between multilateralism Bush-style and multilateralism Clinton-style has not been sufficiently observed. For Bush, it was necessary for the United States to act in concert with other nations, in the setting of the United Nations, but as first among equals. For Clinton, it is necessary for the United States to act in concert with other nations, in the setting of the United Nations, but as one among equals. There is Rwanda, there is Malaysia, there is America. Thus we had action against Iraq and we have inaction against Serbia. When in Brussels a few weeks ago he was asked, he thought rudely, about NATO assistance to Sarajevo, the president said that "we have done everything the United Nations has asked us to do." This was an abdication. And so it was a little delicious when Boutros Boutros-Ghali, who has not exactly covered himself in Balkan glory, informed NATO in the wake of the Saturday slaughter that the decision to strike was theirs to make.

But the administration did not find an opportunity in the secretary-general's change of heart, since it was not looking for an opportunity. Boutros-Ghali robbed American policy of its United Nations cover and delivered it to its European cover. It is commonly said that Bosnia is a European problem, and that the Europeans should do something about it. It is, and they won't. Atlanticism, too, is just an alibi. Last week Lawrence Eagleburger, who aided and abetted the Serbian aggression, opined ruefully on television that "there has to be a time when the Europeans no longer hide behind our skirts." But this is backwards: we are hiding behind the Europeans' skirts. Clinton has abjured America's primacy in NATO just as surely as he has abjured America's primacy at the United Nations. In doing so, he has displayed a terrible misunderstanding of the alliance and its history. And so it was a little delicious when the foreign ministers of France, Holland, and Belgium surprised the White House by calling for the use of force to end the siege of Sarajevo.

The disgusting events in southern Europe are a challenge to American interests and American values. Anarchy is an affront to our interests and genocide is an affront to our values. And the American interests that are implicated by the Serbian war are not only regional, they are also global. The audience for Bill Clinton's prevarications includes Kim Il Sung and Saddam Hussein and Raoul Cedras and Mohamed Farah Aideed and a host of petty fascists in fledgling states who have been wondering about their freedom of action. And what he is telling them all is: act freely, we are busy with ourselves. Clinton does not see that he is making a more recalcitrant world.

The torture of Sarajevo also puts a special pressure on America. For there is a profound sense in which the Sarajevan experiment resembles the American experiment. Sarajevo is a tolerant, secular, multiethnic, multicultural city. For Bosnians, Croatians, and Serbians, for Muslims, Christians, and Jews, the city of Sarajevo was an oasis of decency, a rare and beautiful place where the traditions collided peacefully. There was a time, in the days before his presidency, when Clinton appeared to apprehend the relevance of the Bosnian fate: "Lord of Mercy," he told reporters, "there's 150 different racial and ethnic groups in Los Angeles County. . . . I know that ethnic divisions are one of the strongest impulses in all of society all over the world, but we've got to take a stand against it." The punishment of Sarajevo is the punishment of an American ideal. For Americans in particular, it should be painful to behold.

But this pain is one pain the president fails to feel. Instead the White House shows indifference, and divagation, and timidity, and a sudden anxiety that the terrible pictures on television are becoming a political embarrassment. To be sure, there is outrage. "I know I speak for all Americans," the president said on the day of the massacre in the market, "in expressing our revulsion and anger at this cowardly act." But there is something a little cozy about this outrage. Indeed, we must be careful, when we come to consider the destruction of Bosnia, not to express what we warmly call outrage, if outrage is an expression of surprise. The moral sense can no longer survive if it is surprisable. The will to resist evil must be as grim and as disabused and as perdurable as the will to commit evil. Sarajevo is not an occasion for sentiment. It is an occasion for action. But we have a president who prefers feeling deeply to acting strongly. He is not a bad man. He merely makes goodness look like weakness. Historians will deal harshly with him for the horrors that he has already countenanced. If only he feared historians as much as he fears pollsters.

(FEBRUARY 28, 1994)

The Abdication, Cont'd

THE EDITORS

The Serbs are furiously attacking, and ethnically cleansing, northwestern Bosnia and southeastern Bosnia. "The Serbs are going for it," said a United Nations official about the town of Gorazde, a United Nations "safe area," in which 65,000 Bosnians are trapped and hundreds have already been murdered.

Surprise! But the Clinton administration, according to *The Washington Post,* is "taken . . . by surprise." The administration quickly adjusted to the grim development, though, so that the secretary of defense could proclaim that the United States is "standing firm." What it is "standing firm" about is its refusal to come to the assistance of the Bosnians, politically or militarily. Asked on television about the Serbian assault on Gorazde, the callow William Perry answered that "we will not enter the war to stop that from happening. That is correct, yes." The president was embarrassed by his secretary's remarks. By their clarity, not by their content: he denied that Perry had given the Serbs a green light and then assured them ("we're looking at our options there, but it really depends in part upon what the U.N. mission wants to do there") that they need not relent.

Elsewhere at the Pentagon, the chairman of the Joint Chiefs of Staff, who had once concurred with his predecessor's judgment that the siege of Sarajevo could not be affected by air power, opined that "there were very specific conditions around Sarajevo that lent themselves to the application of air power, conditions that don't exist in any other places in Bosnia today." The situation around Gorazde is "very different," General John Shalikashvili said, and NATO intervention against the Serbs would amount to taking sides in the conflict. The deployment of Ukrainian troops in the area of Gorazde, however, might upset the situation. "While there is debate within the administration over using air power to protect Gorazde and other Muslim enclaves," Michael R. Gordon wrote memorably in *The New York Times,* "there is no dispute over using air strikes to protect United Nations peacekeepers." Meanwhile, in New York, the United States pleaded poverty and blocked the Security Council from sending the full contingent of 10,000 peacekeeping troops that were deemed necessary, until the Clinton administration at the last minute deemed otherwise, to secure the emerging diplomatic rearrangements in the Balkans.

It is a repugnant narrative. What makes it especially repugnant is the self-congratulation that accompanies it. Judging by his comments at his "masterful" press conference on March 24, the president appears to believe that he is the savior of Sarajevo. "Our efforts in Bosnia," he said, "have had a lot of success." Efforts in Bosnia? Success in Bosnia? In truth, Clinton is the man who allowed Sarajevo, and the rest of Bosnia, to become the scene of the greatest crime in the West in fifty years. It was CNN that saved Sarajevo, not Clinton; and nobody saved Bosnia. (In Prijedor, the cavalry is . . . the Red Cross.) There is something especially cynical about the administration's distinction between Sarajevo and Bosnia. This is a war against a country, not a city.

It is risible, moreover, that the administration expects the Serbs to take it seriously. "By standing firm," Perry said, "we've provided the maximum pressure and maximum leverage to getting toward the peace agreement." Substitute "minimum" for "maximum" and he has a point; but he is basking in maximalism. With red lights like these, who needs green lights? Even a perfunctory acquaintance with the Serbian methods of operation would have shown that they would seize on the American preening about Sarajevo to strike elsewhere; and they have.

The lesson of Sarajevo is crushingly simple. It is that it takes a little to accomplish a lot. The siege of Sarajevo was lifted as the result of a threat to use air power and a single small use of it. That's it. No quagmire, no slippery slope, no mission creep. The Serbs do not wish to lose all that they have, cruelly and with our complicity, gained. But the White House does not wish to learn the lesson of Sarajevo. And now it has the additional alibi of being "distracted." So expect Gorazde and other towns to fall, and innocent people to be expelled and killed because they are not Serbian and Christian, and the United States to be surprised, and American officials to mutter about the "peace process." And Clinton, of course, to bite his lip. Those are the only teeth in our Bosnian policy.

(APRIL 25, 1994)

"A Civil War"

THE EDITORS

Last week, in a little town called Bihac, the "collective security" of NATO, the "multilateralism" of the United Nations and the "foreign policy presidency" of Bill Clinton were all exposed for what they are.

NATO's credibility was defeated; but the brandy-sipping circumlocutors in the capitals of Europe also have presided over the defeat of NATO's legitimacy. Since the collapse of the Communist order, the Atlantic alliance has gone begging for a reason for being. Such a reason was to be found in the Balkans, NATO, some of us thought, would stop the killing, or amount to nothing. We now know that it amounts to nothing; or worse, it amounts to an instrument of prevarication and complicity is available to the armed, rampant medievalisms of Europe. NATO used to keep the peace. Now NATO keeps the war. Its secretary-general seems to have been ready to strike the Bosnian Serbs, but the timidity of the British and the perversity of the French were insurmountable. The British and the French are maintaining that in Bihac the Bosnians started it. This is true, but trivial. The Bosnian campaign in the northwestern corner of that former country was, by the standards of the Serbian campaign, only an annoyance, a campaign of hope against hope; and hope lost.

Along the East River, the criminal work of Radovan Karadzic and Ratko Mladic was abetted by other means. Historians will show that the most important allies of the Bosnian Serbs have been the peacekeeping forces of the United Nations. Their strategic role in this conflict has been essentially to act as hostages. They provided the cover that the slaughter needed. After all, NATO will not put the U.N.'s soldiers in danger. This has been the standing alibi for the military inaction of the West, although there are many significant Serbian targets not ornamented by the blue helmets of UNPROFOR; and the alibi works almost every time. The U.N. might as well have deployed women and children. While the U.N.'s apologists insist on a multipolar, pluralistic,

thoughtful post–cold war world in which forceful action must be the consequence of a more or less global consensus, the commander of the Bosnian
Serbs proposes to reporters that "borders are drawn in blood," and proceeds
to prove the proposition.

It is the White House, however, that has behaved most contemptibly. The
administration had begun to lift the arms embargo against the Bosnians, at
least to the extent of no longer enforcing it at sea; but it took only a Serbian
challenge to the "safe area" of Bihac to reverse the administration's course. On
the autumn morning when Americans awoke to such headlines as "U.S. FAVORS
MAKING CONCESSIONS TO SERBS" and "U.S., IN SHIFT, GIVES UP ITS TALK OF
TOUGH ACTION AGAINST SERBS," they learned that their country no longer acts
as a great power. The president had caved, and he didn't even pretend that he
hadn't. His secretary of state was not seen and not heard. His secretary of
defense observed coldly a few days earlier that the conquest of Bosnia was
irreversible. His chief of staff began to describe the Serbian war of aggression
as "a civil war." His national security adviser was on his farm, in the company
of his famous cows and his famous conscience.

Oh, we did send an aircraft carrier to the region, but only to help the U.N.
troops in the event of an evacuation. It fell to Karadzic to tell the truth about
American foreign policy. "The United States sends 2,000 Marines," he said,
"then they have to send 10,000 more to save the 2,000. This is the best way to
have another Vietnam." The man is cruel, but he is not stupid. He speaks the
language that spooks Washington.

Strategically and militarily, Karadzic is wrong. There was never the danger
that Bosnia would turn into Vietnam. The Serbian army is only the Serbian
army, and we are the United States. We have the power to stop the Serbian
advance, not by landing American forces, but by striking a variety of Serbian
positions from the air, and by helping the Bosnians to acquire the strength that
they need for their own defense, and by establishing the tone for a proper
response to genocide. Politically and psychologically, however, Karadzic is
right. We are inhibited, and wavering, and uninterested, and heartless. The
poor Bosnians have no political constituency in this country that might attract
a political handler's attention. The president is up for politics, but he is not up
for history.

The realists will say that Bosnia is only Bosnia, that a quarter of a million
people is only a quarter of a million people. What matters about a stain,
though, is not its magnitude. What matters is its delibility; and if the conquest
of Bosnia really is irreversible, then the stain of Bosnia really is indelible.

(DECEMBER 19, 1994)

Merry Christmas, Mr. Karadzic

THE EDITORS

"One of the rare chances to let the world know the truth": this was what Jimmy Carter promised Radovan Karadzic last week. The abasement took even our breath away. And there was more. "I cannot dispute your statement that the American public has had primarily one side of the story," the mad dove of Plains told the mad hawk of Pale. The difference between the men paled before the similarity. They were collaborators in evil; and when, in a few weeks or a few months, the genocide in Bosnia finally pays off, and a Greater Serbia finally is brought into being, a statue of the vain, meddling, amoral American fool should stand in its every ethnically cleansed square.

Jimmy Carter's reputation for idealism has been one of the great swindles of American politics for two decades. In fact, he is the man in his time who will have done most to damage the prestige of idealism, and the prestige of peace. For peace is never lasting or true when it is based on the belief that there is nothing worse than war; but that is Carter's belief. He practices "conflict resolution," a contentless approach to conflict, for which all parties in all conflicts are like all parties in all conflicts, and there are no conflicts that cannot be fairly ended by compromise. It is the gospel of reasonableness, which is, as the Carter presidency demonstrated, a hapless foundation for foreign policy. And since the world is not reasonable, the world must be misdescribed, as Carter misdescribed "the truth" about the Balkans. Be reasonable, Carter says to the butcher of Sarajevo, as he said to the butcher of Hama; and they, assuring themselves that they have Sarajevo and Hama in their power, are glad to oblige. He provides tyrants with the thing that tyranny cannot provide, which is legitimacy. He brings them even a little pathos, as he sees into the hearts of men who have no hearts.

Sitting between Radovan Karadzic and Ratko Mladic, that is, at the most dishonorable table in the Western world, Jimmy Carter secured from them, according to press reports, the reopening of Sarajevo's airport, "a cease-fire leading to the complete cessation of hostilities," the free movement of aid convoys, "full protection of human rights," and freedom for all people in the region "regardless of age, sex, or ethnic origin to choose where they wish to live." This is an indecent farce. There is no promise that the Bosnian Serbs made to their turtle-necked, brow-furrowed, return-ticketed stooge that they have not made before, and broken. He is elated that they agree to take another look at the "Contact Group" plan, when that plan, as Albert Wohlstetter showed in these pages . . . , is a blueprint for a Greater Serbia. He entertains their plan for a partition of Sarajevo, which they call "the sacrifices around Sarajevo." He talks human rights with them!

But Carter is not alone to blame for his mission. He is, after all, a former president. There is, after all, a current president. Why can't the current president tell the former president to stay the hell out of American foreign policy? The question, alas, is a rhetorical one. The whole country knows the answer. It is that Bill Clinton lacks a spine. This has been especially the case in foreign policy, and especially the case in Bosnian policy. He cannot stand up to Carter, and we are expecting him to stand up to Karadzic. To be sure, his press secretary was quick to "distance" the administration from Carter's analysis of "the truth" by insisting that the Bosnian Serbs are the "aggressors"; but it has been only a few weeks since his national security adviser called the same aggression a "civil war." (And where is Al Gore?)

Here is "the truth." Carter is a menace. Clinton is a sap. Karadzic is a murderer. And unlike the menace and the sap, the murderer knows what he is doing.

(JANUARY 9 & 16, 1995)

--- ✦ ✦ ---

The Abdication, Again

THE EDITORS

This year is the fiftieth anniversary of the United Nations. The celebrations will go on and on, as politicians make banal speeches to command-performance audiences. It is unlikely that Bosnia will appear among their banalities. For it is in Bosnia that the debility of the United Nations has finally been revealed.

There is another Bosnian crisis this week. Not in Bosnia, of course. In Bosnia things are the same, only more so. A Greater Serbia is slowly and steadily emerging by means of a genocidal war. No, the crisis is taking place in the capitals of the Western powers, which are finding it harder and harder to escape the consequences of their policy of appeasement. The doves, you might say, are coming home to roost. And they still don't get it. When the Serbs made hostages of hundreds of United Nations troops last week, a spokesman for the U.N. thundered that "the Bosnian Serb army is behaving like a terrorist organization." But the Bosnian Serb army *is* a terrorist organization, unless you wish to include systematic rape among the terms of military engagement. And the general in command of the U.N. forces in Bosnia demanded of General Ratko Mladic "that he treat the United Nations soldiers in a manner becoming a professional soldier." But General Mladic is *not* a professional soldier. He is a man wanted for war crimes.

Here is what happened last week. The Serbs moved heavy weapons closer to Sarajevo and fired upon it. They have done so before. NATO issued warnings. It has done so before. The Serbs ignored the warnings. They have done so before. NATO launched a trivial attack against a Serb position. It has done so before. The Serbs responded by taking U.N. troops hostage. They have done so before. The only thing that changed last week, in short, was that the latent became manifest. *De facto* hostages became *de jure* hostages.

Also the iconography of the conflict was enriched. There have been many indelible images of the slaughter in Bosnia; last week's pictures of the scattered limbs in the Tuzla café were only the most recent ones. What was lacking, until last week, were images of the West's weakness. Now we have those photographs of those U.N. soldiers chained to those poles. Not exactly a picture of a helicopter lifting off the roof of an American embassy, to be sure; but surely a picture of our humiliation, of the forces of order flouted, of the triumph of tribalism over pluralism, of the lupine post–cold war world in full swing. No amount of "pragmatic neo-Wilsonianism" (the empty locution of Anthony Lake, who prefers the devising of bold foreign policy rationales to the devising of bold foreign policy) will erase these images of Western impotence from the memories of warlords and xenophobes around the world. They have been instructed that this is their time.

Two conclusions are being drawn from the success of the Serbs. The first is that the use of force has failed. "The Bosnian Serbs have now trumped our ace," as former Secretary of State Lawrence Eagleburger told *The Washington Post.* Eagleburger's pronouncement is utterly self-serving; the man was one of the architects of American appeasement in the Bush administration. Still, the Clinton administration will not exactly recoil from an analysis that refuses to

entertain the serious use of real force. For this reason, it is important to understand that we did *not* play our ace in Pale last week.

Though the West has occasionally acted militarily against the Serbs in
Bosnia, the West's response has been fundamentally unmilitary. No sustained
air campaign against the war-making ability of the Serbs in Bosnia was ever
really considered. (The precision of the wee assault on Pale, by the way, shows
what can be accomplished by air power.) Like NATO's previous strikes,
NATO's strike last week was more a demonstration of inhibition than a
demonstration of the lack of it. This was not what the Serbs were fearing. It
was what they were counting on. This trifling retort to the Serbs' violation of
the Sarajevo arrangement played right into the Serbs' hands: it was a military
response so predictably puny that it could serve only as a pretext for a Serb
provocation. It also reassured the Serbs that they will never experience pun-
ishments proportionate to their crimes, and they assassinated the Bosnian foreign minister.

The second conclusion is that we must act forcefully against the Serbs to
help . . . the United Nations. The ministers of the Contact Group (including the foreign minister of Russia, who must have been chuckling) announced
at The Hague that they intended to expand the size of the U.N. mission and
to fortify it with heavier weapons. They said nothing about the nature of the
mission itself. For all with eyes to see, of course, the essential absurdity of the
U.N. mission was made brutally plain last week. The blue helmets are "peacekeepers" where there is no peace in "safe areas" that are not safe. They have
not impeded the war or the genocide. They have impeded only a powerful and
decent response.

Recall that the "safe areas" of Bosnia were supposed to be made safe by the
U.N. There are six such enclaves: Sarajevo, Bihac, Srebrenica, Zepa, Gorazde,
Tuzla. The list of their names is a litany of lament. The U.N. has brought them
little respite. When the Serbs attack, the blue helmets retreat. On May 21, *The
New York Times* described a videotape that captured a Serb atrocity on a Sara-
jevo street: "The crack of a shot echoes in Sarajevo's valley. He [a young Bos-
nian man] falls. He lies on his side. He is curled in an almost fetal position. A
United Nations soldier looks on." In Bosnia, a U.N. soldier always looks on.
Bystanders or hostages: that is what the "peacekeepers" really are.

It cannot have escaped the notice of our policymakers that the U.N. is providing cover for the Serbs, except that the U.N. is providing cover for our
policymakers, too. It saves them from the prospect of action. That is why the
plight of the U.N. stirs them more than the plight of Bosnia. And nobody is
less stirred by the plight of Bosnia than the aloof Boutros Boutros-Ghali, who

put an early damper on international outrage when he called this a "rich man's war." The Bosnians, he said, were less deserving than those under siege, by hunger and by arms, in Africa. And the United States followed the secretary general's recommendation. We sent troops to Somalia and we sent no troops to Bosnia.

It is hard to think of a major crisis since the Second World War in which the president of the United States has wielded less moral and political authority. There are 22,470 U.N. troops in Bosnia, from eighteen countries. Britain has 3,565 men under arms; France has 3,835; Pakistan has 2,978. The United States has none, and the Clinton administration, the same administration that denounces the Republicans as isolationists, regularly boasts about it. In such circumstances, it is impossible for the president of the United States to lead. But he is not chafing. He does not wish to lead. He isn't terribly interested. When his national security advisers met last week in the West Wing, he stayed in the East Wing. He did tell a reporter, though, that "the taking of hostages, as well as the killing of civilians, is totally wrong and inappropriate and it should stop." And also that "I would ask him [Boris Yeltsin] to call the Serbs and tell them to quit it, and tell them to behave themselves."

To behave themselves. And if that fails, to go to their room. Does Clinton grasp that there is evil in the world? And does he understand that he is not the governor of the United States? It is a requirement of his job that he care about matters beyond our borders, matters such as war and genocide and the general collapse of America's role in the world, matters that will not gain him a point in the polls. The joke on Clinton is that he is almost certainly about to be hoist by his own isolationism. The result of the Bosnia policy that was designed to spare the United States all costs in lives and dollars may be a U.N. "extraction operation" that will require the deployment of many thousands of American troops and the expense of many millions of American dollars. *And* Bosnia will have been destroyed. Nice work.

It is time to conclude this sinister farce. The U.N. should get out of the way. Its forces must be withdrawn, so that the Serbs may no longer hide behind them, and then the Bosnians must be armed, so that they can fight their own fight, which is all that they are asking to do. Withdraw and strike, lift and strike. Obviously this is not as simple as it sounds. The withdrawal of the U.N. will mean war; and unless NATO provides protection from the air, for the departing U.N. troops and for the training Bosnian troops, the U.N. withdrawal will expose the Bosnians to the Serbs as brusquely as it will expose the Serbs to the Bosnians, and Bosnia will fall. But there already is war and Bosnia already is falling. Anyway, Bill Clinton and Boutros Boutros-Ghali and John

Major and the rest are not keeping the U.N. in Bosnia to spare it horror. They can live with its horror. They are keeping the U.N. in Bosnia to spare themselves a reckoning with their own failure. For it is they who ordained that Bosnia become a place where it is always too late for justice.

(JUNE 19, 1995)

"It Has Not Been a Good Day"

THE EDITORS

July 11 was a day of history for America. About that, in Washington, there is no disagreement. The history, however, is rather more entangled and embittering than is commonly acknowledged. On the day that the United States recognized Hanoi, Srebrenica fell. The coincidence is beyond irony. For the war in Bosnia proves that the war in Vietnam is not over. It lives, in the premise of the American refusal, pioneered by the Bush administration and perfected by the Clinton administration, to put a halt to the genocide that is taking place in our (the Western, the American, the European) midst.

The reconciliation with Vietnam, overshadowed by a hamlet in Bosnia? It is not as preposterous as it sounds. The war in Vietnam may have been the primal political scene of the generation that produced a president in Bill Clinton, but time does not stop, not even for the 1960s, and foreign policy must be made in the present; and in the present it is southeast Europe, not southeast Asia, where the powerlessness of the United States, morally and strategically, is regularly demonstrated. (The recognition of Vietnam does constitute a strategic challenge to China, except that the Clinton administration never describes China as a power that must be strategically challenged.) And the recognition of Vietnam reminds us again that in the Clinton era, in the era of economicism, there is only one sure way of holding the attention of the only great power on earth: money. If only Bosnia had cheap labor, instead of cheap life.

The fall of Srebrenica happened the usual way. The Serbs laid low for a while; then they attacked a United Nations position; then the United Nations dithered; then, when it was too late, the United Nations ordered a NATO airstrike (or, as the Bosnian prime minister more precisely described it, a "so-called air-strike"); then NATO unleashed its fearsome might and destroyed two Serbian tanks; then the U.N. position collapsed; then a Serbian flag was raised over dead Muslims and fleeing Muslims; then nothing was done.

And there was the usual rhetoric. On the day before the conquest of Srebrenica, the U.N. spokesman in Bosnia, the deliciously named Lieutenant Colonel Coward, told reporters: "It's still a fine judgment as to whether or not the Bosnian Serbs' intent is to continue." On the day after the conquest of Srebrenica, Boutros Boutros-Ghali told reporters: "What is important is that we are condemning the offensive of the Bosnian Serbs against the safe area of Srebrenica and the resolutions of the United Nations." In Washington, Michael McCurry, the White House press secretary, told reporters that "the U.N. mission, fragile though it is, . . . helps keep the citizens of Bosnia alive," though he conceded that "with respect to the protection of this particular eastern enclave, it has not been a good day." And Secretary of Defense William Perry observed that "this raises the question as to whether the U.N. force will be able to stay in Bosnia to perform the humanitarian mission."

Does the word *duh* mean anything to Perry? The question of the U.N. mission in Bosnia was answered a long time ago, except for American and European officials who need the U.N. to rescue them from their duty to rescue. The hapless U.N. troops should quit Bosnia, where they are complicit in a war of aggression. And the United States should lift the arms embargo against the Bosnians—*the arms embargo against the Bosnians:* who cannot see the grotesqueness of those words?—and arm the Bosnians directly or indirectly, so that they can fight for their lives. "I do not see what [aside from force] will stop the Serbs in the other enclaves or in Sarajevo," Jacques Chirac remarked last week. They were the only decent words to be heard.

But none of this will happen in this lifetime, or at least in the lifetime of the Clinton administration in Washington and the Boutros administration in New York. Instead we will hear about consultations in capitals, and rapid reaction forces, and openings in Belgrade. The excruciation of Sarajevo will continue. Zepa will fall, and then Gorazde, and the Serb conquest of eastern Bosnia will be complete. And words of outrage will tire, as often they do, when the evil are more diligent than the good. Good morning, Vietnam. Good night, Bosnia.

(JULY 31, 1995)

Accomplices to Genocide

THE EDITORS

Evil is a mirror, and the evil in Bosnia is a mirror, too. Among the images in the Balkan glass is an image of America, and it is not pretty. The United States seems to be taking a sabbatical from historical seriousness, blinding itself to a genocide and its consequences, fleeing the moral and practical imperatives of its own power. The impression of American indifference and American incompetence is everywhere.

The truth is more textured. A distinction must be drawn between the American government and the American people. The ugliness of the American government cannot be gainsaid. The president and his advisers are not even pretending to be shaken by the expulsions and the exterminations in eastern Bosnia. They are "scrambling," as the papers nicely put it, to keep the United Nations from withdrawing and the Congress from permitting the Bosnians to fight their own fight, because they do not wish to "Americanize" the war. An election is imminent, and the president with the least body bags wins.

The president warns about "overly Americanizing dealings in Bosnia." The secretary of state declares that "lifting the arms embargo, for all the attraction it has, if you do it unilaterally, it means we take a unilateral responsibility here in the United States, and it Americanizes the war, so it's a very bad idea." But the choice, gentlemen, is plain. You Americanize the war or you Americanize the genocide. Since the United States is the only power in the world that can stop the ethnic cleansing, the United States is responsible if the ethnic cleansing continues.

Well, not exactly the United States. The American president is an accomplice to genocide. Not so the American people. The president of the United States does not have the right to make the people of the United States seem as indecent as he is. He has the power, but he does not have the right. The evidence is everywhere that more and more Americans would like to know why we are standing by and doing nothing.

In this country isolationism runs deep, but idealism runs deep, too. The American people are traditionally wary of what their first president denounced as "foreign entanglements," but they are just as traditionally ready for the good fight; and they are not timid. They see what is happening in Bosnia. And just as clearly they see the bankruptcy of the Clinton-NATO–United Nations policy. They are not heartless and they are not fooled.

Would a majority of Americans support an endless and massive invasion of Bosnia by the United States? Of course they would not. But such an invasion is a fantasy designed to frighten us away from the military actions that could have halted, and can still halt, the horror. Would a majority of Americans support a sustained air campaign against the Serb war machine, an immediate withdrawal of the humiliated and humiliating UNPROFOR forces, an arming of the oppressed so that they may defend themselves against the oppressor, and a remorseless diplomatic campaign to raise the costs of this hell for Pale and Belgrade? Of course they would.

There is no assurance that Americans will not die in such an attempt to end the evil. But surely they will not die in vain. They did not die in vain in Somalia either, where hundreds of thousands of men, women, and children were saved from starvation by American troops, though the president stole the significance from their deaths when he cut and ran. In a new study of American public opinion on Bosnia, conducted by the Program on International Policy Attitudes at the University of Maryland, a man in Kalamazoo explains his support (and the support of 63 percent of those polled) for assertive American action even at the cost of casualties: "If we're simply stating that our mission is to prevent these moral atrocities from developing and continuing, for me, once that decision is made, that gives meaning to death. . . . It's important, it's something bigger."

The man was speaking American. Again, the monsters in the Balkans can be stopped by much less than an invasion of American ground troops. (When American troops are introduced into Bosnia to "extract" U.N. forces, though, Bill Clinton will become the first president in American history to commit American soldiers to a war after it has been lost.) But they will be stopped only by force. It is the last hope of Bosnia, and of Americans stricken by conscience, that Bill Clinton and Al Gore and Warren Christopher and William Perry and Anthony Lake can still be shamed into action. For if they cannot be shamed, then they will have shamed us all.

(AUGUST 7, 1995)

Finally

THE EDITORS

The right thing, at last. In the largest military operation in its history, NATO is raining what Boris Yeltsin calls "a cruel bombardment" (we hope that he is correct) on the war machine of the Bosnian Serbs. The military objective of this air and land assault is to make the "safe areas" finally safe, to diminish or to destroy the power of the Bosnian Serb ability to attack them, and so the targets are strategic ones, Serb communications centers, Serb arms depots, and the like. The political objective seems twofold: to bring the Bosnian Serbs to the bargaining table and to rescue NATO, the United States, the United Nations, and the possibility of justice from the international oblivion to which they had just about been consigned by the inaction of the West in Bosnia. At this writing, a NATO spokesman is telling CNN that the strikes are "open-ended," that they will "keep going" until their objectives are accomplished, that they denote "a much more robust role for the NATO alliance" in the Balkans.

The world has been made a little saner, especially for the perdurable people of Sarajevo and Gorazde and Tuzla, who may experience a day, or a week, not in the grip of despair. (Their bitterness will never leave them, but it is a mark of intelligence.) To be sure, the ravings in Pale continue, as Radovan Karadzic swears to Reuters that "we will win in the end," but he, too, detects a reversal of fortune, and so he sent a letter to Jimmy Carter, who sees into his heart, to announce that he is "prepared to negotiate a comprehensive peace agreement on the basis of the current U.S. peace initiative." A new, improved Karadzic is upon us. Mike Wallace has just returned with an exclusive from Pale, where he discovered that Karadzic is a thoughtful and not altogether unreasonable fellow.

The West has found its resolve; and yet there is the matter of the aforementioned bitterness. For there is nothing that justifies military action now that would not have justified military action before. "After four years of tragic and terrible warfare," the swelling State Department spokesman tells reporters, "the time has come to end this war." Well, yes; but there is something a little indecent about the words. Those four years might have been three years, or two years, if the government of the United States had promptly recognized its moral and strategic responsibilities. Before the swelling continues, it is important to understand that this strong retort to the Bosnian Serbs is not a fulfillment of the previous American policy but a repudiation of it. For this reason we support the administration's course of action, but we will not congratulate the administration for it. It is not too little, but it is too late.

Indeed, the success of the NATO campaign rather definitively gives the lie to the axioms upon which the Clinton-Ghali policy was based. We were told that the Serbs were too powerful to be challenged militarily; but NATO planes, and the heavy British and French guns of the Rapid Reaction Force, have shattered the myth of Serb invincibility, just as the Croatian troops in the Krajina shattered it last month, and revealed that the Serb forces are merely the Republican Guards of the Balkans, a threat exaggerated by soldiers and politicians who have their own reasons for opposing the use of American force. We were told that the loyalties that animated the Serb aggression were too intractable to be met by the prosaic instruments of foreign policy, that this was a conflict too ancient, too far from reason, to be resolved by Western intervention; but the élan of the Serbs has evaporated, and Belgrade wishes to be unburdened of Pale, and a season of opportunism is at hand. We were told that the solution to the Balkan crisis is diplomatic, not military; but now it is plain that diplomacy in the Balkans is nothing without the use of force. We were told that Bosnia is not an American problem but a European problem, that the United States must take a "backseat" and not go "out front" in the resolution of the conflict; but it is America that led the onslaught and it is an American diplomat who is shuttling between the capitals that are required for a peace.

And we were told one other thing: that the appeasement of ethnic cleansing would never matter in American politics. The joke is on Bill Clinton. The timidity that was urged on him by his national security advisers turns out to have been not only bad strategic advice, but also bad political advice. And yikes, there are already straw polls in Iowa. So the NATO campaign is also the Clinton campaign. It isn't Churchill, but it's something.

(SEPTEMBER 18 & 25, 1995)

51–49

THE EDITORS

In the first issue of *The New Republic,* which appeared not long after the assassination of the Austro-Hungarian emperor by a Serb radical in Sarajevo, Rebecca West, a formidable student of the Balkans, wrote about the need for "an unsurprisable mind." She was not writing about the Balkans, but the recent history of the wretched region, and of American policy toward it, has made unsurprisability even more urgent, and even more remote. The surprises just won't stop. We were surprised when the Clinton administration did nothing. Then we were surprised when the Clinton administration did something. Now we are surprised by the something that the Clinton administration did.

Operation Deliberate Force, the NATO assault on strategic targets of the Bosnian Serbs, for the purpose of relieving the sadistic siege of Sarajevo and persuading the Serbs to exchange war for diplomacy, was a reversal of American policy. It looked like the end of appeasement. But strange things are happening, or not happening, on the ground. "NATO is operating with one hand tied," a senior U.N. military officer told *The Washington Post.* The magnitude of the NATO action appears to be seriously limited. Many significant Serb assets, including heavily armed front-line units, have been kept off the NATO target list. The reason for this inhibition of force is not only an anxiety about civilian casualties. There is another reason, grimly reminiscent of the Western prevarications of the recent past. As the *Post* reported, "NATO has specifically placed those targets off-limits so as not to be seen as trying to strategically affect the outcome of the war." The largest operation in NATO's history, and it is not to change the balance of power! No wonder the Bosnian Serbs are defiant. "If I were Mladic," that same U.N. officer said, "I would resist to the last."

And even stranger things are happening at the bargaining table. The NATO campaign was designed to produce a diplomatic breakthrough, and it did. On September 8, it was announced in Geneva that the parties to the conflict had accepted a plan that will create a Serbian republic, already named Republica Srpska, on 49 percent of the territory of Bosnia. The armed intervention that was supposed to bring the aggressors to heel, in short, has brought them a new state; and the idea that the new Serb state will not affiliate with the old Serb state, and together realize substantially the dream of a Greater Serbia, is absurd. It is absurd not least because the remaining 51 percent of Bosnia is expressly allied to Croatia. And then the plan becomes truly mysterious. It declares that Serbia and Croatia agree to recognize the existence of Bosnia, and also that Bosnia will retain its seat at the United Nations. But what sort of sovereignty is it that obtains for only half of a country that is confederated with another, more powerful country?

This 51–49 formula has always been rather offensive. Is there anybody who does not see that 51–49 is 50–50 diluted by a little meaningless symbolism, that the Serbs are being rewarded with half of Bosnia for their attempt to conquer all of Bosnia? (It is also a very American formula, in the way that Americans like to sell goods that cost $100 for $99.99.) But there is something even more offensive about the new plan. It is premised on the acceptability of ethnic cleansing; or more precisely, it aims to transform ethnic cleansing from an instrument of war into an instrument of peace. A Faustian plan, if ever there was one.

The quasi-legitimation of ethnic cleansing as a condition of diplomacy began in August, with the Croatian seizure of Krajina and the subsequent expulsion of Serbs from the region. A poetic injustice, but an injustice all the same: this, too, was ethnic cleansing. But the American government was reluctant to condemn the atrocities of the Croatians. It had a use for them. Richard Holbrooke, a restless and intelligent man with an eye for the main chance, explained to his superiors that the ethnic segregation of the region may be ugly, but it makes possible the conflation of political boundaries with ethnic boundaries. Suddenly the fall of Srebrenica and Zepa to the Bosnian Serbs in the east fell into place with the fall of the Krajina to the Croatians in the west. "We ought to use it to our advantage," Warren Christopher said of the Balkanization of the Balkans, "or capitalize on it."

We do not doubt that the war in the Balkans must end with a partition of Bosnia. But why 51–49? And we understand that a peace based on the principle of pluralism may be asking too much. But why a peace based on the principle of racial purity? (It is worth remembering that 50,000 Serbs stayed in Sarajevo to tough it out with 200,000 Bosnians.) A part of the answer, of course, is that the United States wants a quick fix. The president is running for president. But he is also running the country that exemplifies for the world the essential connection between multiethnicity and decency.

(OCTOBER 2, 1995)

Afterword

"One could never have supposed that, after passing through so many trials, after being schooled by the skepticism of our times, we had so much left in our souls to be destroyed." Those words were written by Alexander Herzen in 1848. They almost silence you. *They* did not suppose that *they* had so much left in *their* souls to be destroyed! What basis for bitterness do those words leave us, who have witnessed atrocities of which the nineteenth century only dreamed, who have watched totalitarian slaughter give way to post-totalitarian slaughter, and the racial and tribal wars of empire give way to the racial and tribal wars of empire's aftermath? But bitterness is regularly refreshed. Evil is final for its victims; but for history, evil is not final. And so even we, the famously disabused children of the twentieth century, have something left in our souls to be destroyed.

The "ethnic cleansing" in the Balkans has been a soul-destroying event. It has been so unimpeded. In Bosnia, a war of aggression, motivated by a nationalist and religious ideology, employing mass expulsion, mass rape, and mass murder as the instruments of war, has been successfully waged against a population that has lacked the means to defend itself and been denied those means by the international community as a matter of policy. The past four years have not been kind to certain expectations about the world after the cold war. Some of those expectations were political: that NATO would not abide a war of conquest on its continent; that the United Nations would not be indifferent to a violation of its charter and would not allow its own troops to aid and abet such a violation ("peacekeeping" has become the first Orwellianism of the post–cold war world); that the United States, on the morning after its victory over the Soviet Union, would not retreat from the internationalism of the recent period in its history and refuse to act swiftly and forcefully, on grounds of morality and strategy, against a genocide in Europe.

After the complacency of the Western powers in the early 1990s, an intellectual reconstruction, a restatement of first principles, is necessary. Since the United States is the only country in the world with the force to slow down or to stop such a genocide, the catastrophe in Bosnia is also an American problem, and demands a reckoning of Americans. Surely we did not stand for one thing in the struggle against totalitarianism only to stand for its opposite in the wake of that struggle. What do we represent? What are the responsibilities of our power? What do our values have to do with our interests? What are the purposes of our military strength? What are the consequences of intervention and what are the consequences of isolation? The "bi-polar world" that once provided clear answers to these questions has vanished, but the questions are still good.

At this writing, the U.S. government, for not wholly admirable reasons, is actively, almost frantically attempting to broker a not wholly admirable conclusion to the Bosnian war. Its reasons are not wholly admirable on two counts. First, it has worked up an interest in Bosnia because its lack of interest in Bosnia, and the consequent embarrassments to the Clinton administration, threatened to become an issue in the forthcoming presidential election. Bill Clinton's interest in Bosnia is substantially an expression of self-interest. The president of the United States wants so much to be the president of the United States that he will even act like the president of the United States. As he discovers that the American people admire forceful action in serious crises, Clinton may be expected more and more to assume a role in American foreign policy.

Second, the Clinton administration is disguising realism as idealism. Its policy is not precisely an expression of outrage. The United States waited to intervene against genocide until a change in the balance of power made its intervention less of a leap. In August 1995, Croatia conquered Krajina and completed an ethnic cleansing of its Serbs. This established Croatia as a strategic counterweight to Serbia, and it made the ethnic boundaries of the region seem more like political boundaries. Since the Croatian conquest was useful to the Clinton administration, which needed the Bosnian crisis to disappear in a hurry, it accepted, and even encouraged, the irredentism of Croatia. The atrocities of the Croatians were expedient atrocities. Nobody ever expected Bosnia to win this war. The question was only whether Serbia would win it. Well, Croatia has won it. And the Croatian victory has become the premise of the Bosnian peace process.

It is important to understand that the American-sponsored negotiations do not represent a return to moral and historical clarity. The deal that the United States is promoting is a ratification of the results of genocide, not a repeal of them. By the terms of the deal, known in diplomatic shorthand as "51–49," the Bosnian Serbs will be rewarded with fully half (OK, unfully half) of Bosnia, and they will establish in that conquered and cleansed territory a new Serbian republic which will have the right to affiliate with the old Serbian republic. The other half of Bosnia will be confederated with Croatia. And yet these semi-autonomous, demi-affiliated, hemi-confederated halves of Bosnia will together still comprise a state called Bosnia. Or so the diplomats say. This Bosnia will be a sovereign state consisting of a republic and a sort of republic. The casuistry of the arrangement is a measure of the difficulty of the problem; but it *is* casuistry, and it is hard to believe that such an incoherent entity will long withstand the coherences of ethnic and religious identity that led to this war.

The new American policy in Bosnia is completely consistent with the old American policy in Bosnia in its indifference to the fate of pluralism. The pluralism of Yugoslavia was a complicated matter, to be sure: it required the iron fist of empire, the imperial inhibition of identity, first by Vienna and then by Moscow (and then by the little Moscow that was Tito's Belgrade); and it was the inevitable result of the mottled map of the region, in which ethnicities and religions were so entangled with each other that they could be disentangled only by violence, which is what happened. Still, there were places in Yugoslavia in which pluralism was not only a necessity but also a virtue. The city of Sarajevo in particular seemed like a monument to multiethnicity. Even during the siege of the city, from 1992 to 1995, scores of thousands of Serbs stayed in the city, because it represented a principle and a practice worth suffering for, worth dying for.

Now Sarajevo is a monument to the failure of multiethnicity. There are important conclusions to be drawn, conclusions not only about policy but also about history. The first is that pluralism is not strong when it is a necessity, or a virtue made of a necessity. It is strong when it is a virtue, full stop. To put it differently: a pluralist reality is not the same thing as a pluralist ideality. It is not enough that groups live together and muddle through. They must make an ideal of living together. They must choose decency over authenticity, the threat of assimilation over the threat of persecution. Difference is not to be tolerated; it is to be respected. When it is tolerated, it is not respected.

The war for Bosnia was a war for two objectives: the survival of Bosnia as a state and the survival of Bosnia as a multiethnic polity. The latter objective has now been sacrificed to the former. If there will be peace, it will be a segregated peace. For this reason, the indifference of the American government to the siege of Sarajevo was especially appalling, because it was an American idea that was under siege. Sarajevo was destroyed in a time when the most powerful country in the world was also the most pluralist country in the world; and this most powerful, most pluralist country was idle.

And so the war in Bosnia should serve as a warning about the fragility of pluralism. We are living in a time in which the dream of integration, which was never very popular, is losing its popularity. Hans Magnus Enzensberger recently wrote a book about the "civil wars" of the contemporary world, and subtitled it "from L.A. to Bosnia." Of course, L.A. is nothing like Bosnia (and the war in Bosnia is not a civil war), but it is true that the repudiation of the dream of integration is everywhere. The flight from universalism is universal. Identity is laying waste to the world.

There are large lessons, again, to be learned from the Bosnian catastrophe, whatever the results of the current negotiations. The first is the fragility of pluralism; and the second, alongside the fragility of pluralism, is the unfragility of the past. Too often in the discussion of Bosnia, and more generally of the ethnic and religious conflicts of the contemporary world, we hear about archaisms and atavisms and anachronisms, as if there is something shocking about the survival of all these ancient allegiances. Surprising, and also a little insulting. How was it that so much of the past eluded modernity's grasp? Quietly or unquietly, this stuff was supposed to go. Economic explanations, as usual, explain little: even in advanced societies, where the bliss of bourgeois life was expected to dull or to destroy the passions of gods and groups, those passions are active. Srebrenica is a place in Europe.

We disarmed ourselves with our condescension, with our worship of revolution. Human nature did not change in 1910, as a modern writer said it did; or later. The spiritual needs of individuals take different historical forms, but they are not historical. And the spiritual traditions of groups are not the consequences of underdevelopment. For this reason, development will not transform them. Technology puts new tools at the service of old hungers, that is all. Theocracy was established in Iran with the help of tape cassettes. The air defenses of the Bosnian Serbs have the blessing of the Eastern church. (And cyberspace is a sanctuary of unreason.) These are not archaisms or atavisms or anachronisms. They are the unsimple expressions of individuals and groups who are continuous and discontinuous with what preceded them. Those are the only kind of individuals and groups there are, or have ever been. The past is a part of the present and the present is a part of the past. That is what moderns do not like to see. The ideology of modernity taught that the relationship between the present and the past is a relationship of contradiction; and so we are always startled.

Racial genocide, in the West, in this day and age? You better believe it. And not for the first time, if a day and an age is longer than fifty years. Almost as soon as the character of the war against the Bosnians was clear, comparisons to the war against the Jews were made. In anguish and in analysis, the Holocaust was remembered; and since genocide is not quantitatively measured, the remembrance was right. What has not been sufficiently remarked upon is the impact of the European genocide of the 1990s upon the world picture that was formed in the aftermath of the European genocide of the 1940s. We have been robbed, you might say, of our post-Holocaust innocence.

Post-Holocaust innocence? Let me explain. The enormity of our century marked us with a vanity about darkness. We were the ones who saw, or we were the children of the ones who saw, an evil that would never come again. This belief in the uniqueness of the evil was a tribute to its magnitude (which, again, was not measured only quantitatively). A perverse kind of pride could be found in this experience of finality. "Never again," some of us used to say about the radical, state-sponsored, tribe-happy evil that destroyed the Jews of Europe a generation ago.

Watching Bosnia, from my lucky but cheerless distance, I have understood the secret attraction of that slogan. It flattered us that we had hit bottom; and in this way it held out the prospect of a re-illusionment. For the mind might accommodate such crimes, if it could be sure that they occurred only once; and sure, too, that their occurrence would be received as a warning. But now we know that the Holocaust was not received as a warning. It was received as a precedent. And so we are bereft of the certainty that the worst is over, which was a kind of optimism. For that part of the world that we congratulate as "the West," the post-Auschwitz honeymoon is over. It is one of the consequences of the Serbian terror in Bosnia that we may never again say "never again."

And there is still another lesson that must be learned from the Balkan genocide, another disappointment for those who thought that the Holocaust left the West in a condition of clarity. One reason (but not, alas, the only reason) that the Allies did not take action against the Nazi extermination of the Jews was their ignorance, and then their incredulity. Historians have documented in grim detail the difficult journey to the corridors of Western power of what Walter Laqueur has called "the terrible secret." The facts of the Final Solution to the Jewish Question were not immediately known and they were not immediately believed. And when the world saw the proof of the extermination in 1945, when photographers brought back pictures from the camps, the world was revolted.

Fifty years later, however, there was no "terrible secret." The Final Solution to the Bosnian Question was covered by CNN. The pictures were everywhere, including the east wing of the White House. There was knowledge and there was belief. And yet there was no action. From this we must conclude about the response to genocide that knowledge and belief are not enough. We may know and we may believe that a people is being systematically destroyed and still we may do nothing. Alongside knowledge and belief, there must be a ready will, a lively moral sense, a natural human empathy, an appetite for the battle that is necessary and just.

For Bosnia, these dispositions were developed too late, or not at all. There was no rescue. The diplomacy in Dayton makes the resumption of genocide in Bosnia less likely, but this diplomacy is not to be mistaken for rescue. The goal of these negotiations is the partition of Bosnia, which is a way of giving the remains of Bosnia a decent burial. Bosnia will be interred in a diplomatic contraption so weak, internally and externally, that it will become a standing invitation for the chauvinist powers of the region to finish their work. Even as the preparations in Dayton were being made, the Serbs were proceeding with the ethnic cleansing of Banja Luka and the press was documenting the full horror of what happened in Srebrenica, and also the debt that the killers in Srebrenica owed to the United Nations and NATO. Srebrenica is the new Guernica, the new Lidice. It is only a matter of time before we learn the name of the place that will be the new Srebrenica. The destiny of Bosnia has given heart to the wicked. We will be tested again.

Leon Wieseltier
Washington, D.C., November 1, 1995

Once More by the Potomac

Here is a Jolly Good Fellow,
he's painted the White House yellow.

Here are the Mighty Generals,
bemedaled for fighting memories.

Here are the Hallowed Offices,
groggy with foggy prophecies.

Here are the Strategic Centers,
filled with their caviar emptors.

Here is our Congress, scrupulous
in making their marbles the cupola's.

And here are We, The People;
each one a moral cripple

or athlete, well-trained in frowning
on someone else's drowning.

Joseph Brodsky

Chronology

1990

First multiparty elections in the six republics of the former Yugoslavia. Serbian Communist leader Slobodan Milosevic elected Serbian President.

1991

June: Slovenia and Croatia declare independence. Yugoslav army attacks Slovenia.

July: Yugoslav army withdraws from Slovenia. Serb-Croat skirmishes going on since early 1991 escalate into war between Croats and rebel Serbs, backed by the Yugoslav army, in Croatia.

September: United Nations imposes arms embargo on all of former Yugoslavia.

December: European Community, under pressure from Germany, says it will recognize Croatia and Slovenia.

1992

January: U.N. mediator Cyrus Vance negotiates cease-fire for Croatia.

February: U.N. Security Council sends 14,000 peace-keeping troops to Croatia. Bosnia-Herzegovina declares independence. Bosnian Serbs declare separate state. Fighting spreads.

April: Bosnian Serb gunners begin siege of Sarajevo. European Community, followed by the United States, recognizes Bosnia. Intense fighting in Bosnia.

May: Yugoslav army relinquishes command of its estimated 100,000 troops in Bosnia, effectively creating a Bosnian Serb army. United Nations imposes sanctions on a new, smaller Yugoslavia made up of Serbia and Montenegro, for fomenting war in Bosnia and Croatia.

July: International airlift begins to Sarajevo.

September: U.N. Security Council drops Yugoslavia from General Assembly.

1993

January 2: International mediators Cyrus Vance and Lord Owen unveil plan to divide Bosnia into 10 provinces, mostly along ethnic lines.

February 22: Security Council sets up war crimes tribunal for former Yugoslavia.

March: Bosnian Croats and Muslims begin fighting over the 30 percent of Bosnia not seized by Bosnian Serbs.

April 12: NATO jets begin to enforce U.N. ban on aircraft flights over Bosnia.

April–May: Security Council declares six "safe areas" for Bosnian Muslims: Sarajevo, Tuzla, Bihac, Srebrenica, Zepa, and Gorazde.

May 15–16: In a referendum, Bosnian Serbs overwhelmingly reject Vance-Owen plan in favor of independent Bosnian Serb state.

July 30: Warring sides reach preliminary agreement in Geneva on Union of Republics of Bosnia-Herzegovina with three states and three peoples. Bosnian President Alija Izetbegovic walks out August 2 after Serbs violate cease-fire.

September 1: Geneva peace talks collapse.

December 19: Early parliamentary elections in Serbia called by Milosevic leave his Socialists as largest party.

1994

February 5: Mortar shell slams into downtown marketplace in Sarajevo, killing more than 60 people and wounding about 200 others.

February 9: NATO gives Bosnian Serbs 10 days to withdraw heavy guns from Sarajevo region or face airstrikes.

February 17: Bosnian Serb leader Radovan Karadzic agrees to remove guns from around Sarajevo if soldiers from Russia, a historical Serb ally, join peacekeeping mission.

February 28: U.S. jets, flying for NATO, down four Bosnian Serb warplanes violating "no-fly" zone.

March 18: Bosnia's Muslim-led government and Bosnian Croats sign U.S.–brokered accord, ending yearlong war.

May 13: Five-nation Contract Group announces new peace plan, including a four-month cease-fire and eventual partition of Bosnia.

July 20: Serbs refuse Contract Group plan.

August 4: Milosevic cuts ties with Bosnian Serbs for rejecting plan.

October 29: Bosnian government forces score their biggest victory of the war around Bihac, in northwestern Bosnia. Fierce Serb counterattack follows.

November 21: NATO launches its largest action ever, about 50 jets and support planes attacking Serb airfield, but fail to take out Serb jets attacking Bihac.

November 25: Serbs detain 55 Canadian peacekeepers against further airstrikes. Eventually more than 400 peacekeepers held. NATO attempts airstrike on Serbs near Bihac. Mission called off after U.N. fails to pinpoint targets.

December 20: Former U.S. President Jimmy Carter ends mediating mission with announcement of Bosnian cease-fire.

1995

January 1: Four-month, nationwide truce takes effect. Bihac is never quiet.

April 8: U.S. aid plane hit by gunfire. All U.N. aid flights to Sarajevo canceled.

May 1: Bosnian cease-fire expires. Croatia launches blitz to recapture chunk of land from rebel Serbs. Serbs retaliate by rocketing Zagreb; six killed, nearly 200 wounded.

May 24: U.N. orders Serbs to return heavy weapons to U.N. control and remove all heavy weapons around Sarajevo.

May 25: Serbs ignore U.N. order. NATO attacks Serb ammunition depot. Serbs respond by shelling "safe areas," including Tuzla, where 71 people are killed and over 150 injured.

May 26: NATO warplanes attack more ammunition depots. Serbs take U.N. peacekeepers hostage. Eventually more than 370 seized.

May 28: Bosnian Foreign Minister Ifran Ljubijankic shot down by rebel Serbs near Bihac. France, Britain, and United States send thousands more troops toward Bosnia.

June 2: Serbs shoot down U.S. F-16 over northern Bosnia, release 121 U.N. hostages.

June 3: NATO defense chiefs, meeting in Paris, agree on rapid reaction force to bolster U.N. peacekeepers in Bosnia.

June 6: U.S. envoy Robert Frasure fails to agree with Milosevic after weeks of talks on Serbia recognizing Bosnia.

June 7: Serbs release 111 more U.N. hostages.

June 8: U.S. Marines rescue downed pilot of U.S. F-16. NATO approves new rapid reaction force, but says peacekeepers will leave Bosnia by fall if rebel Serbs don't accept new force. Complex evacuation plan approved.

June 14: All but last 26 U.N. hostages released.

June 15: Government launches offensive to break siege of Sarajevo. Serbs step up shelling of Sarajevo and other "safe areas."

June 18: Last 26 U.N hostages released.

July 11: Serbs overrun Srebrenica "safe area" after last-minute NATO airstrikes fail to stop advance.

July 21: NATO threatens airstrikes if the nearby Gorazde "safe area" is attacked.

July 28: Croatia sends thousands of troops across the border into Bosnia, where they cut Serbian supply lines and threaten a widening of the war.

August 1: NATO extends its threat of airstrikes against rebel Serbs to protect all remaining "safe areas" in Bosnia—Sarajevo, Gorazde, Tuzla, and Bihac. House of Representatives follows Senate on defying arms embargo, sending measure to a certain presidential veto.

August 12: President Clinton vetoes Congressional measure to lift arms embargo.

August 19: Three U.S. diplomats, including Robert C. Frasure, President Clinton's special envoy to the former Yugoslavia, are killed in a car crash while driving on a narrow mountain road to Sarajevo.

August 28: Two shells slam into central Sarajevo market area, killing 37 people and wounding 80.

August 30: NATO launches 50-hour air campaign against Bosnian Serb targets around Sarajevo and other safe areas.

September 5: NATO resumes bombardment of Bosnian Serb targets after four-day pause for negotiation fails to achieve the withdrawal of artillery that has kept Sarajevo under a 40-month siege.

September 8: Croatian, Serbian, and Bosnian Muslim leaders agree to create a Serbian republic within Bosnia-Herzegovina.

September 11: Navy cruiser USS *Normandy* fires 13 Tomahawk cruise missiles into area around Banja Luka.

September 14: Serbs agree to pull back their heavy artillery from Sarajevo exclusion zone.

September 25: Mass graves reportedly found in caves located north of the Muslim city of Kljuc. The remains of more than 500 Muslims reportedly found.

September 26: Croatian, Serbian, and Bosnian Muslim foreign ministers meet at the United Nations and endorse U.S.–brokered peace plan. The plan calls for a collective presidency, a parliament, and a constitutional court.

October 2: Bosnian Serbs reject Bosnian government conditions for cease-fire.

(*Source:* Associated Press and *The New York Times*)

Contributors

FOUAD AJAMI is the Majid Khadduri Professor and director of Middle East Studies at the School of Advanced International Studies at Johns Hopkins University.

JOSEPH BRODSKY was awarded the Nobel Prize for Literature in 1986. His next book, *So Forth*, will be published by Farrar, Strauss and Giroux in January 1996.

ZBIGNIEW BRZEZINSKI was National Security Adviser from 1977 to 1981 and is a counselor at the Center for Strategic and International Studies.

ISTVAN DEAK is Seth Low Professor of History at Columbia University and the author most recently of *Beyond Nationalism: A Social and Political History of the Habsburg Officer Corps, 1848–1918* (Oxford University Press, 1990).

ZLATKO DIZDAREVIC is the author of *Sarajevo: A War Journal* (Fromm, 1993).

ALEKSA DJILAS, a fellow of the Russian Research Center at Harvard University, is the author of *The Contested Country: Yugoslav Unity and Communist Revolution, 1919–1953* (Harvard University Press, 1991).

SLAVENKA DRAKULIĆ is the author of *The Balkan Express: Fragments from the Other Side of the War* (W. W. Norton, 1993).

NIALL FERGUSON is a fellow at Jesus College, Oxford.

MISHA GLENNY is the author of *The Fall of Yugoslavia: The Third Balkan War* (Penguin, 1992).

PATRICK GLYNN is a resident scholar at the American Enterprise Institute. He is the author of *Closing Pandora's Box: Arms Races, Arms Control, and the History of the Cold War* (New Republic Books/Basic Books, 1992).

ANNA HUSARSKA is a contributing editor at *The New Republic*.

CHARLES LANE is a senior editor at *The New Republic*.

ANTHONY LEWIS is a columnist for *The New York Times*.

ARTHUR MILLER'S latest play was "Broken Glass."

CZESLAW MILOSZ was awarded the Nobel Prize for Literature in 1980. His next book, *A Year of the Hunter*, is forthcoming from the Noonday Press.

NADER MOUSAVIZADEH is an associate editor at *The New Republic*.

MARTIN PERETZ is editor-in-chief and chairman of *The New Republic*.

SAMANTHA POWER has been covering the war in the former Yugoslavia since 1993. Her reportage has also appeared in *The Boston Globe* and *The Washington Post*. She is currently a law student at Harvard University.

DAVID RIEFF is the author of *Slaughterhouse: Bosnia and the Failure of the West* (Simon & Schuster, 1995).

LEON WIESELTIER is the literary editor of *The New Republic*.

ROBERT WRIGHT is a senior editor at *The New Republic*.

Index